THE REPUBLICRAT JUNTA

How Two Corrupt Parties, in Collusion with Corporate Criminals, have Subverted Democracy, Deceived the People, and Hijacked Our Constitutional Government

The Republicrat Junta

J. P. Befumo

PDF Edition

Library of Congress Control Number: 2011929137
ISBN #: 978-0-9767489-9-1 Softcover

Cover Art and Book Design by J. P. Befumo

To order additional copies of this book, contact:
Pleasant Mount Press, Inc.
www.PleasantMountPress.com

I dedicate this book to Senator George V. Voinovich, who stood up for his beliefs by pleading—pleading to the point of tears—that he so deeply opposed the appointment of John Bolton as UN Ambassador, and then voted in favor of the appointment, thereby proving himself a thrall of the party structure, and providing my perfect example for the word ***'hypocrite'.***

Something of immense significance has occurred right before our eyes, so note and consider it well. This man has come forward, and in plain view, demonstrated that he is voting the will of his **party***, not his conscience, nor the good of his constituency. This is what the 'two'-party;* ***'Republicrat'***[1] *-dominated government has become.*

Understand this, and every other malfeasance will become crystal clear.

1 "Republicrat" is a portmanteau word comprised of the names of the two main political parties in the United States: the Republicans and the Democrats. The term is used pejoratively by those on both the right and left who allege that the policies of these 'two' parties are, in practice, indistinguishable, and so form essentially one party with two names.

KAKISTOCRACY:

THE GOVERNMENT OF A STATE BY THE WORST CITIZENS[1]

"Political parties exist to secure responsible government and to execute the will of the people. From these great tasks both of the old parties have turned aside. Instead of instruments to promote the general welfare they have become the tools of corrupt interests, which use them impartially to serve their selfish purposes. Behind the ostensible government sits enthroned an invisible government owing no allegiance and acknowledging no responsibility to the people. To destroy this invisible government, to dissolve the unholy alliance between corrupt business and corrupt politics, is the first task of the statesmanship of the day."

—Republican President Theodore Roosevelt–first American to receive a Nobel Prize in any field (Peace Prize recipient, 1906).

1 *Oxford English Dictionary* Second Edition on CD-ROM (v. 4.0) © Oxford University Press 2009.

CONTENTS

PART III – THE JUNTA

PART IV – THE BACK BURNER

PART V –CONCLUSION

Adult Content Warning

Employing slang, obscenity, or profanity in serious nonfiction is a risky proposition, and never one to be undertaken without deep consideration. While the shock value may serve to punctuate a point, the likelihood of offending or distracting the reader, and the danger of compromising the author's judgment and credibility must be balanced on the opposite arm of the scale.

In the final analysis, the only time doing so can be justified is when there is absolutely no alternative in the English language which embodies the specific meaning, nuance, and imagery of the word/phrase under consideration. In terms of the current work, I have decided to take this risk in the case of two essential words:

The first such word is: *scumbag*.

The unabridged *Oxford English Dictionary* (hereinafter referred to as *OED*) includes the following entries:

scumbag coarse slang (chiefly U.S.).
1.1 A condom.
2.2 A base, despicable person. Also as a term of vulgar abuse.

What is a scumbag?

In simple words, the item in question is an inexpensive device that facilitates individual pleasure and self indulgence while preventing the creation of new life. The end result is a flaccid, disposable latex envelope, filled with foul, dead bodily fluids, fit only to be flushed down the toilet. Hence, there is simply no other word in the English language that more appropriately describes people like Bernie Madoff, the biggest swindler in history; Kenneth Lay, whose Enron debacle ruined countless lives; Judge Mark Ciavarella, who sent innocent juveniles to prison in return for cash kickbacks from the operators of the for-profit facility; any lawyer who pulls out all the stops and manipulates evidence to free a child murderer; or, conversely, a District Attorney who suppresses evidence that he *knows* will prove a man innocent; and, indeed, for the vast majority of politicians who currently run our country—just a bunch of *scumbags*.

Then there's the dread 'N-word'—an utterance so powerful that, like the fabled *Tetragrammaton*, its mere vocalization is apt to undo all of creation:

Nigger

In Harriet Beecher Stowe's immortal novel, *Uncle Tom's Cabin*, Simon LeGree says: "I don't go for savin' niggers. Use up and buy more,'s my way... I used to, when I fust begun, have considerable trouble fussin' with 'em and trying to make 'em hold out.... Now, you see, I just put 'em straight through, sick or well. When one nigger's dead, I buy another; and I find it comes cheaper and easier, every way."

It is my judgment that, as ***so*** perfectly reflected in this passage, there is no other word in current English usage that packs quite the power and nuance of this word when it comes to expressing the utter disdain with which our politicians, business leaders, and other scumbags hold the common working person, regardless of race, national origin, or creed. I use the word in this book in the same sense and spirit as John Lennon's *Woman is the Nigger of the World* (1972). A more appropriate verse might be: "The worker is the nigger of the rich." Just as African-Americans were viewed by plantation owners, to the corporations and their greedy officers, managers, and investors, workers are all just a bunch of *their* niggers.

Indeed, our current perversion of Capitalism (which I refer to as AmeriCapitalism), is predicated upon convincing the working men and women that if they only work harder, and sacrifice more, they too will one day be rich, corrupt scumbags like their corporate masters. It takes little imagination to recognize that this promise is as specious as the slave owner telling his property: "Hey, boy, if you work hard and pick lots of cotton, one day you'll be the massah of your own plantation...."

I apologize in advance for any discomfort the use of these terms may incur, and hope the reader will understand that hiding in the shelter of our comfort zones is one of the main reasons we all find ourselves in the predicament we're in today.

Introduction

I'm going to begin this book by suggesting one simple, concise idea for your consideration. I am not asking that you *believe* it; merely that you *ponder* it in the light of the evidence supplied by your own senses, reason, and experience. If by so doing you recognize the slightest ring of truth, then I urge you to read on, for the remainder of this book will substantiate this thesis with such a preponderance of evidence as to preclude any possibility of doubt.

That illuminating disclosure is simply this:

Both the Democrats and the Republicans are peddling the exact same deception; and that bill of goods is that the Republicans represent the interests, values, and will of Conservative Americans, and the Democrats represent the interests, values, and will of Liberal Americans.

Before you decide, consider the following: Since 1960, we have had ten presidents; five Republicans and five Democrats. While there have been some minor variations, these have been largely independent of the party in power, and overall, that trend has been downward for people who actually *work* for a living and produce something of value, and steeply upward for those who advance their interests through other means.

I could throw a bunch of numbers at you, but just a qualitative picture will tell a better story.

My grandfather, who immigrated from Sicily with his family at the age of four, was a printing press operator. On his salary, he owned a two-family home in a nice neighborhood of Brooklyn, NY, and a large country home on ten acres of land in Tuxedo, NY. He bought a new Cadillac every two years, and my grandmother never had to work outside the home in her entire life.

My father, with a high-school education, worked as a lithographer. He also owned his own home from the time I was six, and traded up to a brand new, custom built 4-bedroom, two-story dwelling, in the desirable Round Lake Park neighborhood of Monroe, New York when I was about ten. My mother, also, never had to work, and was able to devote her time to raising myself and my three brothers. We all attended private schools, and my father also drove new cars, albeit more modest models than my grandfather.

We weren't rich by any stretch of the imagination—I often heard the phrase: "we can't afford that," but we always had food on the table, gifts on birthdays and Christmas, clothes on our backs, and furniture for our home.

Ours seemed like a pretty typical lifestyle, at least judging by everyone I knew, and everyone I saw on television.

Since 1960, the home ownership rate in the United States has remained relatively stable having increased 5.6% since 1960 when 62.1% of American households owned their own home. However, homeowner *equity* has fallen steadily since World War II and is now, on average, less than 50% of the value of the home. Moreover, in order to *afford* this cornerstone of the American dream, the vast majority of households depend on multiple wage earners, with children increasingly being raised by others.

Those who consider themselves 'Conservative' frequently identify with family values, so they should consider carefully the fact that in 1960, only 18% of women with children were in the workforce. Currently that number is 71.3%. Granted, *some* of this represents 'career women' who do so by choice, but one need only look at their own friends and neighbors to realize that the vast majority work because they *must*.

Is this an improvement? I don't believe it is.

It's also informative to consider the policies instituted by the 'two' parties; not what they *say* they're going to do, but what actually transpires.

Whether it's Reagan and 'trickle-down', or Clinton and 'free trade', the resultant dynamic is indistinguishable: huge incentives, tax breaks, and outright give aways are funneled to giant corporations, with the justification being that this will encourage them to create more jobs, hire more people, and propel our economy upward. While the rhetoric is invariably "we want to help our *small* businesses," in practice, these financial benefits allow the giant corporations to undersell their smaller, more honest competitors, and ultimately, drive them out of business. Meanwhile, they ship American jobs overseas, and use the threat of further outsourcing to keep their remaining domestic workers compliant through fear for their jobs.

Bill Clinton while signing the NAFTA bill stated: "NAFTA means jobs. American jobs, and good-paying American jobs...." When *performers* like Clinton, Bush Sr., Newt Gingrich, Huckabee, Dole, *et al* set aside their pro-wrestling-style contrived hostilities, join hands, and assure American workers of their bipartisan endorsement, people should sense *something* is seriously amiss.

Here's how 'free trade' *really* works. The laws are designed to encourage giant corporations (you know, the ones who can afford some *serious* political contributions) to move their factories overseas, where labor costs are miniscule, benefits nonexistent, and conditions little better than slavery. In addition to the removal of all tariffs, these sweetheart deals allow companies to 'sell' their own products back to themselves as they cross into the U.S., thereby ensuring that the bulk of their profit remains offshore and untaxable. And all those jobs Slick Willie was talking about? Americans fortunate enough to have jobs at all, now work at places like Wal-Mart, *selling* those high-profit imports, and earning a fraction of what they once did at those 'undesirable' manufacturing jobs that are now in China.

Meanwhile, the stock market soars. Who is benefiting from *that*? Not the guy who's working 60-hours a week to make ends meet. It's the people who are making their money by producing *nothing*. And what do they *do* with that money? Why, they funnel it back to the politicians, who then pass *more* laws benefiting those who support them.

Let's be honest here: Who, precisely, ran our economy (and that of the world) into the ground. Was it *you*? Did all this happen because *you* weren't working hard enough? Was it because *you* were playing slight-of-hand games with investment firms? Was it *you* who were swindling friends and relatives with precarious Ponzi schemes? And, when this disaster occurred, *who* decided that the *only* way to solve the problem was to give massive hand outs (corporate welfare) to the criminals who *caused* the problem? Was It Barack (Democrat) Obama? Was it George W. (Republican) Bush? Or was it Barack Obama, George W. Bush, ***and all*** the other Republican and Democrat cronies who have lived their entire lives on *your* money?

One last question: how much personal wealth did our Republican and Democrat politicians *lose* as a result of the financial meltdown?

Well, as it happens, when the global economy collapsed, congressional members scored big, posting a 16% gain collectively between 2008 and 2009. Moreover, approximately *half* of these humble public servants are millionaires, compared to 1% for society at large in America. Eight members of congress are mega-millionaires, with portfolios in excess of $100 Million. Rep. Darrell Issa (R-Calif.) holds the largest treasure chest, estimated in excess of $300 million. Trailing close behind is Rep. Jane Harman, (D-Calif.) with her portfolio averaging $293,454,761. Rounding out the top three is Sen. John Kerry, (D-Mass.), with $238,812,296.

In 2010, the median wealth of a House Representative was $765,010—up from $645,503 the previous year. The median wealth for Senators jumped up to nearly $2.38 million last year, from a mere $2.27 million a year earlier.

Congressional representatives on balance rank among the wealthiest of wealthy Americans, and boast financial portfolios that are all but unattainable for most of their constituents.

Nice work if you can get it, especially when you consider that the median per capita income in the United States is $25,000...and falling. Who *supports* these laws?

Clinton, Gingrich, Democrats, Republicans....

How many federal lawmakers have had to contend with the financial ills that have befallen millions of Americans? How many of *them* are in danger of losing *their* homes? How many of them are working second jobs to make ends meet (other than their second jobs working for the corporations that fill their pockets)?

Oh, right; remember *them*? We all know that when *Mafia* criminals buy a politician, they expect something in return, and in this case, return on those 'political contributions' is considerable indeed:

Top Ten Corporate Kickbacks

1. **Exxon Mobile**'s 2009 profits totaled $19 billion, but according to its Security and Exchange Commission filings, it received a $156 million rebate from the IRS, even though it *didn't pay a single penny in federal taxes.*
2. **Bank of America** made $4.4 billion in profits last year, after receiving a TARP[1] bailout from the Federal Reserve, *plus*, they received a $1.9 billion tax refund from the IRS.
3. **General Electric** made $26 billion in profits in the United States alone over the past five years, received a $4.1 billion tax refund from the IRS, and meanwhile, has cut 20% of its American jobs in order to move them overseas, where it can expand its U.S. tax evasion. How much did it pay in taxes last year? $0.00.
4. **Chevron**'s IRS refund last year totaled $19 million, while its 2009 profits were $10 billion.
5. **Boeing** received a $30 billion contract from the Pentagon to build 179 airborne tankers, and at the same time, received a $124 million refund from the IRS.

[1] TARP: the Troubled Asset Relief Program, is a program through which the United States government purchased assets and equity from financial institutions to strengthen (bail out) its financial sector through the infusion of some $700 billion in taxpayer money. The program was signed into law by U.S. President George W. Bush on October 3, 2008 as a result of the so-called financial meltdown. While much of this has since been repaid, as anyone with business experience will admit, cash on hand is a valuable resource, especially to those who know how to make money work for them. How many of us have been in positions where we might have turned over lucrative deals if only we had some liquid cash available for a brief period of time? The point here is not whether or not those funds were or will be ultimately repaid, but that their disbursement represents a highly valuable, preferential treatment for a few well-connected corporations that would never be available to others, including the "small businesses" whose interests 'both' parties claim to support. As such, it can only be classified as corporate welfare, and crony capitalism.

6. **Valero Energy** made $68 billion in sales and received a $157 million tax refund check from the IRS. Over the past three years, it has received a $134 million tax break thanks to the oil and gas manufacturing tax reduction. How much of this is showing up in the form of reduced gas prices at the pump?
7. **Goldman Sachs** paid *1.1%* of its 2008 income in taxes, while raking in $2.3 billion in profit. It was compensated for this 'poverty' by being given a TARP bailout from the Federal Reserve and the U.S. Treasury Department.
8. **Citigroup**'s profits last year exceeded $4 billion, but it paid $0.00 in federal income tax, *and* received a TARP bailout from the Federal Reserve and the U.S. Treasury.
9. **ConocoPhillips** generated $16 billion in profits between 2007 and 2009, but was still awarded $451 million in tax breaks because of the oil and gas manufacturing deduction.
10. **Carnival Cruise Lines** made over $11 billion in profits over the past five years, but its Federal income tax rate remained 1.1%.

Most of the people to whom I show these figures react, predictably, with some variation of: "Yeah, our tax laws are broken."

No! They're *not* broken. They're operating *precisely* as intended by the criminals who are purportedly representing the American People. Not the Democrats. Not the Republicans. The Democrats ***and*** the Republicans—that is, the *Republicrats*. They've robbed you, they've raped your children, and if history is any indication, you're going to punish them by voting them back into office; again, and again, and again.

In the words of Theodore Roosevelt, possibly our last great president, and certainly our last *honest* one: "The death-knell of the republic had rung as soon as the active power became lodged in the hands of those who sought, not to do justice to all citizens, rich and poor alike, but to stand for one special class and for its interests as opposed to the interests of others."

If you want it to stop, that power is still within your grasp. Simply stop voting for Republicans and stop voting for Democrats. That power, however, like so many other rights guaranteed by the Constitution, is quickly, insidiously, slipping away. Every year, more and more laws are enacted aimed squarely at removing this threat to *Republicrat* hegemony by making it virtually impossible for any third party to get on the ballot. If you *like* the choices you're offered every November, then by all means, continue to support your favorite *Republicrat*. If, however, this farce seems increasingly like the 'choice' of whether to step into a steaming heap of pig dung or a stinking pile of dog feces, then read on.

The Sowing of Dissention—Divide and Conquer

Just because you disagree with someone on *certain* topics, that doesn't obligate you to differ on *every* issue; just because someone is dead wrong in one belief, that doesn't mean they will err on everything else; just because you *concur* with another on most issues, don't assume they are *always* correct. This absolutist approach does a disservice to others, but mostly, it does harm to *you.* It is also what the *Republicrats* depend upon in order to get you to support schemes that are diametrically opposed to your own interests.

When the 'conservative' deputation of the *Republicrat* Party wants hard-working, blue-collar Americans to oppose workers' rights, their tactic is elementary: simply tell them that 'the liberals' are *for* workers' rights. Next thing you know, Scott Walker decrees that you can no longer engage in collective bargaining. Oh, but we're talking about *public* workers—that's *different*! So, according to some $2-Million/year Senator, *he's* earning every cent, but the guy who collects your garbage, records your deeds, or fights your fires is a greedy gold-brick, living off the fat of the land.

Consider this from a slightly different angle: what that earnest, passionate politician is implying is that those who depend on a labor union to help them negotiate a decent wage for their work are indistinguishable from that apocryphal 'welfare mother' pulling up at the supermarket in her mink coat and Cadillac, clutching a fist full of food stamps. After all, those bleeding-heart liberals are in favor of both, so you'd *better* be opposed.

I don't know about *you*, but if I'm going to reflexively distrust *anyone*, it's going to be that sly, cynical sleazoid, in the $350 haircut, who thinks he or she can pull my strings as if I'm some wooden-headed marionette.

Some years back, at a time when my thinking was about as conservative as it could have been, I found myself in a business partnership with a gentleman who was about as far off toward the left as I was to the right. Although I respected him deeply as a friend, a colleague, and businessman, we disagreed on virtually every political and social topic. I would simply smile and shake my head at his many quixotic causes, protests, marches, and affiliations.

One day he asked me to join him in protesting a plan to convert the nearby Savannah River Nuclear Plant into a 'breeder reactor', capable of generating weapons-grade by-products. Naturally, I refused. For one thing, I strongly favored the expanded use of nuclear power as a peaceful energy source. Moreover, I was fully convinced that real-world situations demanded the maintenance of a nuclear arsenal, and if you want to make nuclear weapons, you need the raw materials, right?

My friend's argument, however, was focused and practical: whether or not you support nuclear power, regardless of your stance on nuclear weapons, there is a vast chasm between having a simple environmental danger in your back yard, and having what would inevitably be a strategic target in any military confrontation.

After considering his point, I was forced to concur, and did in fact join his protest.

The point here is not whether you agree or not. The point is that, if you're an intelligent, thinking human being, you owe it to yourself to consider every issue on its own merits, and make up your mind based on your knowledge, experience, and intuition. To do otherwise is to turn yourself into one of those slogan-chanting automatons from George Orwell's prophetic novel, *1984*.

So, just because the Liberals object to the government trying to crush the unions that protect your rights; to the government trying to reduce the benefits… benefits for which you have already compromised your pay rates—after that same government evaporated your pensions by investing in the big corporations that destroyed the economy, and who are *still* paying no taxes (after being bailed out with *your* tax dollars)—that doesn't mean that you *have* to assume the opposite position from those dastardly *Liberals*.

Consider what the great Theodore Roosevelt said about unions: "It is essential that there should be organization of labor. This is an era of organization. Capital organizes and therefore labor must organize."[1]

Similarly, just because some Conservatives believe that the Supreme Court was (let's be kind and say 'wrong', rather than 'shamelessly corrupt') in ruling that the principle of *Eminent Domain* can be used to take private property from a citizen, not for essential public works, but to give away to a private, profit-making crony, that doesn't mean that you have to knee-jerk your way to the contrary position.

Just keep in mind that the only positions those in government want us to assume are on our knees.

There have always been disingenuous individuals who, in furtherance of their own agendas, will misquote, misinterpret, and deliberately misrepresent the words, writings, or deeds of others. To the extent that anyone accepts these representations without expending the effort to investigate the quoted material firsthand, they make themselves easily-manipulated dupes of those who seek to control them.

[1] In my opinion, Theodore Roosevelt was the last truly competent man of integrity to occupy the White House. I'll be quoting him extensively throughout this book, however, I don't quote a person because I admire them; I admire a person because they express ideas and sentiments with which I agree, usually saying them far more eloquently than I could ever hope to do.

The tactic of reducing every issue to reductionist slogans and sound bites is no more than a cunning tactic to garner support for concepts without allowing those being manipulated to truly understand the complexity of the topics. This is enhanced by presenting a one-dimensional abstraction of an utterly reprehensible foe to symbolize the opposition.

Even *if* someone says something objectionable, indefensible, or just plain wrong on one occasion or on one particular topic, you can no more assume that they are wrong on *every* topic as infer that a person who is knowledgeable in one area is equally competent in all others. It simply does not follow logically.

Consider the case of William Shockley, recipient of the 1956 Nobel Prize in Physics for his invention of the transistor. Later in his life, Shockley made some statements about race, intelligence, and eugenics which were denounced by many as racist. As is often the case, much of what he said was distorted and misquoted, but even if you consider these theories absurd, that doesn't mean the transistor doesn't work.

Many people, of various political persuasions, object to what Ronald Reagan did when he summarily fired air traffic controllers, but this does not mean those same people cannot acknowledge his triumphant contribution to ending totalitarian government in the Soviet Union. Conversely, just because you admire Reagan's economic stands, that does not mean you have to support his decision to allow illegal drug money to be funneled into arming insurgents in someone else's war, in flagrant violation of the law and the will of the legislature.

Unless you think you're dealing with the second coming of Jesus Christ, you are under no obligation to assume that any person on earth is 100% perfect all of the time.

Many years ago, a friend's parents hosted a party at their home for our teenage crowd. One of our group took great delight in reading quotes to my friend's father—a good-natured, but very conservative WW-II combat veteran—without revealing the source. In each case, our host, finding the quotes inspirational and profound, would go through a succession of guesses, naming people he considered admirable: Thomas Jefferson, Teddy Roosevelt, Omar Khayyám.... Finally, our sly quizmaster would confound him by revealing the sources: Chairman Mao, Alan Ginsburg, Timothy Leary....

I have frequently engaged in similar subterfuges: directing unidentified quotations of a conservative source to Liberal friends, and liberal sources to Conservative friends; enjoying their amazement when they learn that they have just agreed with a statement by someone they considered absolutely reprehensible in every respect.

Here's one of my favorites, written in 1999, two years before the 9/11/2001 World Trade Center attacks:

"If we continue on this course of reflexive interventions, enemies will one day answer our power with the last weapon of the weak—terror, and eventually cataclysmic terrorism on U.S. Soil...."

Ralph Nader?

Noam Chomsky?

No, it was Conservative commentator Pat Buchanan, who, after 9/11, continued, writing: "If this Prodigal Nation dues not cease its mindless interventions in quarrels and wars that are not America's concern, our lot will be endless acts of terror until, one day, a weapon of mass destruction is detonated on American soil. What is it about global empire that is worth taking this risk?"

What indeed? The good of the American people? Or is it the interests of criminal multinational corporations whose servants now control every branch of our government?

How about this one:

"Non-violent resistance activities cannot succeed against an enemy that is able freely to use violence. That's pretty obvious. You can't have non-violent resistance against the Nazis in a concentration camp, to take an extreme case...."

NRA CEO and 2nd Amendment advocate Wayne LaPierre?
'White separatist' Randy Weaver?
No, it was well known *Liberal* icon Noam Chomsky.

And is the following not the sentiment of someone our rulers would connive to paint as an abhorrent *Socialist*?

"We wish to control big business so as to secure among other things good wages for the wage-workers and reasonable prices for the consumers. Wherever in any business the prosperity of the businessman is obtained by lowering the wages of his workmen and charging an excessive price to the consumers we wish to interfere and stop such practices. We will not submit to that kind of prosperity any more than we will submit to prosperity obtained by swindling investors or getting unfair advantages over business rivals."

Well, the man who said *that* was the one of those great leaders whose face appears on Mount Rushmore: Republican Theodore Roosevelt.

Here are two quotations, expressing essentially identical sentiments about the infamous 9/11 attacks:

"After 9-11, at a time of enormous global sympathy and solidarity with the United States, George Bush asked, 'Why do they hate us?' The question was wrongly put, and the right question was scarcely addressed. But within a year, the administration succeeded in providing an answer: 'Because of you and your associates, Mr. Bush, and what you have done. And if you continue, the fear and hatred you have inspired may extend to the country you have shamed as well.' On that, the evidence is hard to ignore. For Osama bin Laden, it is a victory probably beyond his wildest dreams."

"George W. Bush gave this response to the question of 'Why do they hate us?': '...They hate our freedoms: our freedom of religion, our freedom of speech, our freedom to vote...' If these analyses are correct, it would appear that Bin Laden and his gang in Tora Bora had simply stumbled onto a copy of the Bill of Rights and gone berserk....We are not hated for who we are or what we believe; we are hated for what we do. It is not our principles that are despised; it is our policies."

The first quote was from self-avowed Socialist Noam Chomsky, the second, from Conservative Pat Buchanan.

Agree or disagree with the conclusions reached, the critical thing to realize is that there are a great many areas about which *real* Liberals and *real* Conservatives concur, despite what the deceitful, self-serving usurpers in Washington would like us to believe.

If one thing should be growing crystal clear, it's that those who now rule our nation are the antitheses of virtually everything this country, and all of its great thinkers and founders stood for and believed; in other words, they are *not* the legitimate government of the Unites States, but rather, the usurpers thereof.

Once again, Theodore Roosevelt demonstrated his perspicacity by recognizing this a century ago: "Behind the ostensible government sits enthroned an invisible government owing no allegiance and acknowledging no responsibility to the people."

One final observation on this topic: It has been my experience that the people who are most adamant in their suspicion of the government, in their self-image as rugged individualists, as patriots, and as lovers of freedom, are often the ones who first fall back on the meaningless, manipulative slogan-based thinking that is inevitably engineered by the very powers they most detest. Bottom line? Think what *you* wish, but *always* ask yourself if you're basing your principles on real facts, or if you're merely repeating what someone else told you that you *should* be thinking.

For example:

Of all the people in this world, the rural Americans *I* have known are amongst those who would be best able to live without oil. They know how to chop wood, plant the land, ride a horse, dig a well, hunt and fish, and in most ways be self-sufficient. They couldn't care less if the internet works or not, would just as soon toss that cell phone and their land lines as well, and indeed, might actually be a lot happier with that kind of lifestyle.

But *not* if all the fish are dead, the game is gone, and your land and water are poisoned.

Yet these are the folks whom politicians—Republicans *and* Democrats—have manipulated into supporting policies with precisely these results. Is *this* what you want for yourself and your children?

British Petroleum's Deep Water Horizon disaster happened because politicians said that environmental reviews were unnecessary, and the risks were negligible.

They were wrong.

Now President Obama, in an effort to serve his party and save his failing political career, is about to give additional offshore drilling leases to Shell, waiving environmental review, because… "the risk is negligible." Simultaneously, the Republicans are pushing to remove *all* environmental oversight, and grant even more leases. I guess *this* is where you find bipartisan agreement—they *all* agree that *your* interests are worth less than zero, while those of the corporations who fill their pockets are inviolate.

I *think* I'm like a lot of other Americans. I tend to be conservative on some issues, liberal on others. Some are vitally important to me, whereas others merely represent a personal predilection or bias. I have friends from virtually every religious, ethnic, racial, and social background. I have a friend whose name, when it appears in the newspapers (as it often does), is inevitably prefaced with: "millionaire philanthropist…," and friends who live without electricity or indoor plumbing. I have friends who volunteer for Greenpeace, and a friend who is a card-carrying member of the John Birch Society. I consider Dennis Kucinich and Ron Paul, Noam Chomsky and Pat Buchanan, Ralph Nader and the late William F. Buckley all to be honorable, sincere, educated, well-informed men. I think each of them is dead-on-target with respect to some issues, and totally wrong on others, but I am pretty certain that each of them speaks their heart and their conscience.

So why, then, does it seem as if those who purport to be representing us in government often appear to be going out of their way to convince us that our friends and neighbors are either imbeciles, enemies, or the very embodiment of evil?

Why indeed!

One might think that they seek to perpetrate some insidious indirection to deliberately deflect our attention from what *they* and their cronies are actually up to!

George Washington was unambiguous in his distrust of manipulation by political parties, writing that it: "agitates the community with ill-founded jealousies and false alarms, kindles the animosity...[and] opens the door to foreign influence and corruption, which find a facilitated access to the government itself through the channels of party passions. Thus, the policy and will of one country are subjected to the policy and will of another."

Wise man, old George. How much of this country has been *sold off* to foreign interests? To China? To the Arab countries? And precisely *who* made the sales and profited thereby? Not the Democrats *or* the Republicans; it was the Democrats *and* the Republicans—you know, the guys who tell you that a vote for anyone *except* one of them is a vote *wasted.*

Alexander Hamilton addressed this issue, writing that: "Foreign influence is truly the Grecian horse to a republic. We cannot be too careful to exclude its entrance. Nor ought we to imagine that it can only make its approach in the gross form of direct bribery. It is then most dangerous when it comes under the patronage of our passions, under the auspices of national prejudice and partiality."

Finally, I think it's worth reiterating the Theodore Roosevelt quote from the front matter of this book:

"Political parties exist to secure responsible government and to execute the will of the people. From these great tasks both of the old parties have turned aside. Instead of instruments to promote the general welfare they have become the tools of corrupt interests, which use them impartially to serve their selfish purposes. Behind the ostensible government sits enthroned an invisible government owing no allegiance and acknowledging no responsibility to the people. To destroy this invisible government, to dissolve the unholy alliance between corrupt business and corrupt politics, is the first task of the statesmanship of the day."

Once again, I urge the reader to think back, in terms of their own wellbeing, and measure the results against the rhetoric and the actions of those who have been making these decisions in our name. Our greatest national resource was once our self-sufficiency. We could forge our own steel, build our own cars, manufacture our own appliances, construct our own furniture, weave our own cloth—with the hands of our own workers—and were dependent on nobody else for our own survival. Can we say the same thing today? And who has benefitted from the pillaging of this greatest resource? Is it the workers who now sit idle, their jobs shipped off to India and China, while the politicians accuse them of deliberate sloth? Or is it those whose profits were maximized by exporting those jobs, and those in government whom they bribed to make doing so the law of the land?

How many politicians start their rhetoric with: "I believe the American people are intelligent enough to…."

Really? Or is *this* the most cynical statement of all? For only if they believed the exact opposite, would these blatant prevaricators continuously apply these tactics in order to attain and maintain their positions of authority.

Every now and then, one of them betrays the true contempt in which they hold their constituency, such as when a Republican politician advocated "dumbing down" their political propaganda in order to appeal to "truckers and farmers…."

Indeed? I've known quite a few truckers, farmers, and others who actually *work* for a living, and while many lack the privileged background that facilitates a degree from Harvard or Yale, most of them had more common sense, and, more important, more integrity and decency in one work-toughened finger than most politicians and lawyers have in their entire well-pampered bodies.

In the words of Theodore Roosevelt, "There is not in all America a more dangerous trait than the deification of mere smartness unaccompanied by any sense of moral responsibility."

With the antagonism, vitriol, and downright abusive rhetoric between those nominally labeled 'Liberals' and 'Conservatives' at historical levels of vehemence, any attempt to bridge so vast a chasm would seem an exercise in futility. Nonetheless, I am convinced that it is an undertaking that *can* be accomplished. Moreover, it is one that is absolutely critical if we, as a nation, are to shake off the cynical, manipulative forces that deliberately seek to set one American against another in order to preclude any unified challenge to the hegemony, treachery, and even treason that is anathema to every citizen.

When the committed Liberal hears the word 'Conservative', what do they see? Men in white hoods burning crosses in remote wooded glens; 'skinheads' with swastikas engraved on Neanderthal brows; bloody children carried from devastated federal buildings; gay-bashing politicians caught playing footsy in bathroom stalls or vacationing with their rent-a-boys; physicians murdered in church by crazed gunmen for performing legal medical procedures.

And utter the word 'Liberal' to any self-respecting Conservative, and you invoke images of drugged-up flower children, scoffing at capitalist values while living off of Mom and Dad's money; commie forces ransacking house-to-house in search of contraband firearms; construction projects halted while courts deliberate on the impact to some endangered snail species; murderous, rabid rapists set free by whimpering social workers to continue their crime sprees; terrorists coddled for fear of violating their civil rights while their Liberal supporters open wide our borders to invite in ever more insidious criminals; homosexual recruitment in our elementary school curriculum....

How could such natural enemies even *endure* each other's presence, much less find common ground for dialog and debate? Judging by the behavior of those who purport to represent us, the answer must be: *no way*! Indeed, this is the message they deliberately contrive to communicate, both by their rhetoric and their actions. But is it necessarily so?

`No, I don't expect the denizens of middle America to sign on to the nationalization of all businesses, the elimination of private property, and the establishment of free-love hippie communes as the basic social structure. And I suspect we'll have a long wait if we expect Liberals to embrace a rollback of the Civil Rights Act, a return to segregation, or the mandatory teaching of Creationism as the sole permissible model of the origin of mankind.[1]

However, when it comes to, say, the imposition of a police state, I daresay that the majority of people from all persuasions would unite in opposition. We'll explore this specific topic in greater depth later, but for now, I'll toss out a couple of observations to ponder:.

For all you Liberal folks, read the words of Noam Chomsky, one of the greatest Liberal minds of our time: "Non-violent resistance activities cannot succeed against an enemy that is able freely to use violence. That's pretty obvious. You can't have non-violent resistance against the Nazis in a concentration camp, to take an extreme case...."[2]. Do you really think that, in the final analysis, there is *anything* that will prevent such subjugation *except* the prospect of armed resistance? *That*, my friends, is the *real* intent of the Second Amendment.

And for those of a more Conservative bent, satisfying as it might be to see the bad guys thrown into some deep black hole from which they might never emerge, what do you suppose is the inevitable result when the government (which, as you are already aware, cannot be trusted) is permitted to suspend *your* constitutional rights, arrest and hold you without charge, abscond with your property so you can't afford to mount an effective defense, and subject you to whatever treatment they desire, just by assigning a *label* to you. Perhaps it works to your satisfaction when that label is 'terrorist', or 'drug kingpin', but how about when it's 'anti-government extremist,' or 'white supremacist', or 'radical tax protester', or 'survivalist gun-nut'? And if you think this could never happen, just ask Randy Weaver. (See p.53)

[1] And, for the religious orthodox, do you think science is too complex to be the mechanism through which the God who invented *all* science to have worked His miracle of creation?

[2] Noam Chomsky, *Chronicles of Dissent: Interviews with David Barsamian*, Common Courage Press, 2002.

"Naturally, any conqueror is going to play one group against another. For example, I think about 90% of the forces that the British used to control India were Indians.... But forget the Third World, just take a look at the Nazi conquest of nice, civilized Western Europe, places like Belgium and Holland and France. Who was rounding up the Jews? Local people, often. In France they were rounding them up faster than the Nazis could handle them."[1]

At the risk of sounding like a paranoid conspiracy theorist, I contend this is precisely what our rulers are doing when they encourage divisiveness between Americans. This is why the *insiders* on both sides *love* all the Michael Moores, and Glenn Becks, and Rush Limbaughs. By distilling the truth into concentrated propaganda points, they fan the sparks of our basic value system into a conflagration beside which the cool analysis of reason stands no chance.

Who is the government of the United States?

It is against the law to encourage or incite the overthrow of the legitimate government of the United States. For example, the U.S. Code of Law, Title 18, Part 1, Chapter 115, Section 2385, "Advocating Overthrow of Government" states:

Whoever knowingly or willfully advocates, abets, advises, or teaches the duty, necessity, desirability, or propriety of overthrowing or destroying the government of the United States or the government of any State, Territory, District or Possession thereof, or the government of any political subdivision therein, by force or violence, or by the assassination of any officer of any such government; or

Whoever, with intent to cause the overthrow or destruction of any such government, prints, publishes, edits, issues, circulates, sells, distributes, or publicly displays any written or printed matter advocating, advising, or teaching the duty, necessity, desirability, or propriety of overthrowing or destroying any government in the United States by force or violence, or attempts to do so; or

Whoever organizes or helps or attempts to organize any society, group, or assembly of persons who teach, advocate, or encourage the overthrow or destruction of any such government by force or violence; or becomes or is a member of, or affiliates with, any such society, group, or assembly of persons, knowing the purposes thereof—

On the other hand, Thomas Jefferson, in paragraph two of the Declaration of Independence, wrote:

[1] Noam Chomsky- *Keeping the Rabble in Line: Interviews with David Barsamian*, Common Courage Press, 2002..

"Governments are instituted among Men, deriving their just powers from the consent of the governed—That whenever any Form of Government becomes destructive of these ends, it is the Right of the People to alter or to abolish it, and to institute new Government, laying its foundation on such principles and organizing its powers in such form, as to them shall seem most likely to effect [sic] their Safety and Happiness. Prudence, indeed, will dictate that Governments long established should not be changed for light and transient causes; and accordingly all experience hath shewn [sic], that mankind are more disposed to suffer, while evils are sufferable, than to right themselves by abolishing the forms to which they are accustomed. ***But when a long train of abuses and usurpations, pursuing invariably the same Object evinces a design to reduce them under absolute Despotism, it is their right, it is their duty, to throw off such Government, and to provide new Guards for their future security."*** (My emphasis)

In a similar vein, Jefferson wrote: "When the government fears the people, there is liberty; when the people fear the government, there is tyranny."

Obviously, this is an area in which there exists considerable ambiguity, and personally, I would not care to be at the defense table in any resultant legal proceedings. So, just to be clear, I will state unequivocally that I fully support the *legitimate* government of the United States, as defined in the Constitution and amendments thereto, and consider that document to represent the primary definition of our government. Activities, agencies, and additional laws passed under the provisions of The Constitution, insofar as they are not inconsistent with the Constitution, collectively comprise the legitimate legal system of the United States of America.

It is the obligation of every citizen to either:

1. Support the legitimate government of the United States,
2. Work to change that government within the mechanisms provided by the Constitution, or
3. Renounce their citizenship, and relocate to a different country more consistent with their views.

Nevertheless, it is not only our right, but, indeed, our duty, to repel hostile invaders, *restore* that government, and to remove and punish any groups that have usurped it, using whatever means are necessary.

But amidst all of the various different, often opposing perspectives, is it even possible to unambiguously define what would constitute legitimacy in government? I contend that it is far easier than some would lead us to believe. I would propose that the legitimate government of the United States consists of those who demonstrably uphold and implement The Constitution. Conversely, laws, agencies, and activities that are antithetical to the provisions of The Constitution represent sedition, and those who subvert the Constitution by perpetrating such deeds are, by definition, insurgents and traitors.

Of course, there are myriad issues that were never, and could never have been, anticipated by the framers of the Constitution; things like electronic privacy, stem cell research, ownership of space.... These were gifted men, but they were not gods, nor were they even *perfect* men. As many will point out, their initial model denied rights to women, denied humanity to an entire race, and codified innumerable other inequities. However, what they *did* accept was their own fallibility, and they consequently included robust mechanisms to allow the Constitution to meet unanticipated requirements. Today, women *can* vote because, on August 18, 1920, the Nineteenth Amendment to The Constitution remedied that initial error. Similarly, human beings who had been kidnapped and brought to this country in chains, as property, were freed by the Thirteenth Amendment in 1865. True, much suffering was endured during the interim; nobody claims the system is perfect, but it *is* workable, if honestly and diligently applied.

In his 1949 masterpiece, *1984*, George Orwell wrote that "It does not matter whether the war is actually happening, and, since no decisive victory is possible, it does not matter whether the war is going well or badly. All that is needed is that a state of war should exist...."

Similarly, in the current *Republicrat Junta*, the perpetual skirmishes over a spectrum of issues are completely irrelevant as far as those in power are concerned. Their sole value is as a distraction, keeping the eyes of the electorate so fixed upon their enemies/neighbors, that they will overlook the continual chicanery of those whom they have elected to represent them. The reason, of course, is that *any* substantive alteration of the *status quo* would negatively impact the *real* interests of 'both' parties: the continued growth of multi-national corporations, in both wealth and political power.

The purpose of this book, therefore, is to explore the many ways in which the various sides agree—or *would* agree, if they weren't being so shamelessly manipulated so their knee-jerk reaction is always: "if *he/she* is for that, then *I'm* against it!" For those areas on which we will never agree (and there *are* many), I think it's possible for us to at least begin to understand that those holding opposing beliefs may actually have reasons for their positions, even if *we* have reached alternative conclusions.

What will emerge is that all honest men of integrity have far more in common with each other, and with the will of the majority of the American People, than with any member from either deputation of today's corrupt ruling junta.

I firmly believe that if we can all approach this topic with open minds, the inevitable result will be a level of outrage that will allow us to join forces, even if temporarily, and finally oust these treacherous prevaricators who have seized control of this noble nation, and take back what is rightfully *ours*!

PART I

SERFS AND ELITES[1]

[1] This section excerpts and expands upon the 1998 monograph *A Nation of Serfs and Elites,* by Paul Befumo. Reprinted here by permission of Montanans For Due Process.

Natural Law

If we are to judge by the words and actions of those who purport to represent us in government, it would appear that the American people are *so* polarized in their beliefs that no agreement will ever be possible. Indeed, the outright rancor that seems to exist between factions is easily as vehement as that which has led to many a bloody conflict throughout history.

Are we *really* so drastically different in our most essential moral and ethical beliefs, or have we been deliberately manipulated into this divisive state? And if such is the case, who is responsible, and what might their nefarious purposes be?

Achieving such an understanding is the purpose of this book, and I shall begin by suggesting some basic premises upon which honest, thinking individuals of many persuasions *can* agree. You may dispute some of these conclusion; that's fine, and if an honest dialog ensues, such is the manner in which people of good faith understand and resolve their differences. I feel confident, however, that these are observations that most people will not be inclined to simply dismiss out of hand.

So, in order to establish a baseline for discussion, and for the discussions that will follow in the remainder of the book, I begin with the following:

Self preservation is the first law of nature. Man, along with most other forms of life, share the natural drive for self preservation. Only man, through his uniquely developed ability to describe the world around him through language, has endeavored to codify the law of self preservation, along with its essential corollaries, as 'rights'. The right to self preservation is a person's right to protect and preserve his or her own life, as well as the lives of those closest to him. This right to self preservation, combined with man's ability to alter his immediate environment, gave rise to the concept of property. In order to ensure his chances of survival, man, through his *labors* and *efforts*, creates wealth where none previously existed. The fruits of a person's labor become his exclusive possessions, although he may, *at his discretion*, elect to share such possessions with others of the community. This is the origin of property. Whether this consists of a tool fashioned *by the work of one's own hands*, crops raised from the earth *through one's labors*, or some other form of wealth resulting from an individual's industry coupled with the raw materials from his environment, the object of a person's individual efforts become his exclusive property. Property is first accumulated for the purpose of ensuring survival, and later, for the purpose of increasing one's comfort and enjoyment of life. Property is one common incentive to labor.

The essential points here, as emphasized, are those related to property arising from *individual effort*. To the extent that one is helped by one's neighbors, the results must be considered common to a greater or lesser extent, whether this is accomplished in the form of wages, or apportionment of the property created. When this wealth results from the substantial endowment or subsidies from a public institution, the generated wealth belongs, in part, to that institution and its owners. If that institution is a government, then part of that wealth must be returned to *the People*.

Businesses, including corporations, convert abstract concepts into commercially viable products as a result of the vision and insight of their founders, enabled by capital from forward-thinking investors. To the extent that this is the sole source of their wealth, it is right and proper that the results be distributed amongst those who facilitated its accumulation. However, when this wealth is also dependent upon collectively owned resources, such as public lands, or is based on publicly-funded research and development, such as the internet or subsidized private laboratories, then, once again, a proportional component of the profit belongs to *the People*.

Any attempt to deny the People their just return is fraud and/or theft.

The prerogative to make choices respecting one's life and property, in the furtherance of self preservation and happiness, is also claimed as one of the self-evident rights belonging to all humankind: this is the right to *liberty*. Liberty is that right to make the critical choices that affect our lives, accepting the consequences visited upon us by those choices as the inevitable laws of nature dictate. In the context of society, liberty is the freedom from restraint, under conditions essential to the equal enjoyment of the same freedom by others; it is freedom regulated *to the minimum essential degree necessary to protect the freedom of others*. This concept of liberty also finds itself as the theological cornerstone of most of the world's religions: the free will of man.

The opposite of liberty is slavery.

The rights to life, liberty, and property are rights with which we are born. They are the natural rights of man, inherent in our natures as human beings. They are not granted to us by society or by government. They are not a gift based on the generosity or benevolence of some man or group of men. These fundamental rights must nevertheless be *claimed* by those who wish to exercise them. The inevitable result of failing to claim these most fundamental rights is that their existence will be ignored or denied. Those who fail to claim their natural rights as men risk being treated as the property of others, rather than as human beings with a birthright of freedom. Those who do not claim their rights risk enslavement.

Fundamental, natural rights *are never privileges*, granted by a government or other group, and susceptible to being taken away at the whim of the grantor. Those who attempt to characterize *rights* as *privileges* do so in order to deny their existence, and to strip away those rights completely. Those who speak of our rights as if they were privileges have as their objective the plunder of our property, and our eventual enslavement.

These natural rights—life, liberty, and property—constitute the basis for all forms of society created when free individuals come together to form groups. Individuals form groups for the purpose of furthering and protecting these fundamental rights. Forces that seek to abrogate these rights are *ipso facto*, enemies of life, liberty, and individual expression.

Society and Government

To illustrate how the furtherance of these fundamental rights forms the basis of society and government, let us consider a group of people in an isolated state, sequestered from all others. These individuals come together to form a *society*, in order to combine their common resources, thus increasing their chances for achieving mutual objectives. By doing so, they increase efficiency, ensure their mutual survival, and enhance their chances for achieving happiness. The formation of *society* promotes these goals in a *positive* way, by uniting their needs. Voluntary cooperation to further the goals of the participants is the true meaning of *socialism*.

The isolated hermit, living alone in the wilderness, availing him– or herself of no tools, supplies, or any items produced by any other human being, is the *only* individual existing completely outside of social support. Even animals that cooperate in order to ensure the survival of the group, colony, pack, or herd, are participating in socialism.

After formation of society, the same group of people will form a *government* in order to unite their common authority to protect their lives and property, along with their liberty, through rules of *law*. Again, they do so to ensure their survival and their chances of achieving mutual goals and individual happiness.

Law is the tool of government. Government promotes happiness *negatively*, by restraining those who would *violate* the fundamental rights (i.e., life, liberty, and property) of their neighbors. The purpose of government, and therefore of law, is not to *cause* justice to prevail, but rather, to *prevent* injustice from reigning. Justice is the absence of injustice. The sole function of government, and therefore the law, is to prevent violation of our lives, liberties, and property by greedy or power-hungry individuals and groups.

It is essential not to confuse government and society. An objection to something being done by government is not the same as an objection to it being done by other social forces. An objection to government-enforced equality of result is not the same as an opposition to equality of opportunity for all. All of the charitable, altruistic aspirations of politicians may very well be worthy pursuits; however, they are endeavors that should be undertaken and implemented by individuals and voluntary groups, of their own free will, not forced upon unwilling people through the police power of the state. They must not be funded by the ostensibly legal pillaging of private property by the government.

Society at large can choose to engage in any philanthropic pursuit conjured by the imaginations of altruistic individuals. Government, however, has its sole legitimate function in preventing the *violation* of the lives, liberties, and properties of its constituents. It is *not* empowered to promote individuals' happiness, security, or comfort in any manner whatsoever.

Government at its best is a necessary evil; at its worst, an intolerable one.

The Authority of Government

The following axioms describe the authority of government, as it is derived from the consent of the governed:

1. Government has one, and only one, *legitimate* purpose: the protection of the lives, liberty, and property of the governed.
2. The scope of the authority delegated to the government cannot exceed the scope of authority of those making the delegation; the People as a group cannot delegate authority that they do not have as individuals to begin with. For example, no individual has the right to define a 'person' as being anything other than the normal, commonly understood concept of a human being. No normal human being would contend that General Electric, or British Petroleum, or Massey Energy is a human being, and hence, no government has the right to do so either.
3. The delegation of authority to government by the People is *conditional*; when government usurps, exceeds, or abuses its delegated authority, the delegation is revoked, and the government loses any legitimate authority to govern.

The aforementioned rights to life, liberty, and property are naturally limited with respect to each individual. They are limited to that extent necessary to protect the corresponding rights of others. Liberty is freedom from restraint, under conditions essential to enjoyment of the same freedom by others; that is, my right to swing my arms ends where my fist intersects your person. Unfortunately, not everyone respects the rights of their neighbors. In the primal state of nature, every person has the authority to use whatever force is necessary to protect their lives, liberty, and property, thus ensuring their survival. This moral authority to protect our natural rights from those who would usurp them is as fundamental as the rights themselves.

Once people gather into a voluntary society, they may make the choice to delegate their authority to protect these natural rights. Such delegation is the basis of the power and jurisdiction of government. Government derives its power from the consensual delegation of authority to those who constitute the government. Again, the people cannot delegate authority they do not have as *individuals* to begin with.

Since every individual has the natural authority to protect their lives and their property, a group of individuals can delegate the authority to government to protect the lives and property of the People as a whole; however, no individual has the right to determine that someone else has accumulated too much property, *through their own effort and resources*, and therefore take some of this property and give it to a poorer, less fortunate neighbor. Neither can any government legitimately claim the authority to redistribute wealth among its citizens, *regardless of whether or not the majority of its citizens agree with such a policy.*[1] There is simply no legitimate basis for the delegation of such authority to government in the first place. Any exercise of government police power to take what belongs to one citizen in order to give it to another, is not only an abuse of power, but a usurpation of the fundamental rights of its individual citizens. Once a government exercises such authority, it can no longer claim its constituents as the source of its authority. At that point, a government's power is coming from other sources, such as aristocratic prerogative, the threat of violence, or brute force.

For many, the mention of "redistribution of wealth" invokes images of Marxism, the Bolshevik Revolution, and the welfare state; in which the honestly earned property of those who have worked hard to acquire it is stolen and given to those who, for whatever reason, do not enjoy such advantages. However, redistribution of wealth also occurs when property is taken from citizens and given to huge corporations in the form of subsidies, tax exemptions, grants, low-interest loans, bail-outs, and so forth. Then, adding insult to injury, these corporations pay their top executives unjustifiable compensation, while simultaneously exporting jobs overseas, *and* then returning large parts of this plunder to the government in return for enacting laws that perpetuate this upward redistribution of wealth. Thus, the property of the People is forcibly appropriated, and applied to programs which work *against* those same People. Examples include curtailing the rights of the unions formed by the People to protect their interests, opposing safe working conditions, fighting against a fair minimum wage, or protecting the property of the People from irresponsible damage through pollution in the relentless pursuit of profits. Calling this 'capitalism' is no less than a cynical application of blatant propaganda to justify what is essentially government-sponsored plunder.

[1] *This* is why the framers of our Constitution implemented our government as a Republic, rather than a Democracy. In a true democracy, the majority may easily morph into mob rule, denying the natural rights of the minority.

When any government *exceeds* the limits of power that it may naturally claim in any free society, forfeiture of its authority and legitimacy is automatic. Unfortunately, forfeiture of its *police power* is not. When a government forfeits its rightful claim to authority, the task remains for its People to document the usurpation of power, reclaim their rightful authority, and reconstitute a new government that will protect their rights.

Unfortunately, governments that exceed their authority, and which rule by force to the detriment of fundamental individual rights, seldom relinquish their grip on power peacefully. One need only consider the recent events in Egypt, Libya, and other Middle-Eastern nations to see the lengths entrenched despots will take to maintain their illegitimate power. The duty of the People at such a juncture is to either *convince* their government to relinquish power, or *compel* them to do so by the threat or application of force.

The Rule of Law

The *Rule of Law* means the use of known principles or laws without the intervention of discretion in their application. The Rule of Law did not begin in the United States. Men have placed the rules of their society into writing for thousands of years. The Code of Hammurabi, considered the oldest set of written laws promulgated by man, dates from approximately 1790 B.C. This code was carved into stone pillars that were available for all to see. Accessibility to the law *by the People* is of primary importance, because access to the laws is a prerequisite to holding the public accountable for *obeying* those laws. The efficacy and advisability of the Rule of Law has been proven over thousands of years, and was recognized early in our country's history. "The government of the United States has been emphatically termed a government of laws, and not of men."[1]

Early in the history of organized society, those who favored justice and fairness, and opposed tyranny and enslavement, understood that in order to achieve these ends, it was essential to put the rules of society into writing and make them accessible to all. In the absence of the Rule of Law, living in society is like sitting down to a card game where you aren't told the rules before the game starts, and in which the dealer can change the rules as the game progresses. In such a game, the inevitable result is that you will lose the stakes you bring to the table. In a society without the Rule of Law, the dealer is the government, and the inevitable result is that you will lose your property and your liberty.

The Rule of Law means that:

1. We agree on certain rules,
2. We write them down for all to see, and
3. We, through our courts, apply them equally to all individuals, exempting no one.

[1] Chief Justice John Marshal, *Marbury v. Madison,* 1 Cr. 137 (1803)

The Rule of Law is the necessary prerequisite for constitutional government. Under the Rule of Law, written rules have absolute supremacy over the discretion of individuals.

The Rule of Law presupposes that words have readily accepted *meanings*. If 'never' could mean 'sometimes'; if 'all' could mean 'some'; or if 'shall' could mean 'may'; then there would be no point in writing down the rules that we intend for the governance of society. Where the Rule of Law is implemented, we have objective decision making in government, or *a government of laws, and not of men.*

The basic set of written rules that is supposed to govern *our* society is the United States Constitution. This set of rules defines the limit of government's power, and elaborates on the fundamental rights of *individuals*[1] that the government may not abrogate.

The Constitution also specifies a strict procedure that the People must follow if they wish to *change* the rules by amending the Constitution. Obviously, Constitutional government of any kind presupposes a society that accepts the principle that written laws must be followed, regardless of whether or not those entrusted with enforcing or applying the laws agree with them. To have Constitutional government, we must first accept the Rule of Law as its foundation. We must also agree that the words in the Constitution have specific meanings. If the meaning of a word has changed over the centuries, we look to the meaning of that word at the time of the Constitution's adoption to determine its present scope. It should be stressed that our language has *not* changed significantly since the adoption of the Constitution, and the meanings of the most important terms remain constant. For example, the word 'all' is just as inclusive today as it was in 1791; it allows for *no* exceptions. Likewise, the meanings of words like ***NO***, ***NONE***, and ***SHALL*** have not changed over the past two hundred years. The definition of some other words *have* changed, but mostly through the effort of unscrupulous judges, lawyers, and politicians to change our laws without resorting to the necessity of amending the Constitution. Nevertheless, the meaning of those words when the Constitution was adopted is easily determined, and doing so does not require a degree in law, history, or linguistics.

Every judge, lawyer, lawmaker, and law enforcement official in our country swears an oath to support our Constitution, to recognize it as the supreme law of our land, and to uphold *only* those laws that are in conformity with the Constitution. To violate his oath by subrogating the Constitution to conflicting legislation, or by ignoring its safeguards to further any other policy, is a usurpation of the only legitimate form of government recognized by the People. Disregarding or ignoring

[1] As every reasonable, literate person can easily perceive, corporations are *not* individuals, the findings of the Supreme Court notwithstanding. Those who have supported this seditious decision justify their ruling by a deliberate misinterpretation of the *Marbury v. Madison* decision, in which they *claim* that the words of the Constitution mean whatever the Supreme Court *says* them mean, regardless of any contrary apparent meaning! As we shall demonstrate throughout this book, this proclamation, by Chief Justice Oliver Wendell Holmes, marks the moment when *the Republicrat Junta* executed an overthrow of the Constitutional government of the United States of America.

the Constitution, or treating its mandates with indifference, is essentially a *coup d'etat*. Purposely violating one's oath of office to uphold the Constitution as the supreme law of the land is akin to levying war against the legitimate, Constitutional government. Violating one's oath of office adheres to and aids the enemies of Constitutional government; in other words, it is nothing short of *treason*.

The Lawyers

No discussion regarding the Rule of Law is complete without scrutinizing the role of lawyers in society.

Most decent people are not motivated by obtaining unfair advantage or power over others, but rather, are content to apply themselves to their work, hoping to improve their situation as a result of benefiting from the fruits of their labor. However, there always exists an element of society that, when given the opportunity, will seek to benefit from the work of others, to find some edge without honest effort on their own part, and to gain control over their neighbors. When a society adopts written laws, it creates a potential role for any person who can position themselves to 'interpret' the law for others who, supposedly, are incapable of understanding it themselves.

Early in the history of any society, the law is not complex, and can be understood by the average citizen, for whom it is in fact written. One example from antiquity was the Mosaic Law, which consisted of ten commandments that the people could comprehend without the necessity of an 'expert' to interpret it for them. Likewise, our Constitution can be understood by any American with average intelligence and minimal education.

When the laws are simple, there is little need for 'experts' to interpret and apply them. Thus, those who contrive to make themselves the guardians or interpreters of the law must first render the law sufficiently complex so that it is beyond the comprehension of the common person. This is the strategy of the lawyers. It is an ancient tactic that has been employed successfully to disenfranchise and deprive the People of the protections intended by written law.

In some societies, civil and religious law are integrated, and the interpreters of the law are the Priests, Mullahs, and Ayatollahs. When civil and religious law are separated, those who connive to make themselves the custodians and interpreters of the law are called lawyers.

Prior to the separation of civil and religious law in Judeo-Christian society, lawyers were known as 'scribes'. They were members of an elite, learned class in ancient Palestine who served not only to transcribe religious texts, but also as jurists, teachers, and interpreters of Judaic law. They were condemned at that time for actions which are essentially identical to those of today's lawyers:

"Woe unto you, lawyers! For ye have taken away the key of knowledge: ye entered not in yourselves, and them that were entering in ye hindered."
—(Jesus of Nazareth, *Luke 11:52*).

Just as they do today, lawyers in ancient times made the law their exclusive province, and through subterfuge and deceit, prevented non-lawyers from accessing and employing the truths embodied therein. Then, as now, lawyers set up a system of additional laws whose sole purpose was to hamper the application of the essential laws, whilst simultaneously exempting themselves from the burdens they created for others:

"Woe unto you also, ye lawyers! for ye lade men with burdens grievous to be borne, and ye yourselves touch not the burdens with one of your fingers."
—(Jesus of Nazareth, *Luke 11:46*).

The remainder of this book will prove, beyond any shadow of doubt, that the Republican and the Democratic parties, in collusion with corporate criminals, have in fact conspired and executed an illegal overthrow of the Constitutional government of the United States through the passage of unconstitutional legislation, and must be dealt with accordingly if liberty and the Rule of Law are to be restored to this great nation.

The motives of the priestly classes of the past and those of today's lawyers are identical: to prevent the law from being accessed by the people; to pervert the law for the benefit of their keepers and their clients; to undermine the positive nature of written law so that the lawyers can organize and gain the advantage of ruling their fellow men at their sole discretion.

Our society is no exception. The history of the lawyers in the United States traces its roots to England's corrupt lawyer's guild.[1] Today, discretionary rule, rather than government under the Rule of Law, is exercised by the *Republicrats*, along with a wealthy elite who purchase the their acquiescence and complicity. Together they comprise a ruling aristocracy that abrogates the fundamental rights and liberties our law was designed to protect.

[1] A guild is an association of people with a common occupation or business, whose purpose is to further the common aims and interests of *its members*, including the *monopolization* of their trade, and the prevention of honest competition from those outside of the guild.

One cannot fully understand the treachery of lawyers without an analysis of the lawyers' cartel,[1] commonly known as the *Bar Association*.

The Bar has as its true objective the undermining of the Rule of Law, beginning with our Constitution. The reason for doing so, and for abolishing self-government in general, is simple and obvious: Lawyers see themselves as an elite; a veritable aristocracy in a supposedly classless society. The promotion of elitism is an underlying theme of the indoctrination to which every law student is exposed early in law school. A class system, with members of the Bar and their wealthy, influential clients at the top of the pyramid, is the inevitable result of the Bar gaining absolute control over the law.

Consider these facts: The lawyers' cartel has total control of the judiciary branch of government on both the state and federal level. Every judge and lawyer is a member of this nefarious organization. On both the state and federal level, the legislative branch of government is dominated by members of the Bar. At the executive level, every state Attorney General, every county prosecutor, the U.S. Attorney General, and most of their underlings are members who have *sworn allegiance*[2] to this organization whose objectives are demonstrably at odds with the United States Constitution. Our current President (Obama), and his wife, are both members of the Bar, not to mention thousands of bureaucrats with discretionary decision-making authority.

The list of proven criminals who emerged from this cartel include Richard Nixon; Spiro Agnew; Bill Clinton; Lewis (Scooter) Libby, convicted of perjury and obstruction of justice in the Valarie Plame Affair on March 6, 2007; Jack Abramoff, convicted in 2006 of mail fraud and conspiracy; Steven Griles, former Deputy to the Secretary of the Interior, who pleaded guilty to obstruction of justice and was sentenced to 10 months in prison; Brian J. Doyle, Deputy Press Secretary in the United States Department of Homeland Security, indicted for seducing a 14-year-old girl on the internet who was actually a sheriff's deputy, and sentenced to 5 years in prison, 10 years of probation, and registered as a sex offender.... The list of Bar Association members who were convicted of serious crimes while infiltrating the United States Government would itself fill an entire book.

If *any* other trade union or cartel had so thoroughly infested our government, the People would certainly recognize the remarkable conflicts of interests this entailed. If the Teamsters Union, or the Teacher's Union, or the United Auto Workers had so infiltrated our government that they were able to brazenly pass

[1] A cartel is a combination of producers of any product or service who join together to control its production. Cartels are supposedly restricted in the United States by anti-trust laws. The Bar Association, through its complicit judges, has exempted its members from these laws, and has formed an illegal modern-day cartel that controls all aspects of our law. Unlike modern-day trade unions, guilds and cartels are not voluntary organizations; membership is mandatory if one wishes to engage in the cartel's self-defined area of exclusivity. This illegal cartel is known as the Bar, and consists of the American Bar Association, and each of its associated state Bar Associations.

[2] Recall the words of Theodore Roosevelt: "We can have no '50-50' allegiance in this country. Either a man is an American and nothing else, or he is not an American at all."

laws making it impossible for any but their own members to be judges, officers of the court, or hold any number of other positions upon which the Bar Association has laid claim, the People would certainly have objected, if not revolted; yet, the Bar Association has so deceived our populace that they have accepted government domination by the lawyers' cartel and their wealthy, well-connected clients as the natural order of things.[1]

Early in the law school indoctrination process, prospective cartel members are instructed in a case known as *Marbury v. Madison*. Based on this case, law students are told that the U.S. Supreme Court has the authority to determine what the U.S. Constitution says, regardless of its apparent meaning. The following quote, *taken out of context,* is presented to students as the holding in the case: "It is emphatically the province and duty of the judicial department to say what the law is." Young law students are *explicitly instructed* that regardless of its apparent meaning, the Constitution means whatever the Supreme Court *says* it means.

The deceptive process of 'interpreting' away Constitutional protections is common knowledge among our legislators (most of whom are members of the Bar Association themselves), as well as among the membership of the Bar as a whole. Although each side loudly decries the practice of 'legislating from the bench', the truth of the matter is that *all of them* are complicit in the obstruction of our Constitutional rights, all of them are completely aware of the methodology, and all of them challenge the practice only when applied in opposition to their own personal interests. It is has long been widely known that the U.S. Supreme Court is "able to achieve almost any result in the field of constitutional interpretation which it considers desirable...."[2] While it is tempting for citizens to applaud this practice when implemented by 'one of *our* guys', careful analysis will reveal that in *every* case, this chicanery favors only those involved in the illegal exercise of power, and *never* the interests of the People.

Even ***if*** *Marbury v. Madison* actually stood for such a seditious proposition (which it does not), it would be nothing more than an attempt to usurp Constitutional government, and should be dismissed as such. The fact that it is being misused, and *deliberately misinterpreted* in this way is clear and unequivocal evidence of *treason* by those who have entrenched themselves in Washington in place of the legitimate government they have overthrown.

In reality, *Marbury v. Madison* stands for no such proposition. The complete text of this landmark case is seldom presented, rarely cited, and almost never examined. What this case *does* state is that *when* there is a conflict between the Constitution and a *legislative act*, the Supreme Court

[1] Even if we were to accede some formal education in the law as prerequisite for engaging in these monopolized practices, it should be noted that any individual who graduates from an accredited law school with a Doctor of Jurisprudence Degree is, by definition a lawyer. However, in order to engage in the *practice* of law, one must *also* be an attorney, which the cartel has *defined* as having been initiated into their private cabal.

[2] Senate document No. 170 of the 82nd. Congress, 1952

has the authority to make the final determination of whether the law complies with *Constitutional limitations*. More importantly, the case also states that: ***"the framers of the Constitution contemplated that instrument, as a rule for the government of courts, as well as the legislature."*** This statement, in plain English, should be comprehensible to any literate American, without the necessity of cunning lawyers to twist its meaning into something totally unrecognizable. This aspect of the case is totally ignored. It is the Bar's *perversion* of the holding in this case that underlies the outright fraud that the Bar has perpetrated on the American people, and the *treason* it has instigated against the legitimate constitutional government of the United States.

How did the Bar get away with so mind-boggling a deception? The answer is that the Bar, and the conniving lawyers who comprise it, are expert at creating the appearance—the illusion—of justice, while in fact implementing its diametric opposite. What American with even a modicum of political awareness *hasn't* stood aghast at the utter, blatant, Kafkaesque miscarriages of justice that pass for due process in our so-called courts of law? To understand this snide, cynical, deliberate contempt for the American people, one need only read the American Bar Association's own so-called 'code of ethics', which has as its prime directive, the promotion of "the appearance of respectability."

Yes, those are *their own words*, and they are quite appropriate at that. The *only* possible reason for promoting the "appearance" of respectability, like the *illusion* of justice, is if *true* justice and respectability do not exist, are not desired, and in fact, are actively suppressed. The *last* thing the illegal *Republicrat Junta*, and its primary instrument, the American Bar Association want to promote is *genuine* respectability or justice; and here again, this is a truth that is apparent to every American, regardless of their political affiliation. Any truly respectable person charged with upholding the law would have no choice but to immediately expose the *Republicrats'* fraud to the American people. Of course, there are *some* who have *tried*—honest men like Pat Buchanan, Ralph Nader, Ron Paul, or Dennis Kucinich— but their voices are universally marginalized through a deliberate and insidious program of misquotes, misrepresentation, and misinformation.

Only scoundrels, legitimately deserving of popular contempt, would need to promote the *appearance* of respectability, rather than respectability in fact and practice. Respectability in fact, like honesty and trustworthiness, would run counter to their *real* objective of undermining the Rule of Law and abolishing the Constitution. Like the *appearance* of respectability, the *Republicrats* want only the *illusion* of a Constitution.

As irrefutable evidence of the degree of success the *Republicrats*, in collusion with the Bar Association, have had in usurping the Constitution, we shall present three Constitutional rights that they have brazenly eradicated: the right to assistance of counsel, the right to a trial *by* jury in *all* criminal cases, and the requirement that our monetary system be based on silver or gold. (In **Chapter 36—**

The Indictment, we will prove that this illegal *Republicrat Junta* has, in fact, scornfully violated virtually *every* section of the United States Constitution.)

The Constitution guarantees the right of the People to have *any* person they choose assist them in court. This was the first Constitutional right the lawyers' cartel had to scrap. To this end, the Bar Association, through its member judges, interpreted the word "counsel" in the Sixth Amendment to mean "attorney-at-law" (which is, by definition, a member of their cartel).

The word *counsel* can be found in any dictionary, and its primary meaning is *not* "attorney-at-law." In fact, it means *any* person who gives advice. Indeed, the *Republicrat* judges deliberately *ignore* the fact that the Judiciary Act of 1789, §35, allowed for assistance by *either* "counsel *or* attorneys at law." This represents *prima facie* proof that the term "counsel" is not, nor was it ever synonymous with the term "attorney at law." Those judges who found otherwise were either ignorant of the Judiciary Act (highly unlikely), or *lied* in their sworn duty to accurately interpret the law, in which case they are guilty of treason, as are any who knowingly perpetuate this deception.

In addition to ensuring that only fully-corrupted inductees of their cartel could assist a person in court, the lawyers also perverted the term *assistance*.

The counsel guaranteed by the Sixth Amendment is an *aid*, not an agent of the ruling junta interposed between an unwilling citizen and his or her right to have help in court. One who is *assisted* by another remains in control, and bears ultimate responsibility for their own representation. One who is *represented* by another relinquishes all responsibility and control to the representative (the Bar-controlled attorney). As a result, the *Republicrat*-dominated Bar Association has stripped *the People* of their fundamental Constitutional right to have an *independent* person *of their choosing* help them in court. In its place, they have given us one of two choices: We can either proceed on our own, with no assistance whatsoever, in a deliberately obfuscated environment where the very language has been redefined beyond any recognition, or else relinquish all control to an agent of the illegal ruling junta, whose integrity is dubious at best, and whose independence is non-existent. ***STRIKE ONE!***

A second instance in which the Republicrat-dominated Bar Association has blatantly abrogated the Constitution pertains to our right to a jury trial in all criminal cases. Article III, Section 2, clause 3 of the United States Constitution states that "the trial of *all* crimes, except in Cases of Impeachment, shall be *by* jury…." Amendment VI begins: "in *all* criminal prosecutions, the accused shall enjoy the right to a speedy and public trial, *by* an impartial jury…." To anyone other than a criminal usurper of the Rule of Law, these provisions would be absolutely clear: anyone put on trial for a crime is entitled to a trial by jury. Period.

The *Republicrat*-infiltrated Supreme Court, however, asserted in *Duncan v. Louisiana* that *some* crimes and offenses are *not* subject to the Sixth Amendment jury trial provision, and that "crimes carrying possible penalties up to six months do not require a jury trial." In other words, they summarily denied this provision of the Constitution, without the required procedure of amending the Constitution,and in so doing, proved themselves once again to be illegal usurpers, and not representatives of the legitimate government of this nation; that is, they, and anyone who knowingly has perpetuated this seditious action, are guilty of treason.

Moreover, they have surreptitiously replaced the notion of trial *by* jury, as guaranteed by both the Sixth and the Seventh Amendments, with the disparate notion of a trial *with* jury. To understand both the distinction, and the motivation for so seemingly innocuous a substitution, we must once again remind ourselves of the deliberate obfuscation of the language of the law that allows *only* members of the lawyers' cabal to interpret the meaning thereof. (Similarly, at one time in Great Britain, the law had to be spoken in *Latin* during legal proceedings, thereby ensuring that the common person would never truly know what was being said, or be able to dispute any point of law.)

When laws are simple and direct, as ours were *intended* to be, the jury is quite able to determine the meaning and applicability of the law in a given circumstance, without the judge instructing them in obscure and counterintuitive 'meanings'. In such an environment, we have a trial *by* jury. Contrast this to our current standard of a trial *with* jury, in which frustrated jurors, whose reason and logic tell them one thing, must find precisely the opposite because the judge has instructed them the equivalent of 'up' meaning 'down'. People today are frustrated with the legal process, and are told that the problem is that there aren't *enough* laws, when precisely the opposite is true. ***STRIKE TWO!***

Nearly every important protection of individual rights guaranteed in the Constitution has been perverted or abolished by the *Republicrat* members of this illegal and treasonous cartel. Consider the requirement that our monetary system be based on silver or gold.

The Constitution of the United States unequivocally states that nothing *except* silver or gold shall be accepted as payment in tender of debt. In the early part of our history, before the *Republicrat coup d'etat* and the corruption that has resulted, efforts to undermine the gold/silver standard were attempted and rebuffed on numerous occasions, for the ability to 'float' currency gives those in power unchecked capability to manipulate the economy to serve their own ends. After the takeover of the courts by the *Republicrat Junta*, the gold standard was summarily scrapped, and our currency was allowed to 'float' against other world currencies, in furtherance of the agendas of the *Republicrats* and the elite groups whose interests they serve. The Constitutional mandate of a sound monetary system based on silver or gold remains; it is simply ignored by this illegal ruling junta. Indeed, in this instance, these traitorous hounds have not merely *ignored* the Constitution, they have deliberately *reversed* it, thereby making a criminal out of anyone who obeys this tenet of the law of our land:

TITLE 18 > PART I > CHAPTER 25 § 486. Uttering coins of gold, silver or other metal: Whoever, except as authorized by law, makes or utters or passes, or attempts to utter or pass, any coins of gold or silver or other metal, or alloys of metals, intended for use as current money, whether in the resemblance of coins of the United States or of foreign countries, or of original design, shall be fined under this title [1] or imprisoned not more than five years, or both.

This alone provides indisputable *prima face* evidence for the prosecution for treason of anyone who proposed, endorsed, or enforces this law. This ability to clandestinely manipulate the economy has only one goal: it permits real wealth to be accumulated by those connected individuals and organizations favored by the corrupt ruling junta, while the average citizen is made to suffer the deprivation that ensues. Without delving into details, suffice it to say that the dire 'financial meltdown' of 2008 could never have occurred if this aspect of the Constitution had not been illegally overruled. ***STRIKE THREE!***

These are but three examples among many showing how this illegal ruling junta has usurped our Constitution and the rule of law. Although we have not been overrun by an invading army, or experienced an overt *coup d'etat*, the Constitutional government of the United States, formed in 1791, has, by every measure or standard, been overthrown.

If this seems like hyperbole or exaggeration, just ask yourself whether we are truly governing ourselves under the United States Constitution; or are we, in fact, being *ruled* by men of influence who, at their sole discretion, have disregarded the very foundations of the Rule of Law? Is it hyperbole to characterize the *Republicrat*-dominated power structure, and the secret, elite groups they serve, as an invading force that has overthrown lawful, Constitutional government?

You be the judge:

Former Supreme Court Justice Charles Evans Hughes fired the first salvo in this takeover when he ruled: "We are under a Constitution, but the Constitution is what the judges say it is."

LIAR! HYPOCRITE! TRAITOR!

The Constitution is a document, composed of *words;* words that have definite and ascertainable meanings that any literate citizen can understand.

Supreme Court Justice Oliver Wendell Holmes conspired in this treason by asserting that the Supreme Court exercises the "sovereign prerogative of choice...."

Hey! Whoa! Back up there a moment! WHAT kind of prerogative?
Sovereign, ***you say?***

Sovereign: *2a : possessed of supreme power *a sovereign ruler**
*b : unlimited in extent : ABSOLUTE c : enjoying autonomy : INDEPENDENT *sovereign states**
3 : relating to, characteristic of, or befitting a sovereign.
4: One who has supremacy or rank above, or authority over, others; a superior; a ruler, governor, lord, or master (of persons, etc.). Freq. applied to the Deity in relation to created things.
In later use suggestive of sense 2 a.

The *OED* defines democracy as: "Government by the people; that form of government in which the *sovereign power resides in the people....*"

The *legitimate* government of the United States, as described by our Constitution, *has* no individuals imbued with such prerogatives. Any individual or group laying claim to sovereign prerogatives is, by definition, acting in opposition to our Constitution—in other words: a traitor.

Under Constitutional principles, *anyone* attempting to assume such powers *must* be regarded as legitimate targets of whatever forces in our country are responsible for defending us from invaders, be they our standing armies, or the militia of armed citizens. It is not merely our moral option to rid ourselves of such tyrants, it is our *legal obligation* to do so!

In creating a monopoly of the practice of the law, the cartel of renegade lawyers known as the Bar, and specifically, those members in government who are nearly all *Republicrats*, must answer to the people whom they have deprived of access to justice. When our court system fails to protect the fundamental rights guaranteed in our Constitution, who is to blame if not those who deliberately conspired to circumvent those laws? When the *Republicrats* took over our courts and our government, they made themselves solely responsible for the government's failures and violations of the law, and solely answerable for any and all misdeeds perpetrated in the name of *the People*.

Law is supposed to protect the lives, liberty, and property of those who delegate the law-making authority to their government. The law is intended to guarantee each individual the free, inoffensive use of his or her abilities for self improvement and self expression. Law is organized justice. All that can be required of our law, and of our government, is the absence of plunder. By the 'absence of plunder', we mean the abstinence from taking or despoiling the lives, liberty, and property of the members of society.

Law necessarily entails the use of force (enforcement), but force may only be legitimately used for the limited purpose of protecting the natural rights of all *natural persons*. As soon as the law is extended beyond this purpose, it is perverted, and is inevitably turned *against* the People in favor of the few, the powerful, the well-connected. Thus, no matter how altruistic the motive, the use of law for purposes such as bailing out massive corporations, whose criminal greed caused their own problems, is fatal to those legitimate purposes for which it was originally intended. Law must be just, not philanthropic, nor corrective, nor economically manipulative. When law is applied outside its intended purposes, it inevitably acts against the liberties of individuals.

Our law, as perverted by the *Republicrats*, has been transformed from an instrument for the protection of liberty and property into its opposite: an instrument of legitimized but unlawful plunder. Plunder has been organized by law in our country for the sole benefit of those who make, interpret, and enforce the law: the lawyers, politicians, and their contributors. We, the plundered classes, are encouraged to organize, but *not* for the purpose of stopping the plunder and restoring the proper Rule of Law. Instead, we are manipulated into organizing in order to attain political power, and *participate* in the plunder of our neighbors. An obvious example of this is the infiltration and co-opting of the Tea Party movement, originally formed to oppose government corruption; and the insidious manipulation of its members' frustrations into support for illegal statutes curtailing the natural rights of public-sector *workers*. Meanwhile, the 'Dem' contingent of the *Republicrat* ruling class uses this obvious injustice to manipulate *its* constituencies not against those who are truly responsible, but against their neighbors who have themselves been deceived into supporting these iniquities.

The result of law becoming an instrument of organized plunder by this *Republicrat Junta* is that we, as a society, are losing from our consciences the distinction between justice and injustice. Why should we respect the law when the law itself, along with those who are charged with its safekeeping, are worthy only of our deepest contempt, rather than our respect? Our law and our morality contradict one another. We are maneuvered into the untenable position where we must either abandon our moral sense, or lose our respect for the law. It is an impossible choice, because either way, we lose.

Most of us equate law with justice. We tend to believe that anything that is 'lawful' is also legitimate. The lawyers and politicians—the perverters of our law—have used this tendency to make their plunder appear just, by sanctioning it under law. They have done this by enacting laws that steal property from one person in order to give it to another, more favored entity, and *we* accept it because the theft is sanctioned by law. Not only have we been led down a path into monopolization, restriction, and servitude, but we have defended these institutions despite being their victims! Under the pretense of protection, regulation, and bail-outs, the law has stolen the property of the many and given it to a sinister and mendacious few.

Plunder by force or subterfuge is called theft, larceny, burglary, swindling. Plunder under color of law can take the form of 'economic regulation', 'too big to fail', 'corporate subsidies', bail-outs, tax exemptions, and a plethora of other noble-sounding, but ultimately self-serving programs.

Consider the sophistry of this elite: our purported representatives in government, and the scheming lawyers; the supposed defenders of law. They would have us believe that by organizing their plunder, and presenting it as the only hope for saving the economy (which they themselves have driven into the dust), we will comply, albeit grudgingly, then turn around and blame each other, rather than the true source of the problem. The nature of their deceptive reasoning is apparent. The law, diverted from its true purpose, now violates the fundamental rights of liberty and property instead of protecting them. It has become a source of hatred and conflict, undermining and fragmenting our society instead of strengthening it; and *this* is precisely their intent. By fostering divisiveness among honest, well-meaning citizens, they aim to prevent recognition of the true source of our ills, and the general uprising such a realization would and should inevitably promulgate.

If Americans actually realized what has been done to them, their freedom, and their beloved government, the result would make the French Revolution look like a candle-burning vigil by comparison; and rightly so. As these favored groups begin to fear the righteous wrath of those whom they have wronged, they seek to further fragment opposition with accusations of 'class warfare'. But we must remind ourselves that this nation was designed to be a classless society! Hence, their great fear as that honest citizens might realize that these self-serving enemies of humanity have, in fact, instituted an elite, ruling class, from which they have excluded all by their own hand-picked members. Indeed, 'class warfare' is precisely what the situation demands, and it should be a war fought with pitchforks, axes, and machetes, and culminating at the guillotine, leaving the streets running red with the blood of these traitorous enemies of the People!

One need only look to the first century of our nation's history to see the true source of wealth in society: the freedom to pursue our dreams, free of government control; the right to possess the fruits of our labor; and individual responsibility for individual actions. As a society, we will never again enjoy the degree of freedom and prosperity known to past generations unless we eliminate legal plunder by ousting the illegal and subversive *Republicrat Junta.*

There can be no half-way measures to dealing with legal plunder perpetrated by a dishonest, intransigent, ruling junta. Limited legal plunder, like universal legal plunder, is incompatible with the Rule of Law, and inimical to our

Constitution. *No* plunder is the principle of justice, peace, harmony, and success. Legalized plunder of any sort is the principle of inequity, strife, decline, and corruption. In the end, it leads to servitude, or worse. Institutionalized legal plunder is causing our society to lose the ability to distinguish between justice and injustice, leader and criminal, right and wrong. Legal plunder denies the very reality that presents itself before our eyes. Worst of all, it has resulted in our society losing all moral sense, as well as respect for the law.

We need not look very far back in history to find a society that was in a similar predicament.

Pre-war Germany had been subjected to perversions of justice similar to those experienced by U.S. citizens today. It was the end of the Weimar Republic, and German society of the 1930s and 1940s had lost its ability to distinguish between lawful and unlawful acts, as well as between right and wrong. When the Nazis came to power, their 'laws', calling for the extermination of vast groups of people, were enforced by the civil authorities without question, while the majority of the German people stood idly by and watched; complicit through inaction.

There was a time when those who controlled our legal system had consciences, and upheld the Constitution and the Rule of Law because it was their sworn duty. It was the right thing to do. Today's leaders, however, are no different than Doctor Hans Frank, President of the *German* Bar Association, and Nazi Minister of Justice, who said: "Formerly, we were in the habit of saying: this is right or wrong; today we must put the question accordingly: What would *the Führer* say?"

Today, the entire nation has been indoctrinated to go along with whatever the Supreme Court says, regardless of whether it is right or wrong; legal or illegal; loyal or seditious.

In yet another deliberate subterfuge engineered to sow division amongst citizens, *Republicrats* have set their sights upon the Second Amendment as the centerpiece of their campaign of misinformation and misdirection. While 'one side' presents itself as 'pro-gun', and the other, 'anti-gun', make no mistake; both sides are heavily motivated to eliminate this final threat to their complete power grab.

Much has been made of the meaning of each individual word and phrase in the Second Amendment—this so-called analysis most often resembling former President Bill Clinton's quibbling under oath over the meaning of the word "is." Once again, the Constitution was written by honest men whose aim was to record their intent in the clearest possible language, rather than to obfuscate, as we have come to expect from our current so-called leaders. Nevertheless, if there is *any* question as to their motivation, one need only examine the political circumstances surrounding the formation of this nation to derive a clear answer.

The colonists—not an organized army, not a formal National Guard unit—just groups of angry citizens…with guns…after being pushed beyond the limits of endurance by an overbearing, unresponsive tyrant, had, after decades of peaceful petitioning, demonstrating, pleading, and reasoning, finally resorted to the last option available to them: They took up arms against the oppressive British government. At great personal risk, they had overcome the most powerful fighting force on earth, and were in the process of drafting a Rule of Law that would preclude any possibility of future subjugation.

While most citizens of the fledgling nation did, indeed, rely on their firearms to put food on the table and to repel hostile attackers, this was by no means the primary motivation for inclusion of the Second Amendment. Once again, the *Republicrats* have schemed to obscure this concept, which rightfully strikes fear into the heart of any totalitarian force, through the specious argument that the word 'militia' was intended to refer to the 'National Guard'. We need only examine the circumstances surrounding the formation of the nation, as well as the other writings that reveal the most pressing concerns of the drafters of the Constitution to discern their intent.

Virtually every recorded document we can access from that time proves that the overwhelming concern of the Founding Fathers was to protect the People *from* the government they were in the process of forming. A frequently overlooked historical fact is that a great number of Americans wanted to crown George Washington *king*. He refused, indicating that they had not fought simply to replace one despot for another. Those charged with forming this new nation sought, above all else, to prevent this country from being turned into another totalitarian society, which is precisely what the *Republicrats* are already far advanced toward accomplishing.

Now, as then, prudent people must regard force as the absolute last resort. Nevertheless, if history and current events teach us anything, it's that there will always be tyrants who will yield to nothing less; and they will always be served by amoral mercenaries, under the guise of legitimate law enforcement, who are more than willing to murder their fellow citizens in service to the *dictator du jour.* Libya, Egypt, Syria, Tiananmen Square…even Kent State, Ruby Ridge, Waco Texas, and Hurricane Katrina provide telling examples.

Former American Bar Association president R William Ide, III revealed himself as an enemy of Constitutional government by creating a project to assist cities, counties, and states in drafting new and increasingly restrictive disarmament laws. He vowed that the lawyers' cartel would fight any challenge to such laws. He urged supporters of the Constitution to "admit there is no Second Amendment guarantee" of an individual's right to own firearms. His words would have fit seamlessly on the lips of Heinrich Himmler, who proclaimed that "Germans who wish to use firearms should join the SS or SA—ordinary citizens don't need guns, as their having guns doesn't serve the state."

One of the first things the Nazis did after taking power was to cement their control and preclude resistance by disarming the German people. Similar programs were instituted in the newly-formed Soviet Union, in The People's Republic of China, and in virtually every other situation where dictators endeavored to preclude resistance to their nefarious agendas.

While, in our country, the Republican contingent of the ruling *Republicrat Junta* pay lip service to their support for Second Amendment rights, a close analysis of their actual positions reveals their true agenda, which, like their Democrat counterparts, is the ultimate removal of any threat to their illegal political hegemony. Were this not the case, why have they not stood up and countered these attacks on the Constitution with the truth, which is:

The Second Amendment is not about hunting furry little critters, nor is it about defending your domicile from the occasional burglar looking take your stuff. The Second Amendment is about defending your freedom against power-hungry organized criminals who will be deterred by nothing less than competitive combat capabilities. This means if their 'police' (amoral, masked mercenaries) are capable of attacking the People with automatic weapons, tanks, or explosive devices, the People must be able to defend themselves with similar armament. This is not extremism, it is simply good sense. Moreover, a domestic peace keeping force does not employ such ordinance against citizens, only an illegal occupying army does.

As usual, propaganda and mischaracterization are the weapons of choice in this concerted assault on our ability to resist tyranny.

To those targeted for manipulation by the Democrat contingent of the junta, the opponents are portrayed as uncouth, uneducated, ignorant, violent, racist troglodytes who long for the days of frontier justice and shootouts at the OK Corral. As an example, recall Episode #38 of *All in the Family,* in which Archie Bunker espouses his theories about gun control in a television editorial:

"...Now I wanna talk about another thing that's on everybody's mind today, and that your stickups and your skyjackings, which, uhh, if that was up to me, I could end the skyjackings tomorrow. All ya gotta do is arm all your passengers. Your skyjacker, he knows all the passengers are armed, and he ain't got no superiorarity[sic] there, and he ain't gonna dare to pull out no rod. And then your airlines, they wouldn't have to search the passengers on the ground no more, they just pass out the pistols at the beginning of the trip, and they just pick them up at the end! Case closed."

Who in their right minds *wouldn't* be concerned about such armed idiots?

On the 'other side of the aisle', the Republican division of this duplicitous junta promote their own grotesque distortions, portraying all liberals as naive idealists at best, and devious communist infiltrators at worst. Small wonder folks react with "…from my cold, dead fingers…!"

Obviously, there are *some* individuals who fit these extreme stereotypes. Sarah Brady, Chairperson of Handgun Control, Inc., stated explicitly that their task "can only succeed when those who would resist us have been totally disarmed." Conversely, the people who decided to blow up the Alfred P. Murrah Federal Building in downtown Oklahoma City in on April 19, 1995, regardless of their objectives, or moral outrage at whatever motivated their actions, demonstrated a lack of judgment that cannot be disputed, no matter what your political orientation. However, I have known gun-owning Conservatives all of my life, and to my knowledge, *none* has ever shot another human being, other than those ordered to do so as soldiers. Conversely, I have known, and do know, a great number of political Liberals, and many of them are gun owners, and staunch supporters of the Second Amendment. We need to step back and ask ourselves whether we are being led by people of integrity with real, honest concerns, or being manipulated by sinister forces whose primary aim is to prevent the American people from recognize their many commonalities, shared threats, and mutual enemies.

The message to honest people of integrity on both the right and the left is simply this: if you want the 'other side' to stop heeding the blatant propaganda, and stop judging *you* by inaccurate stereotypes, you must be ready to suspend your credulity and suspicion and offer *them* the same benefit of the doubt. Maybe your original suspicions *will* be confirmed; perhaps they will be repudiated—in either case, you'll have the certainty that you made up your *own* mind, rather than allowing yourself to be brainwashed and manipulated by groups whose agendas both sides *know* to be suspect.

The Crossroads of Freedom and Servitude

Liberty is the freedom of every individual to make full use of his or her faculties, so long as doing so does not harm other persons in their pursuit of that same self-expression. Liberty is free choice, coupled with acceptance of responsibility for one's actions. Liberty requires the utter and complete destruction of *all* despotism. Liberty requires restricting the law to its only legitimate sphere: organizing the right of individual self-defense, and punishing violations against persons and property. Liberty has been thwarted throughout history by an elite who desire to set themselves above their brothers and sisters in order to arrange, organize, and regulate the lives of others in accordance with their own ideas, agendas, and ambitions. Even the most benevolent rulers still embody the arrogant desire to rule. A prerequisite to ruling is the destruction of liberty.

In essence, anyone who aspires to be a *career politician* is, by the very fact, unfit to serve.

What should we do when the Rule of Law is suspended by those charged with its safekeeping? What *must* be done when the people who exercise power over our lives do not play by rules based on respect for liberty and property? Isolated cases of such abrogation of the Rule of Law can be addressed more simply than when it permeates society and government as a whole. The solutions, however, as well as the moral justification for invoking them, are basically identical. Indeed, similar situations have occurred several times in our nation's history, and provide precedents for how citizens must respond.

The Vigilance Committees

While vigilantism is rightly regarded with prudent apprehension, it is *not* synonymous with vicious lynchings, mob rule, and denial of due process, as it is often portrayed by those who fear any challenge to their pseudo-legal hegemony. When all legal avenues have been subverted by an unjust power, true justice can only be recovered through a *responsible* implementation of locally established authority.

For example, Montana in the 1860s was heavily influenced by the quest for gold; however, it was by no means the lawless frontier portrayed in fictional accounts of the era. The vast majority of people in that time and place had both knowledge of, and respect for, the Rule of Law, and for its necessity in protecting their lives and property. In the Bannack and Virginia City vicinity, however, something went seriously amiss with the legal system. Indeed, a situation analogous to what we see today in our nation as a whole had emerged:

The law had been subverted into an instrument of plunder. Both law enforcement and the judiciary had been infiltrated by greedy, self-serving individuals, contemptuous of the Rule of Law, individual liberty, and private property. The system, in other words, had been taken over by those whose only objective was despoilment. The law had been subverted into an instrument of injustice, with the governing authorities using the power delegated to them by the people for the sole purpose of pillaging people's property, rather than protecting it. The very lives and futures of every citizen were at stake.

At that juncture, the power previously assigned to the government reverted back to the People of the Montana Territory, who formed *vigilance committees* for their own defense. This demonstrates a fundamental tenet of self government: when the Rule of Law is abrogated, the authority previously delegated to government automatically reverts back to the people. At that point, those who have conspired to apply discretionary rule for the purpose of depredation become no more than any other invading force; entitled to the same consideration and treatment as a personal attacker, members of a foreign invading army, or unlawful combatants. In Montana, that is precisely the consideration and treatment the usurpers of the law received.

The freedom fighters took action, invoking their fundamental right to protect their lives and property. Once it was established that the Rule of Law had been abrogated by those who purported to act under color of law, the course of action justified by the circumstances was clear. Swift retribution is, and always has been, the only remedy with respect to blatant tyranny.

The citizens formed a tribunal, pledging to render impartial justice to friend and foe, without regard to personal prejudices. They deliberated to ascertain the nature and severity of the crime, and united to repress disorder, punish the crimes, and prevent their society from collapsing into the throes of anarchy or despotism. It was soon widely known that the People had spoken, and had proclaimed that organized plunder under color law would not be tolerated.

Although twenty-one of the worst criminal politicians were executed, it is important to note that Judge Smith and J. Thurmond, the judge and lawyer who assisted the brigands in using the law as an instrument of their plunder, were merely banished. Hence, this was clearly *not* some violent frontier lynching, as some have portrayed it, but rather, an application of self-government in its purest and most appropriate form.

Nor were the freedom fighters of Montana the first group in our history to assert their natural rights and authority in order to protect their lives, liberty, and property. Much earlier in our nation's history, similar groups in communities throughout New England and the Atlantic states, known as the *Committees of Safety,* joined forces to consider charges against agents of Great Britain, and ultimately formed an authority authorized to call the colonial militias into action.

The Vigilance Committees of Montana and the Committees of Safety in pre-revolutionary America took enormous risks and shouldered grave responsibilities in order to stand up for their basic human rights. They must certainly have had to ask themselves some difficult questions before asserting their rights for the purposes of freedom and self-preservation.

There was another time in our history, other than the first (successful) American revolution when the People realized that the ruling government had become of force of oppression and domination.

While the sanitizers and rewriters of history have gone to enormous lengths to portray the second American revolution, also known as the Civil War, as a battle to end the dastardly injustice of slavery, this is an historically inaccurate and deliberately deceitful portrayal. Indeed, while moral individuals in both the North and the South had long decried the evil of this inhumane institution, no overt efforts, or even threats, had been made by the government to eliminate it.

The specific grievances that motivated secession are complex, and clearly beyond the scope of the current treatise, but essentially, the Southern States rebelled against the usurpation of their rights under the Constitution as sovereign states. It's critical to remember that, until that time, the United States had been a *voluntary* confederation of independent states, rather than the mandatory monolith, maintained by force of arms that it has since become. Ever since, our federal government has acted swiftly to crush any movement aimed at increasing the rights of the people and their States, or limiting federal control. Indeed, the status of the States more closely resembles the coerced 'participants' in the former Soviet Union, held together solely by threats of force, and eager to assert their independence as soon as that central authority began to crumble under its own ponderous weight, than the decoupled, largely autonomous units described by the Constitution and intended by its authors.

Today, anyone who seriously challenges federal hegemony is threatened, suppressed, driven into poverty, or imprisoned, often without anything resembling due process. If they persist, our federal government has repeatedly demonstrated that it will not hesitate to use its tactical 'police' forces to murder its opponents. Although the government euphemistically refers to these forces as 'law enforcement' personnel, by any honest, impartial appraisal, they are in fact a well-equipped standing army used to exterminate U.S. citizens who threaten federal hegemony. Everyone has seen them, heard of their tactics, and knows of the results of their assaults. Dressed like Gestapo, in black uniforms, faces masked like the criminals they are, they descend upon and eradicate any opposition to the ruling junta. These are manifestly *not* dedicated protectors of the public, whose objective is to 'serve and protect'. They are a mercenary force, compensated with cash, unanswerable power, and often the spoils of their engagements in the form of cash and drugs, who could give less than a rat's ass where their orders originate, or whether they are legal, moral, or justified. These are people who would just as happily confiscate a Japanese American's property and send them to a concentration camp, round up Jews and herd them into cattle cars for extermination, or rape and torture anyone identified by their tyrannical masters. Mere hints of their true nature and agendas escaped their generally successful cover-ups in the form of events like Waco Texas, Ruby Ridge, and a handful of others; but we can be certain that what has come to light is merely the tip of a far more insidious iceberg. Here are just a few representative examples:

On May 13, 1985, supposedly responding to complaints by neighbors about unsanitary conditions, police attacked a primarily black back-to-nature group known at *Move*. Though aware that the building housed many women and children, the police lobbed tear gas canisters at the building, fired 10,000 rounds of live ammunition at the house in two hours, and finally, a police helicopter dropped a four-pound bomb made of C-4 plastic explosive and Tovex, a dynamite substitute, onto the roof of the house without any prior warning.

Figure 1: Police tactics against American citizens?

The resulting explosion caused the house to catch fire, igniting a massive blaze which eventually destroyed 65 houses. Eleven people—six adults and five children—were killed. Hundreds were left homeless. The firefighters were prevented by police from putting out the fire, based on allegations that firefighters were being shot at; a claim that was later proven false.

Figure 2: Rubble is all that remains after the Move bombing.

Mayor W. Wilson Goode was compelled to appoint an investigative commission called the PSIC or MOVE commission. It issued its report on March 6, 1986, denouncing the actions of the city government, and stating that: "Dropping a bomb on an occupied row house was unconscionable."

Figure 3: Bodies being removed from the rubble of the Move bombing.

Of course, nobody from the government or the police force was charged criminally. In a 1996 civil suit in US federal court, a jury ordered the City of Philadelphia to pay $1.5 million to a survivor and relatives of two people killed in the incident. The jury found that the city used excessive force and violated the victims' Constitutional protection against unreasonable search and seizure. Philadelphia was given the sobriquet "The City that Bombed Itself."

Oh, but they were *black radicals….*

Then there was the debacle at Ruby Ridge: Randy Weaver, a former Green Beret, was the victim of a federal entrapment scheme intended to recruit him as an informant against a white separatist group, with which it was subsequently revealed he had no connection. The government purported that he sold two shotguns with shorter-than-legal barrel lengths to an undercover informant, who later admitted he was "just in it for the excitement." (Weaver maintained that the shotguns were legal when sold, and had been subsequently shortened by the buyer.) Based on erroneous and falsified evidence, several hundred heavily-armed federal agents surrounded the Idaho cabin where he lived with his Wife, Vicki, 14-year old Son, Sammy, daughters Sara (16), Rachel (10), and Elisheba (10 months), and friend Kevin Harris. The government agents operated under Rules of Engagement (ROE) that essentially amounted to "shoot to kill," and this was precisely what they did.

Figure 4: Staging area prior to the assault on Randy Weaver's family.

Figure 5: 14-year old Sammy was shot in the back and killed.

Figure 6: Wife Vickie was shot in the face by a government sniper.

Randy's wife Vickie was shot in the face by a government sniper from a distance of 200 yards as she stood on their porch, holding their infant daughter in her arms, before the eyes of her husband and other two daughters. Randy's 14-year-old son (who *was* armed) was *shot in the back* as he tried to flee their attackers. Randy Weaver and Kevin Harris were both severely wounded. Weaver was ultimately acquitted of all charges except missing his original court date and violating his bail conditions. Charges against the federal agents, including manslaughter, were summarily dismissed. Weaver and his surviving children were 'compensated' in the amount of $3,100,000.00.

Oh, but *he* was a white separatist gun nut!

'White separatist', 'gun nut', 'drug kingpin', 'cultist'—these are common government labels used to justify abrogation of Constitutional rights and even the murder of United States citizens. Calling a religion a "cult" and putting out false information across the media about "child molesting" and "weapons caches" is exactly the same technique that was used by the Nazis to portray the Jews as filthy, disgusting people, so they could be rounded up and killed without further justification. It is the same technique used by every tyrannical government, to kill any unpopular and potentially vocal adversarial group.

On September 29, 2011, Anwar al-Awlaki, an American citizen purported to be the "mastermind" behind various "terrorist" events was summarily executed by a CIA-directed remote-control drone. Awlaki, an American citizen, had been convicted of no crime, either in the U.S. or any other country. The only direct evidence against him consisted of emails and web postings in which he talked about the religious justification for attacks against an enemy of his religion. Even IF we had direct evidence that he had actually flown one of the aircraft into the World Trade Center, and somehow, miraculously, survived, there is no individual or agency in the United States authorized by the Constitution to execute an American Citizen without due process. If our forces are capable of finding him, and incinerating him from afar, then they must certainly be capable of capturing him and giving him the trial to which he is entitled by law. While it is tempting to dismiss the case because *we have been told* that he's a very bad man, I'm inclined to ask how many Americans actually KNEW him? How many actually READ the alleged rhetoric that was SO inflammatory as justify his murder? How many would be willing to bet their lives that he wasn't merely another individual that this illegal government found it convenient to eliminate? Once we open this Pandora's Box, what is to prevent the government from doing the same thing to someone ELSE they don't like, and then mounting a smear campaign to justify their action? Maybe that person is a Neo-Nazi, or a Klansman, or maybe he's a so-called 'eco-terrorist' who has torched a few SUVs, or rescued some animals from an experimental facility. Maybe it's a peaceful but outspoken critic of Obama, or Clinton, or Bush, or Reagan. Does it matter? Will you ever be able to tell the difference? Maybe . . . it will be . . . YOU!

Connecting a person with an unpopular movement, or attaching to them an emotionally charged label; or calling a religion a "cult" and putting out false information across the media about "child molesting" and "weapons caches" is exactly the same technique that was used by the Nazis to portray the Jews as filthy, disgusting people, so they could be rounded up and killed without further justification. It is the same technique used by every tyrannical government, to kill any unpopular and potentially vocal adversarial person or group.

For example, on February 28, 1993, the federal government commenced a 50-day siege on the Branch Davidian ranch at Mount Carmel, a property located 9 miles east-northeast of Waco, Texas. The purported justification was a barely coherent hodgepodge of unsubstantiated accusations of cult activities, gun violations, and sexual abuse of children; all of which were subsequently proven baseless. Indeed, what was portrayed as a Jonestown-style cult, the Branch Davidians, trace their origins back to a 1930 schism from the Seventh-day Adventist Church. Many of the members of the group at the Waco facility had been involved with the Davidians for several generations, and many had large families.

The Davidian members were well known locally and had cordial relations with other locals. Neighbors who had known the Branch Davidians for fifteen years or more described them as "good Samaritan" types, who helped their neighbors and were kind and friendly. Normal people, good neighbors. Certainly the kind of folks you'd rather have living around you than murdering thugs, or gang-members engaging in ruthless drive-by shootings. Ask yourself which are more similar to the government's subsequent actions.

In a January 5, 1992 interview by Martin King of Australian TV show *A Current Affair,* King asked the group's leader, David Koresh: "Would you use a gun if someone trespassed?" Koresh replied: "They come in here with a gun and they start shooting at us, what would *you* do?"

This exchange apparently promulgated the Bureau of Alcohol, Tobacco, and Firearms (BATF) to obtain a warrant to search the premises for illegal weapons. According to the Affidavit presented by BATF investigator David Aguilera to US Magistrate Dennis G. Green on February 25, 1993, the Branch Davidians had purchased many *legal* guns and gun parts from various *legal* vendors. Deliveries by UPS of *legally purchased* firearms and parts had been accepted and paid for at Mount Carmel Center by Woodrow Kendrick, Paul Fatta, David Koresh or Steve Schneider. These purchases were traced by Aguilera through the normal channels used to track *legal* firearms purchases from *legal* vendors. None of the weapons and firearms were illegally obtained nor illegally owned by the Davidians; however, Aguilera affirmed to the judge that in his experience, in the past, *other* purchasers of such *legal* gun parts had modified them to make illegal firearms. The search warrant was justified not on the basis there was *proof* that the Davidians had done anything illegal, but on the basis that they *might* be modifying legal arms into illegal arms.

Could? Might? Others? Was this adequate justification for a massacre of innocent men, women, and children? In retrospect, we can only conclude that, according to the Clinton Administration, the answer was 'yes'.

The BATF also alleged reports of automatic weapon fire, but when confronted with this accusation, residents Steve Schneider and David Koresh showed the county sheriff department a "Hellfire" device—a quick-firing trigger sold with a BATF letter *certifying* that the device was *not* a machinegun, and was, in fact, completely legal.

The Davidians, like many other law-abiding American citizens, partly supported themselves by trading at gun shows and took care always to have the relevant paperwork to ensure their transactions were completely *legal*.1 Davidian Paul Fatta was a *licensed federal firearms dealer* (FFL) and the Davidians operated a *legal* retail gun business called *The Mag Bag*.

[insert as footnote: Contrast this with the ATF's Operation Fast and Furious, in which government agents coerced gun dealers to illegally sell guns to Mexican drug cartel members, purportedly in order to trace their flow. Many of the guns, of which they promptly lost track, were subsequently used to murder civilians, and even American border police.]

On July 30, 1992, BATF agents David Aguilera and Jim Skinner visited the Davidians' gun dealer Henry McMahon, who tried to get them to talk with Koresh on the phone. Koresh offered to let the BATF inspect the Davidians' weapons and paperwork, and asked to speak with Aguilera. Aguilera declined to speak with him. Sheriff Harwell told reporters he had urged law enforcement officials to talk with Koresh, "Just go out and talk to them, what's wrong with notifying them?"

The BATF, however, had already decided on a more confrontational course of action. Between February 25 through 27, BATF agents sought and obtained training for the raid from Special Forces instructors at Fort Hood, Texas, by making a false claim that David Koresh was operating a methamphetamine lab. This provided the drug nexus necessary to obtain military assets under the "War on Drugs".

These facts alone suggest that those at the Waco facility had good reason for paranoia.

Contrary to BATF claims that Koresh could not be captured outside the compound because he had been holed up for weeks, multiple witnesses confirm he was in town as recently as four days before the assault. Witnesses included a store owner providing receipts containing Koresh's signature, a doctor who had treated him for back pain and a bar manager who saw him eating lunch and having a beer.

Like many Sundays at Mt. Carmel, morning prayers on February 28, 1993 were followed by breakfast. Victoria Hollingsworth had been cleaning up when asked to go to the room where they met for Bible study and worship. She waited there with the other women and many of the children until David Koresh came in. There was silence. He said, "They're coming. Get back to your rooms and watch. Don't do anything stupid. We can work this out."

The BATF attempted to execute their search warrant on that Sunday morning. Any advantage of surprise was lost as a reporter, who had been tipped off about the raid, asked for directions from a U.S. Postal Service mail carrier who was coincidentally Koresh's brother-in-law. Koresh then told BATF agent Robert Rodriguez, who had infiltrated the Branch Davidians (to his astonishment, as he was not aware that his cover had been blown), they knew a raid was imminent. The agent made an excuse and left the compound. When asked later what the Davidians had been doing when he left the compound, Rodriguez replied, "They were praying."

Figure 7: UH-1 HUEY Gunship - Standard 'police' issue?

Figure 8: Detail of UH-1 HUEY Gunship armament. - just the thing for women and children.

Three army Huey gunship attack helicopters were purportedly used as aerial distraction, but recent disclosures by witnesses report that they "came in with machine guns blazing, strafing the buildings as if they were attacking some Viet Nam village."

On the third floor, 75-year-old Margaret Lawson and 77-year-old Catherine Matteson gathered children in a schoolroom to get them away from the gunfire and bombs going off below. Suddenly the ceiling erupted with a burst of machinegun fire from the helicopter gunships. The elderly women shielded the children with their own bodies. Miraculously, none of the machinegun fire struck anyone in the crowded room. Elsewhere, the machinegun fire killed Peter Gent, Peter Hipsman as he lay in bed, and Winston Blake as he sat on the edge of his bed, eating French toast.

When the two old ladies managed to escape the compound with the children, they were arrested, charged with murder and thrown in jail.

Now pause for a moment and contemplate just what kind of 'police officer' would interpret his oath to uphold the constitution, or his duty to "protect and serve" to include indiscriminate heavy machine gun fire into a building full of women, children, elderly people . . . ? What would be his justification if (as is almost never the case) he was brought before any legitimate legal tribunal? Was he 'only following orders'? Was this not the same excuse offered by many Nazi prison guards . . . guards who were subsequently convicted and hanged? Have we become *so* calloused to violence against our fellow citizens that we are prepared to accept the word of a government we *know* to be deceitful that these citizens *deserved* to be summarily executed? Are we more inclined to give the benefit of the doubt to lying, jack-booted thugs than innocent women and children?

During this siege, four BATF agents were killed. Although it is not known with certainty who fired the first shots, early information suggested there might have been an accidental discharge of a weapon, possibly by a BATF agent, causing the BATF to respond with fire from automatic weapons. Other reports claim the first shots were fired by the BATF "dog team" sent to neutralize (kill) the dogs in the Davidian kennel. A recent videotape by Linda Thompson entitled *Waco, the Big Lie*, purports to prove that those BATF agents were not killed or shot at by Branch Davidians, but rather, shows the agents going into the compound through an upstairs window. It then shows another BATF agent, positioned on a roof, actually shooting in through the window where the other agents had just entered. Thus, it appears pretty certain that the four BATF agents were killed by 'friendly fire'.

Figure 9: BATF agents entering the Branch Davidian building (despite official claims that no such entry had been attempted). Why are we inclined to take the word of proven liars over that of innocent victims?

While not standard procedure, BATF agents had their blood type written on their arms or neck after leaving the staging area and before the raid because it was recommended by the military to facilitate speedy blood transfusions in the case of injury. Clearly, the government was *planning* an armed conflict.

During the first shots, Koresh was wounded.

David Thibodeau, a Waco survivor, was interviewed on *A Current Affair*, a national television show, on May 3rd, 1993. He declared that one of the members of the Branch Davidians, Wayne Martin, a Harvard-trained attorney, called 911 shortly after the federal agents stormed the compound. He was put through to another agency, and the person said, "Well, hi boys, how y'all doin' out there?"

Wayne Martin pleaded for them to stop shooting, screaming into the phone, "We're getting shot at. We're getting killed. Here they come again!" and "That's them shooting, that's not us!"

Since all 911 calls are preserved, it should be easy to confirm this phone call, but as *Current Affair* reporter Mary Garafolo stated, "It has become a controversial recording that the police *refuse to release* to the press." There was absolutely no response to that emergency 911 call. Does withholding this recording sound more like a matter of national security, or a simple cover-up?

Following the BATF's failed initial attack, the FBI settled in for a lengthy siege. During the standoff, government propaganda was released to the press asserting that: "[Koresh is] your stock cult leader…. They're all the same. Meet one and you've met them all. They're deeply disturbed, have a borderline personality disorder and lack any type of conscience…. No one willingly enters into a relationship like this…. So you're talking about deception and manipulation (by the leader), people being coached in ever so slight increments, pulled in deeper and deeper without knowing where it's going or seeing the total picture."

Around the 40th day of the siege, the wounded Koresh sent a message that the children and babies were out of milk. Two relief efforts to bring baby food to the Mt Carmel compound were turned back. Two people, one of them Gary Spaulding from South Bend, Indiana, were arrested for trying to take the food past a roadblock. When he posed the direct question to the FBI headquarters, "Has it come to this? Does the United States government want babies to starve to death?" The answer was, verbatim: "Yes."

The FBI hinted that the Davidians might commit mass suicide, as had happened at Jonestown (where 918 people killed themselves at their leader's behest), although there was no evidence of any such intent or preparations. U.S. Attorney General Janet Reno approved recommendations by the FBI to mount an assault after purportedly being told that conditions were deteriorating and that children were being abused inside the compound. Over the next several months, however, Reno repeatedly changed her story as to the reason for approving the final tank-and-gas attack. Whereas she initially alleged that the FBI had told her that Koresh was sexually abusing children and beating babies (the FBI later denied evidence of child abuse during the standoff), she later claimed that Linda Thompson and her one-woman "Unorganized Militia of the United States" was on their (her) way to Waco to aid or attack Koresh. Ultimately, when President Clinton suggested continued patience, Reno countered that the FBI was tired of waiting; that the standoff was costing a million dollars a week; and that the Davidians could hold out longer than she was willing to wait. Clinton later recalled: "Finally, I told her that if she thought it was the right thing to do, she could go ahead."

The siege ended 50 days after it began, with agents attacking with tanks and setting the compound ablaze. Seventy-six people died in the fire, including more than 20 children, two pregnant women, and the sect leader David Koresh. Janet Reno's 'concern for the wellbeing of the children'? See for yourself:

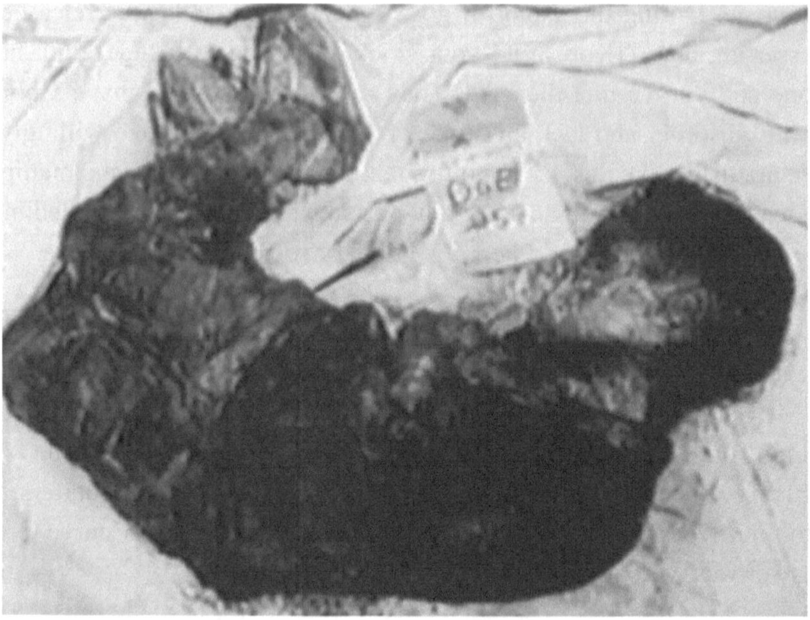

Figure 10: Burnt body of child after Waco attack.

Figure 11: Remains of victim after Waco attack.

Figure 12: Children killed by government forces at Waco.

In the subsequent investigations, government reports were revealed to contain numerous distortions and outright lies. In August, 1999, documents were uncovered which indicated that during the raid on the Branch Davidian compound, the FBI employed flammable tear gas canisters. This revelation contradicted previous assertions of the FBI and the Department of Justice that the government had done nothing that could have contributed to the start or spread of the fire.

Figure 13: Conflagration caused by government forces at Branch Davidian compound

Contrary to BATF's stated concern for the children and women, agents fired wildly into the building, often being seen on videotape crouching behind cover, holding machine guns over their heads and 'spraying' the building with bullets.

Since it's often those on the political right who are most inclined to accept the official government accounts, it's only fair to ask: did THESE children not have some right to life? Are the accounts of THESE particular Christians to be summarily discounted, in favor of the words of a government, and an administration, that you already distrust? An administration led by a man who was subsequently impeached for lying under oath? Are you more inclined to believe the words of armed thugs who don't dare show their faces, who think nothing of firing machine guns into buildings full of civilians? Finally, are you willing to take this abhorrent stance simply because some of your fellow citizens (the 'liberals'), with whom you happen to disagree on other issues, might feel this represents an atrocity of the first order?

Figure 14: US Army Tanks deployed against citizens at Waco: "We're from the government; we're here to help...." Which part of Posse Comitatus do you suppose was ambiguous?

A new documentary contends that federal agents used an explosive device to blast a gaping hole in a bunker holding women and children. The two-hour film also asserts that government agents fired bullets at the *rear* of Mount Carmel building as it burned on the last day of the siege, in order to prevent escape. The intent was clearly to ensure that there would be no evidence and no witnesses.

Indeed, taking only what the government has *admitted* to having done—the spraying of CS gas into the compound at the women and small children—U.S. Congressman Ron Paul reminds all Americans that: "CS gas is banned under the Paris Convention on chemical warfare. The U.S. could not use it in war. It is illegal, but they would use it against their own citizens."— The Washington Times, April 23,1993.

Figure 15:The Posse Comitatus Act is a United States federal law (18 U.S.C. § 1385) passed on June 18,1878. The Act prohibits Army and Air Force personnel and units of the National Guard under federal authority from acting in a law enforcement capacity within the United States,except where expressly authorized by the Constitution or Congress. "Posse Comitatus? We don't need no steenking Posse Comitatus!"

Well, those were crazy armed cultists, so it's *okay* to attack them with tanks and helicopter gunships!

One can only wonder, what next? Nerve gas? Biological weapons? A tactical nuke? Think what you want about the group or their principles, but dropping bombs on American citizens, on American soil? Is this the action of a police force, or a standing mercenary army, bent on murdering opponents of the ruling junta?

Victims of Waco Attack

1. Katherine Andrade, 24, American
2. Chanel Andrade, 1, American
3. Jennifer Andrade, 19, American
4. George Bennett, 35, British
5. Susan Benta, 31, British
6. Mary Jean Borst, 49, American
7. Pablo Cohen, 38, Israeli
8. Abedowalo Davies, 30, British
9. Shari Doyle, 18, American
10. Beverly Elliot, 30, British
11. Yvette Fagan, 32, British
12. Doris Fagan, 51, British
13. Lisa Marie Farris, 24, American
14. Raymond Friesen, 76, Canadian
15. Sandra Hardial, 27, British
16. Zilla Henry, 55, British
17. Vanessa Henry, 19, British
18. Phillip Henry, 22, British
19. Paulina Henry, 24, British
20. Stephen Henry, 26, British
21. Diana Henry, 28, British
22. Novellette Hipsman, 36, Canadian
23. Floyd Houtman, 61, American
24. Sherri Jewell, 43, American
25. David M. Jones, 38, American
26. David Koresh, 33, American
27. Rachel Koresh, 24, American
28. Cyrus Koresh, 8, American
29. Star Koresh, 6, American
30. Bobbie Lane Koresh, 2, American
31. Jeffery Little, 32, American
32. Nicole Gent Little, 24, Australian, pregnant
33. Dayland Gent, 3, American
34. Page Gent, 1, American
35. Livingston Malcolm, 26, British
36. Diane Martin, 41, British
37. Wayne Martin, Sr., 42, American
38. Lisa Martin, 13, American
39. Sheila Martin, Jr., 15, American
40. Anita Martin, 18, American
41. Wayne Martin, Jr., 20, American
42. Julliete Martinez, 30, American
43. Crystal Martinez, 3, American
44. Isaiah Martinez, 4, American
45. Joseph Martinez, 8, American
46. Abigail Martinez, 11, American
47. Audrey Martinez, 13, American
48. John-Mark McBean, 27, British
49. Bernadette Monbelly, 31, British
50. Rosemary Morrison, 29, British
51. Melissa Morrison, 6, British
52. Sonia Murray, 29, American
53. Theresa Nobrega, 48, British
54. James Riddle, 32, American
55. Rebecca Saipaia, 24, Filipino
56. Steve Schneider, 43, American
57. Judy Schneider, 41, American
58. Mayanah Schneider, 2, American
59. Clifford Sellors, 33, British
60. Scott Kojiro Sonobe, 35, American
61. Floracita Sonobe, 34, Filipino
62. Gregory Summers, 28, American
63. Aisha Gyrfas Summers, 17, Australian, pregnant
64. Startle Summers, 1, American
65. Lorraine Sylvia, 40, American
66. Rachel Sylvia, 12, American
67. Hollywood Sylvia, 1, American
68. Michelle Jones Thibodeau, 18, American
69. Serenity Jones, 4, American
70. Chica Jones, 2, American
71. Little One Jones, 2, American
72. Neal Vaega, 38, New Zealander
73. Margarida Vaega, 47, New Zealander
74. Mark H. Wendell, 40, Americ

Very often, an event can be better understood by the events that transpire after it. Who benefits? Was any controversial legislation passed or proposed that would destroy Constitutional liberty?

Two weeks after the massacre at Mount Carmel, John Chafee, a senator from Rhode Island, called for a new law that would institute a nationwide ban on hand gun ownership. It would prohibit the sale, possession, importing, and exporting of hand guns. Had Chafee's proposal become law, it would have torn a huge gap in the 2nd Amendment of the U.S. Constitution, which says, "...the right of the people to keep and bear arms, shall not be infringed."

Who wants to disarm citizens?

Well, clearly, it's difficult to be the dictator of a nation with 200 million guns around. Every man in Switzerland is *required* to have guns in his home, including assault rifles. Crime in Switzerland is almost non-existent. During World War Two, Hitler wanted to invade Switzerland. The Swiss told him that he could send his army across the border, but none of his officers would return. Hitler gave the order to invade Switzerland several times, but his officers simply would not obey. Switzerland remained safely neutral throughout the war.

One final piece of this insidious puzzle:

On 5/17/2011, the Supreme Court decided that the armed enforcers of the Republicrat Junta didn't have enough latitude when it comes to violating citizens' Constitutional protection against unreasonable search and seizure. In an 8-1 Ruling, they decreed that police no longer need a warant to kick in a door if they "suspect evidence is being destroyed."

When you open the door for the kinds of abuses we've just examined, that door is not only open for those whom you *don't* like; it's open for *everyone*.

- Move: Black Radicals
- Ruby Ridge: White Separatists
- Waco: Christian Cultists
- Japanese interment: Asian Citizens
-

Of course, the ruling junta *always* has a good reason—unsanitary conditions, a 'child abuse' cult, renegade Indians, people who *look like* our enemies.... The end result is the same: If we allow them to do so, they will use the same kind of force against anyone they please. In every case, the propaganda is identical: Americans are brainwashed into believing that these actions are justified because the victims...aren't like them.... Make no mistake: unless you are the kind of complacent, compliant, docile, brain-dead worker drone they want (or a rich elite), the time will come when they come for you, but by then it will be too late.

Figure 16: Japanese internment camp.

Figure 17: Japanese-American *citizens* being rounded up by US Troops. (It's okay, though. They were only :"following orders.")

The Difficult Decisions Before Us

We, as a nation and as a people, stand poised at a juncture not unlike that faced by our heroic and venerated predecessors. Like our Founding Fathers, we are faced with difficult questions, whose answers will determine the moral justification for any course of action we must, of necessity, undertake.

Are *We, the People of the United States,* being governed in accordance with the principles of the U.S. Constitution? If not, did *We, the People* knowingly and willingly surrender constitutional self government to an unanswerable, all-powerful ruling junta? If we are no longer governed under a Constitution, *and* we never willingly surrendered our right to a duly constituted government, what rules should govern our actions in restoring constitutional government to our land?

The answers to these questions are self-evident. *We, the People of the United States,* are no longer being governed in accordance with the principles of the U.S. Constitution. *We, the People,* never knowingly and willingly surrendered constitutional self government. The *rules* that govern our actions in restoring constitutional government to our land are precisely the same rules as prevailed when we declared our independence from the rule of Great Britain over two centuries ago.

As responsible, civilized individuals, we are morally obligated to petition our government for redress of our grievances, and to pursue every peaceful means to reinstitute our constitutional self government, before we resort to the legitimate exercise of our prerogative as a People to abolish this illegal junta and reestablish the constitutional government that is our right. However, if and when our repeated petitions are met with repeated injuries, we are obliged and justified in restoring constitutional government by *whatever means are necessary.*

This underscores a central tenet of self government: When the Rule of Law is abrogated, the authority to exercise force to protect fundamental rights reverts back to the People. At that point, those who persist in applying discretionary rule for the purpose of plunder become no more than an invading force, entitled to the same consideration as a personal attacker or an invading army. (Indeed, one might argue that, unlike an invading army, *these* usurpers are 'unlawful combatants', and are therefore not entitled to the normal humane treatment prescribed by the Geneva Conventions.) The only considerations remaining at that juncture are pragmatics and tactics.

Thus far, *all* lawful, peaceful means of righting the wrongs inflicted on our people have been ineffectual. Our petitions have been ignored. Appeals to our courts have been summarily dismissed on the most specious pretenses. Our elective processes have been subverted by corrupt influences of wealth and power. What are passed off as free and fair elections are little more than referendums on the lesser of two evils, so much so that the majority of eligible voters no longer even bother to exercise their elective franchise. The protection of our Constitution, and, moreover, of written law itself, has been laughed to scorn by traitors in black dresses who have the unmitigated audacity to bestow upon themselves the title of *Your Honor*.

The administration of retribution by self-constituted authority is, *in societies governed by the Rule of Law*, an affront to dignity, an outrage to due process, and an abomination on mankind. *In societies governed by the Rule of Law,* it is also wholly unnecessary. But, if our country *was* governed by the Rule of Law, would we repeatedly hear about nonviolent offenders being sent to prison for lengthy terms while corporate criminals, whose profit-driven abrogation of mandatory safety measures at mines and oil rigs, lead to the death of hundreds of innocent workers, are rewarded with tax incentives and preferential legislation? Would peaceful organizations be infiltrated, their telephones tapped, at the public's expense, solely because they have the temerity to question the government's iniquities? Would innocent citizens be susceptible to having the doors of their homes kicked in, their pets killed, and their families terrorized by BATF, DEA, and IRS thugs? Would so-called 'law enforcement' agencies murder men, women, and children with bombs, tanks, helicopter gunships and machine guns? If our society *was* governed by the Rule of Law, would its *de-facto* government engage in the systematic plunder of property accumulated through years of patient, honest toil, only to channel it to greedy cronies who already control 99% of this nation's wealth? In a society where the rule of Law exists, could genuine justice and morals be rendered powerless, and the law be subverted into an instrument of government plunder by the lawyers and judges who masquerade as its guardians?

I think not.

This ruling *Republicrat Junta*, while presenting itself as guardian of the law, is the sole force that has abolished that very Rule of Law; and as a result, the resort to self-constituted authorities to restore constitutional government, and to administer true justice, becomes our duty.

The *Republicrat Junta* has legalized theft. It has painted its murder of innocent men, women, and children by a military force acting against citizens in their own homes, as legitimate and necessary police actions. The formulation of self-constituted authorities for the protection of family and property is not only an option justified by our natural, inalienable right to life, liberty, and property, but our duty to ourselves, our neighbors, and our posterity.

Our nation was once the cornerstone of liberty. This was not the result of groveling before the British crown, or carrying endless petitions to indurate despots, although petition we did; until it was clear that our requests would continue to be ignored. Rather, it was the outcome when fearless brothers and sisters in arms took the necessary measures to protect their lives, liberty, and property, and establish the Rule of Law in their fledgling society.

- Is it legally and morally justifiable for citizens to form self-constituted authorities to restore the Rule of Law today?
- Is it legally and morally justifiable for citizens to punish traitors, murderers, and members of an invading force who have taken over their country and overthrown their laws when they catch them red-handed?
- Or must they wait for 'properly sanctioned enforcers of the law', when none exist?
- Must they be compelled to try the usurpers of our Constitution in courts owned and controlled by the criminals themselves, where the unjust results of sham proceedings are a foregone conclusion?
- Should those who have abolished our laws, stolen our property, and sanctioned the murder of our citizens be made to account for their actions?
- Or should they be permitted to bestow upon themselves unlimited immunity for their traitorous and deplorable acts?

The choice is ours, and it must be made soon

The injuries and disadvantages that we sustain by our continued tolerance of an illegitimate federal government are all too apparent, and too numerous to list. It is our duty to ourselves, our posterity, and to mankind as a whole to put an end to this pernicious criminal *Republicrat Junta*, whose continuation threatens to separate us truly, not into independent states, but into diverse special interest groups that are each manipulated into mutual suspicion, and induced to threaten the rights and liberties of the others, until none of us will retain the liberty to control our own lives. *The Republicrat Junta* fosters our division, not our unity, for in unity would we oppose their contumelies. *The Republicrat Junta* promotes our separation into fragmented ethnic, religious, and social groups, for well they know that *to divide is to conquer.* Their conquest is not yet complete, but their stranglehold grip grows tighter by the day.

Pragmatic Considerations

If and when we finally accept the reality that we are *not* being governed by a legitimate constitutional government, but ruled by a consortium of forces foreign to our Constitution, what then? The moral justification for abolishing a government inimical to our basic liberties is clear; but what about the practical implications of opposing a firmly entrenched, intransigent junta with virtually unlimited resources that is bent on reducing us to utter poverty and servitude within the time span of one or two generations?

Force of arms should always be the last resort to deal with such a threat. Have we yet arrived at that irrevocable juncture?

We have repeatedly petitioned our legislature and our courts. Our petitions are consistently ignored, and our efforts rebuked. We have repeatedly claimed our rights under our Constitution, and are laughed at in our courts by judges who have nothing but contempt for individual rights. Our representation in government is undermined by powerful corporate forces who line the pockets of politicians with *our own money.* So blatant has their utter contempt for the Rule of Law become, that they have granted the rights provided to *the People* by the Constitution to the corporations who all but own them, while simultaneously curtailing the rights of the People themselves! It would seem that the time for reconciliation, like a chimerical delusion, has dissipated into the wakefulness of harsh reality, with the *Republicrat Junta* having forced the choice upon us.

There may, however, yet be a ray of hope, albeit a dim one; but if we fail to take advantage of this slim window of opportunity, we will shortly be left only with the choice between slavery and armed conflict.

While there is still time, we *must* exercise what freedom we still have to vote *every* Democrat and *every* Republican out of our federal, state, and local governments.

Our secret power, which the *Republicrats*, and their complicit corporate-owned media have worked hard to suppress, is that we *do* have choices—*many* choices—and even the worst of them is far superior to the *Republicrat Junta* that has in every sense violated our Constitution, assaulted our freedoms, and raped due process in all aspects of our government.

Whether you are conservative or liberal, from the North or the South, a person of faith or a confirmed atheist, there *is* a party that will reflect your beliefs and your priorities in an honest and forthright manner; and there *will be* a candidate who will tell you what he or she actually believes, rather than what they believe you want to hear.

The *Republicrats*, with the help of their complicit corporate-owned media, have relentlessly worked to convince the American public that a vote for a third-party candidate is a wasted vote, and that such candidates are nothing but 'spoilers'.

In fact, precisely the opposite is true.

The *only* truly wasted vote is the one cast for either of the two deceitful, carefully packaged, hand groomed, corporate-owned candidates who will inevitably enact the same illegal policies. The specific lies and promises are different, but the end results are identical, and *we, the People*, are inevitably the losers.

I encourage every honest, thinking person to take a long, hard, honest look at the last fifty years or so, since, let's say, the administration of Eisenhower. Other than the window dressing, has there *really* been any difference between either component of the *Republicrat junta*?

Johnson, Democrat, deceived the American public about the events in the Gulf of Tonkin in order to justify a war that nobody wanted, and which ultimately cost hundreds of thousands of lives, decimated our economy, fractured our society, while enriching the corporate interests that profiteered from the war, and then funneled huge segments of their plunder to the politicians who made it all possible.

George W. Bush, Republican, deceived the American public about the connection between Iraq and the 9/11 attacks, and about the existence of WMDs, in order to justify a war that nobody wanted, and which ultimately cost hundreds of thousands of lives—both American and Iraqi—eroded our international reputation, and plunged our economy into debt; all the while enriching the corporate interests that profiteered from the war, and then funneled huge segments of their plunder to the politicians who made it all possible. Indeed, as Noam Chomsky so astutely observed: "Somebody's paying the corporations that destroyed Iraq and the corporations that are rebuilding it. They're getting paid by the American taxpayer in both cases. So we pay them to destroy the country, and then we pay them to rebuild it."

Then, of course, there was Richard Nixon and his partner in crime, Spiro Agnew, whose crimes were so overwhelming that they resulted in our nation being headed by a president who wasn't elected at all.

Is a pattern emerging here? What further evidence is needed?

Even our most beloved political figures, John F. Kennedy and Ronald Reagan, engaged in various illegal, immoral, and unjust acts that ultimately harmed the American People and served the interests of the ever more powerful corporate structures.

If any doubt whatsoever still remains, I invite every citizen, of any age, to try this one simple exercise:

Think back as far as your memory can go, and recall what life was like in your earliest recollections. Maybe that's the 1950s, perhaps the 1960s or even the 1990s, and ask yourself two questions:

1. Are things now better or worse for *me and my family* than they were then?
2. Has the progression been more or less linear, that is, have things gone progressively up– or down–hill, as opposed to our just going through a momentary negative blip?

The result of this exercise will prove beyond any question whether the *Republicrat Junta* has been working for your benefit, or to your detriment.

Of course, I could be wrong—it *has* happened from time to time. But if that's the case, what's the *worst* that could happen? The 'other' guy might get in for one election cycle. That, too, has happened before, regardless of what side you happen to be on, and if your memory is accurate, I am confident you will conclude that nothing actually changed, did it? You voted for George W. Bush—he bailed out greedy corporate interests and engaged in a costly war that decimated our economy. You voted for Obama? *He* bailed out greedy corporate interests and continued a costly war that continues to decimate our economy. Kennedy, Johnson, Nixon, Ford, Carter, Reagan, Bush I, Clinton, Bush II, Obama...have *your* circumstances followed an upward or a downward trend, regardless of *which* flavor or *Republicrat* has been in power?

There's a saying that the definition of stupidity is repeating the same mistakes over and over and expecting a different result every time.

How about we all try something *different* for a change? Let's throw these *Republicrat* scumbags out now, while we can still do it without bloodshed. What *we* fail to accomplish with ballots, our *children* will have to do with their blood.

Terrorists, Turbans, and Three-piece Suits

In early 2011, the centennial anniversary of the tragic Triangle Shirtwaist Factory fire was commemorated by extensive media coverage, much of it observing the numerous parallels between the plight of workers then and now. That March 25, 1911 blaze killed 146 workers. Exit doors had been locked because the owners, Harris and Blanck, feared theft, which, they later admitted, might have cost them fifteen or twenty dollars a year. As a result, escape was impossible, and many of the victims plunged to their deaths from the ninth– and tenth–floor windows rather than endure the slow, agonizing prospect of live incineration.

Louis Waldman, later a New York State assemblyman, witnessed the carnage, and described it as follows:

"Horrified and helpless, the crowds—I among them—looked up at the burning building, saw girl after girl appear at the reddened windows, pause for a terrified moment, and then leap to the pavement below, to land as mangled, bloody pulp. This went on for what seemed a ghastly eternity. Occasionally a girl who had hesitated too long was licked by pursuing flames and, screaming with clothing and hair ablaze, plunged like a living torch to the street. Life nets held by the firemen were torn by the impact of the falling bodies...."

One man was seen kissing a young woman at the window before they both jumped to their deaths. This poignant imagery invokes the more recent memories of people throwing themselves from the twin towers following the dastardly attack of 9/11/2001, as well it might.

The righteous indignation that resulted from the attack on the Trade Center has, indubitably, changed the entire world. Indeed, as evidenced by the recent murder of two elderly Sikh gentlemen, so vehement has our hatred and fear of 'the terrorists' grown that some Americans are willing to murder people for simply wearing the same kind of hat as our perceived enemies.

While these acts of violence against innocent strollers, cab drivers, and convenience store clerks are patently indefensible, our rage at the terrorists who inflicted such extensive death and destruction on our fellow citizens is understandable and proper. But what about those *other* terrorists? What *about* those greedy scumbags who locked their workers in that factory, and the myriad others of their ilk? What about the Massey Energy Company, British Petroleum, Union Carbide, and all the others whose myopic focus on profit, and attending indifference to human safety, have resulted in even greater loss of life and property (other than that of their investors, of course)?

Is it the sheer scale of the individual disasters that catch and maintain our attention; the 2,752 people who died in 2001, versus the 146 in 1911? Was the 1911 disaster 1/20th as horrifying as 9/11, based simply on the number of lives lost? Should we, perhaps, scale these numbers in terms of the populations then and now? The population of the United States was 93,863,000 in 1911, versus 281,421,906 as of the 2000 census, so, applying those corrections, 9/11 still remains 6.29 times worse than 1911. Does *that* make it feel better? Would it make a difference if 918 people had perished in the Triangle fire, or if Trade Center body count was reduced to one sixth?

Of course, such numeric comparisons make little sense, other than, perhaps, to those who would only find them convincing if we were to analyze the catastrophes in terms of their impact on rich white males, in which case, the Triangle fire can be dismissed as completely meaningless.

On that journey from window to pavement, each victim was totally alone—a tragedy of ***1***.

Although the World Trade Center attack captures our attention by virtue of the video images depicting the massive loss of life, industrial terrorism, in the form of outright disregard for human life in the quest for profit, has racked up equally appalling numbers. Triangle and many similar cases of callous indifference led to the formation of labor unions; their objective, to afford some measure of protection to those who couldn't afford to hire armed Pinkerton thugs to brutalize and murder the opposition.

In the U.S. alone, 10,000 deaths occur each year due to 'routine' industrial 'accidents'; another 100,000 deaths occur due to occupational disease; and 30,000 deaths and 20,000,000 serious injuries result from unsafe consumer products. (These numbers exclude an estimated 90 percent of cancers which may be environmentally induced.)

Triangle Shirtwaist, Bhopal, Massey's Upper Big Branch Mine disaster, BP's Deep Water Horizon, the Texas City Refinery explosion (also BP)...a cursory *Google* search on "Industrial Disasters" reveals that over the past century or so, well over a hundred thousand deaths, more than a million serious injuries, and incalculable financial losses,[1] have resulted from industrial incidents in which accepted safety practices were deliberately circumvented in order to maximize profits.

Certain occupations are inherently dangerous, and it must be assumed that those who engage in such activities tacitly accept the attendant risk; however, this in no way exempts those in charge from their obligation to ensure the safety of those whose risks beget the company's profits.

Even if we give the companies benefit of the doubt by assuming that they were only *ten percent* culpable, we're still looking at acts of *industrial corporate terrorism* twice as egregious as the much-touted WTC attack. Does it *really* make a difference to the victims whether the terrorists wear Bedouin robes and headgear, or Brooks Brothers suits and Rolex watches? Is it more reprehensible if *their* 'cause' is misguided vengeance rather than abject personal cupidity?

It seems pretty prophetic that now, a hundred years after the Triangle Shirtwaist Fire, the same nefarious degenerates are regrouping, and their primary targets are the workers, and the organizations that protect them; their cynical tactic: marketing blatant exploitation as the downtrodden's best interests.

In his excellent book *The Great Betrayal, How American Sovereignty and Social Justice Are Being Sacrificed to the Gods of the Global Economy,* Pat Buchanan begins with the following 1913 quote from Hilaire Belloc: We're not…approaching Socialism at all, but a very different state of society...in which Capitalist class shall be even more powerful and far more secure…a society in which the proletarian masses…shall change their status, lose their present legal freedom, and be subject to compulsory labor." In other words, *wage slavery*. And the really sad part is that workers everywhere are being deceived into supporting their own enslavement!

Exporting jobs overseas isn't *really* related to domestic job losses, they tell us. Mexicans picking lettuce are stealing American jobs, but greedy multinationals that outsource jobs aren't (and neither are illegal domestic servants working on the estates of the wealthy and powerful). The very rich growing richer, while the middle class struggles to survive, is the natural order of things, and will one day trickle down to everyone. Cutting public education, while the rich send *their* spoiled whelps to private schools, is *not* intended to perpetuate dynasties, and ensure that *they* remain overlords, while *your* children will always be asking:

"You want fries with that, Sir?"

Yeah, sure. And if you believe that, then the road to *Ebay* riches is simply a matter of sending your last $29.95 to the people running that late-night infomercial…*BUT WAIT! ORDER IN THE NEXT TEN MINUTES, AND WE'LL*

[1] While some relatively small negative impact may affect the investors whose interests *caused* the disasters, the brunt of the financial burden is passed on to the consumer-victims themselves.

ALSO SEND YOU THIS HANDY DANDY GUIDE TO GETTING RICH BUYING FORECLOSED PROPERTY WITH NO MONEY DOWN!

Does this model sound more to you like Capitalism, in which every person is capable of benefiting from the fruits of his or her savvy, hard work, and determination, or the establishment of a permanent, entrenched ruling class, in which those born into privilege have all the opportunity, and others are relegated to lives of servitude and deprivation?

Just how gullible do they think we *are*; and, how correct are we going to prove them to be? Do you believe in The Bible? How about Matthew 7:16?

" Ye shall know them by their fruits..."

Just tune down the sound and look at the pictures:

1961: An average household income was $6,691 (which translates to about $34k in today's dollars), with one partner working outside the home, and the other dedicating full time to managing the household, raising the children, and so forth. 38.8% of the breadwinners had achieved only an 11th grade education. The home ownership rate in the United States has remained relatively stable, having increased 5.6% since 1960 when 62.1% of American households owned their own home. However, homeowner *equity* has fallen steadily since World War II and is now less than 50% of the value of homes on average. In other words, in 1961, one could achieve this critical element of the 'American Dream' (home ownership) through hard work, with one partner working, and earning the equivalent of $34k/year. Parenthetically, I recall the year JFK was assassinated, 1963, overhearing my parents' talking about financial matters. My father, I discovered, had recently received a raise, and was earning $10,000/year, and they were considering the purchase of a brand new, 2500 square-foot, two-story home in a new subdivision for $25,000. Scaling as above, how many people today, earning, $50k/year can purchase a brand hew home for $125,000? Certainly not in any neighborhood where I would care to live!

Are things better for your family than for your parents'?

For whom ***are*** things better?

For many of us, the instinctive reaction is to look around at all our *stuff*—stuff our parents always said they couldn't afford—and answer: "Sure, I'm *way* better off than my parents." But look a bit closer. How much of that stuff do you really *own*? My parents had a 20-year mortgage on a home in Brooklyn, New York, which they bought for $26,000, circa 1967. (Thy sold that house in the early 1990s for about $150,000, and today it's probably worth about $3/4 Million.) If they had any other credit, it was with Sylvio, the grocer, My father drove a 1963 Ford Falcon, which he had bought brand new for $1,900, cash.

How much of an average American's income goes to paying off credit used to purchase items other than house and car? Indeed, how many of us have to use credit to buy essentials needed for simple survival?

Remember that old song *Sixteen Tons* (by Tennessee Ernie Ford), in which the beleaguered coal miner laments: "I owe my soul to the company store"?[1]

Is this not remarkably similar to the system under which most of us have come to live? You are encouraged to increase your indebtedness to the same consortium of corporations for which you work, so that you have decreasing options to extricate yourself from the web. If you lose your job, they will repossess your car, your house, and all of the belongings that you have erroneously come to regard as your own. You can't even retreat to your own land and regroup by hunting and fishing, because they have passed laws preventing you from doing so except by license, and during a few weeks each year. Should you decide to eschew electricity, in all likelihood your home will be deemed unfit for habitation and confiscated. Of course, if you fail to pay your taxes, huge portions of which are used to subsidize the giant corporations (your owners), 'your' belongings are similarly taken from you.

Indeed, the more deeply you follow this insidious labyrinth of connections, the more your state of being resembles simple slavery. They want you to do their work, so they can prosper, and they're not going to let go until you are used up. As Simon LeGree said:

"I don't go for savin' niggers. Use up and buy more,'s my way... I used to, when I fust begun, have considerable trouble fussin' with 'em and trying to make 'em hold out.... Now, you see, I just put 'em straight through, sick or well. When one nigger's dead, I buy another; and I find it comes cheaper and easier, every way." *(Uncle Tom's Cabin* by Harriet Beecher Stowe).

Moreover, the greater your indebtedness, the less you can leave to *your* children; the better to ensure that they, too, are well-chained chattel.

The drastic rise in income inequality since the 1960s has received considerable attention in policy debates. This is a complicated issue, made more so by propaganda that strives (successfully, for the most part) to paint any efforts at analysis in terms of communist wealth redistribution. But what does a *real* Conservative (i.e. one who hasn't sold his integrity to the highest corporate bidder) say about the situation?

"The children of Kenneth Galbraith's *The Affluent Society,* they live in spacious homes in tree-line suburbs, send their kids to schools where parking lots are packed with the latest models...This is 401K America, where tax-exempt

[1] "Company Store" is a reference to the so-called 'Truck system', an arrangement in which employees are paid in commodities or some currency substitute (referred to as scrip), rather than with standard money. This limits employees' ability to choose how to spend their earnings—generally to the benefit of the employer. As an example, scrip might be usable only for the purchase of goods at a "company store" where prices are set artificially high.

pension funds fatten yearly like cattle, and the Dow knows no ceiling.... On the other side of the national divide...the forgotten Americans left behind...a land of middle-class anxiety, down-sized hopes, and vanished dreams.... They played by the rules, but the promise was unfulfilled.... In building their new world, our elites treat fellow Americans as obsolete equipment. Economic insecurity is here to stay, they say, a condition of the Global Economy.... Rarely, however, do they themselves share that pain.... The decline and fall of Middle America was neither preordained nor inevitable. It was engineered in Washington D.C. Wages have fallen and the standard of living of American families has stagnated because of a basic law: the law of supply and demand. The price of labor has been dropping because the supply of labor [overseas] has exploded."[1]

Supply and demand. Is this concept really too complex for the average American to grasp?

I've heard Mr. Buchanan called a great number of things, some less than complementary, but never 'socialist', or 'liberal'.

"Most Americans endorse the ideal of equal opportunity, and many interpret this ideal as requiring that children from different backgrounds have an equal chance of achieving economic success. Most Americans also recognize that children whose parents have 'all the advantages' are more likely to prosper than children whose parents lack these advantages."[2] Nevertheless, when austerity programs are implemented, public education is inevitably among the first casualties, along with school lunch programs, and all those other troublesome 'entitlement' programs.

Of course, the manipulators of public sentiment try to implant an image of black women in fur coats, driving their Cadillac to the supermarket where they buy fillet mignons with their welfare checks, in the hope that you won't notice that the benefits they're cutting are the ones that would have helped *your* kids to have some chance of a better life than you've had.

You want fries with that, Sir?

Very few rational people would argue that a person *shouldn't* be entitled to the fruits of their honest labor, intelligence, foresight, and general savvy. If you're smart, resourceful, and work hard, you *should* be able to prosper. On the flip side, the proliferation of property seizure laws seems to argue that most Americans also agree that evildoers should *not* be permitted to profit from their ill-gotten gains. Again, sounds perfectly reasonable. The problem arises when we lose sight of precisely *who* is defining what constitutes honest income versus nefarious booty. As a result, the guy who gets caught with a dozen pot plants in his back yard will

1 Patrick J. Buchanan, *The Great Betrayal-How American Sovereignty and Social Justice Are Being Sacrificed to the Gods of Global Economy,* Boston, Little Brown. 1998, pp. 6-15

2 *The Changing Effect of Family Background on the Incomes of American Adults* By David Harding, Christopher Jencks, Leonard Lopoo, and Susan Mayer. 2002.

have all of his possessions confiscated, while the 'suit' whose corporate policy results in the deaths of dozens of workers, or thousands of civilians; or whose investment fraud brings the world's economy crashing down around us, gets…tax breaks.

One needn't be a mathematician or an economist to recognize that when our Supreme Court decrees, on one hand, that corporations are the same as citizens, while at the same time, allowing a company like General Electric to make $14.2 *billion* dollars profit in the United States alone and pay no—yes, that figure is ***$0.00*** in taxes, something is seriously amiss. At the same time, legislatures in Wisconsin and elsewhere vote to strip public workers of their rights to collective bargaining. This is like the Sheriff of Nottingham telling the peasants that Robin Hood is the reason they are all living in poverty.

What they tell you is that this allows the big corporations to "create more jobs." What they *won't* tell you is that those jobs are in places where the workers can be abused and exploited in ways we will not (or, once upon a time, *would* not) tolerate for our fellow citizens, with the resultant profits going to…those who are already rich. Once again, *this* is not what was intended by the system we know as *Capitalism*! This is a blatant, cynical, misuse of terminology to facilitate the establishment of what is essentially a feudal system. *Their* children are the elites, *your* children are, and will remain, their serfs.

Once again, listen to what Pat Buchanan, a *real* conservative, has to say: "Under both parties, the U.S. Government has stacked the deck against the American worker…. Both parties have collaborated in the sellout. In embracing free trade, Democrats betrayed their workers. In worshiping this golden calf, Republicans turned their back on their history, tradition, and greatest men." Is it any wonder that Democrats *and* Republicans do everything they can to distort his words, and ensure that nobody will listen to what he *actually says*? Instead, the web is rampant with misquotes, fragments taken out of context, and outright fabrications carefully crafted to destroy the message and demonize the man. If I had to recommend only two books that every sincere, concerned American, Liberal or Conservative, should read, they would be *A Republic, Not and Empire*, and *The Great Betrayal*, both by Patrick J. Buchanan. Instead of heeding what those with a demonstrable axe to grind are telling you to think, get it directly from the source, and make up your own mind. It's high time we finally figured out as a society that greed promotes exploitation, not market efficiency; inequality, not opportunity.

So come on, Scott Walker, tell the people once again how they ought just eat cake when they can't afford bread. Hopefully they'll eventually learn from the French Revolution, and give you, and others like you, their just desserts.

Figure 18 - If 'CLASS WARFARE' is what they ***want***, then let it begin ***here!***

World Peace Through Free Trade?

To understand the motivations behind free trade, we need to go all the way back to 1913, and Cordell Hull, Congressman, Senator, and longest-serving Secretary of State in U.S. history. Hull, who received the Nobel Prize in 1945 for his role in establishing the United Nations, was a man of high ideals, who saw free trade as a means for binding nations together in harmony and peace. He decried the government battles over protective tariffs, which he believed were "fought on the home grounds that high tariffs or low tariffs were good or bad for the United States as a purely domestic matter. There was little or no thought for their effect on world peace."[1] His objective was to replace tariffs with…taxes on Americans' income; an agenda that reached fruition when Hull authored the federal income tax laws of 1913 and 1916 (the first appearance of income tax in America), and the inheritance tax of 1916.

Hence, it is an unequivocal fact that *you* pay income tax so that rich swindlers can rake in massive profits through international commerce.

Following WW-II, with the birth of the Cold War, politicians argued that we could best win over less developed nations as allies by *buying* their loyalty with trade concessions; a strategy that was not without some merit. At the time, it *seemed* indisputable that the American steel, automobile, machinery, and electronics industries were *so* highly developed and *so* efficient that no trade protection was even necessary. Hence, in the words of Pat Buchanan, "A policy pursued out of Cold War necessity would be perpetuated out of peacetime habit."[2] To this assessment I would add: "and expanded through abject avarice."

But are simple complacency and liberal ideologies the *only* forces at work here?

[1] Cordell Hull, *The Memoirs of Cordell Hull*, vol.1 (New York, Macmillian. 1948), p82.
[2] Patrick J. Buchanan, *The Great Betrayal-How American Sovereignty and Social Justice Are Being Sacrificed to the Gods of Global Economy* (Boston, Little Brown. 1998), p29.

It has historically been argued that common, honest working men do not start wars, but rather, rich powerful ones who wish to get richer and more powerful at the expense of their peons' blood. If this is the case, then free trade may indeed be the path to world peace. The numbers speak for themselves. Worldwide, the rich are richer than ever, the poor are both poorer and more numerous than ever, and the middle class is rapidly vanishing. Why spill the blood of one's serfs, when one can more profitably simply work them to death, while appropriating what little property they might have managed to accumulate?

Although politicians *have* been known to lie, the numbers do not:

The salaries of top US CEOs, which averaged 30 times the average worker's wage in the 1970s, had reached 263 times the average worker's pay by 2010.

How do they justify those outlandish pay checks?

In many cases, by revenue generated as a result of the kinds of sleazy manipulations that sent the world's economy crashing in 2008.

And who *pays* the price of these shenanigans?

Those workers, who make 0.38% of the criminals who *caused* the disaster, of course. Is the worker who constructs a Ford Pinto worth 0.38% as much as the greedy executive who decided it was cheaper to pay off families of the people who were burned to death than to redesign and recall the faulty vehicles? And, when profits declined as a result, who got laid off? Greedy executives, or honest workers?

By comparison, the average Japanese CEO makes 1/6 of what an American CEO does, which is only 16 times that of the average Japanese worker. Are American CEOs *that* much more valuable than their Japanese counterparts, or that much more greedy? Are American workers that much *less* valuable than their bosses, or merely held in that much greater contempt? With a bit of numeric normalization, it turns out that the average Japanese worker makes 2-1/2 times what an American worker does.

The average total annual compensation of an S&P 500 CEO in 2010 was $11,358,445 (yes, that's over *eleven million dollars a year*). The combined total CEO pay for the top 299 companies ($3.4 billion) could support 102,325 median workers' jobs.

A huge share of the nation's economic growth over the past 30 years has gone to the top one-hundredth of one percent, who now make an average of $27 million per household. The average household income for the bottom 90 percent of us? $31,244.

Interestingly, a recent study (Norton & Ariely, 2010) shows that most Americans (high income or low income, female or male, young or old, Republican or Democrat) have *no clue* how concentrated the wealth distribution actually is.

Since financial wealth is what counts as far as the control of the *Republicat*-dominated government goes, we can say that just 10% of the people *own* the United States of America. Wealth, of course, is the most direct facilitator for exercising power. That's obvious when we think of donations to political parties, payments to lobbyists, and grants to experts who are employed to think up new policies beneficial to the wealthy. Wealth also can be useful in shaping the general social environment to the benefit of the wealthy, whether through hiring public relations firms or donating money for universities, museums, music halls, and art galleries. Moreover, stock ownership can be used to control corporations, which of course have a major impact on how the society functions—even more so since the *Citizens United* decision/disgrace.

Conversely, while wealth leads to power, so too does power generate even more wealth. Those who control a government use their position to feather their own nests, whether that means a favorable land deal for relatives at the local level, a huge federal government contract for a new corporation run by friends who will hire you when you leave government…or a Supreme Court decision favoring big corporations over citizens.

Think this trend is the exclusive doing of the Republicans? Think again. The average income of the top 400 tripled during the Clinton Administration and doubled during the first seven years of the Bush Administration. So, by 2007, the top 400 averaged $344.8 million per person, up 31% from an average of $263.3 million just one year earlier. Conversely who do you suppose were among the most vocal supporters of Bill Clinton's 1994 GATT treaty? None other than supposed 'conservatives' Newt Gingrich and Bob Dole, both of whom eagerly signed on to this unilateral disarmament of America's industrial base.

If you dare to question how such a large gap is justified, the *Republicrat Junta* will condescendingly explain that these CEO's *deserve* their outlandish compensation packages because they 'generate wealth'. However, a more credible explanation is provided by Edgar S. Woolard, Jr., retired CEO of DuPont, and currently chair of the New York Stock Exchange's executive compensation committee:

"The compensation committee [of the board of directors] talks to an outside consultant who has surveys you could drive a truck through and pay anything you want to pay, to be perfectly honest. The outside consultant talks to the human resources vice president, who talks to the CEO. The CEO says what he'd like to receive. It gets to the human resources person who tells the outside consultant. And it pretty well works out that the CEO gets what he's implied he thinks he deserves, so he will be respected by his peers. The board of directors buys into what the CEO asks for because the outside consultant is an 'expert' on such matters. Furthermore, handing out only modest salary increases might give the wrong impression about how highly the board values the CEO. And if someone on the board should object, there are the three or four CEOs from other companies [on the board] who will make sure it happens. "

And for *you*?

Well, you and your *unreasonable* union demands are blamed for the destruction of the economy; and brain-dead voters are manipulated into supporting legislation to curtail those troublesome collective bargaining rights.

Of course, it's scarcely worth mentioning that the federal government has its own heavy hand in this mix. In 1952, the year of my birth, federal income tax claimed 3% of the average family's income. Today it is over 25%. What are you *receiving* for this 'contribution to society'? How about...slavery?

Those who consider themselves 'Conservative' frequently identify with family values, so they should consider carefully the fact that in 1960, only 18% of women with children were in the workforce. Currently that number is 71.3%. Granted, *some* of this represents 'career women' who do so by choice, but one need only look at their own friends and neighbors to realize that the vast majority work because they *must*. We react with righteous indignation to the stories of wicked slave owners separating slave women from their children by selling off these valuable assets, but fail to recognize the similarity in our own supposedly free society.

In the words of Pat Buchanan: "These are Middle America's rewards, as our elites force-marched the nation into the Global Economy of its dreams. And what has happened to the most productive and self-reliant republic in history?

- "Where the United States ran trade surpluses every year from 1900 to 1970, we have now run trade deficits for twenty-six straight years. *[Between 1996 and 2004, the US deficit increased by $650 billion, from 1.5% to 5.8% of GDP. It reached $497.8 billion in 2010.]*
- "Our total merchandise trade deficit since 1980 is more than $2 trillion. In 1996 it was $191 billion, larger than the budget deficit. *[The U.S. merchandise trade deficit with China alone has surged from $10 billion in 1990 to an estimated $273 billion in 2010.]*
- "Imported manufactured goods in 1996 equaled 51 percent of all manufactures MADE IN THE USA.
- "The world's greatest creditor nation had become its greatest debtor. *[Our 2010 national debt was $13,050,826,460,886.97 (thirteen TRILLION dollars).]*
- "Since 1970, the dollar has lost two-thirds of its value against the Japanese yen and the German mark.

[1] Patrick J. Buchanan, *The Great Betrayal-How American Sovereignty and Social Justice Are Being Sacrificed to the Gods of Global Economy* (Boston, Little Brown. 1998), pp, 11-14.

- "In 1962 manufacturing accounted for 29 percent of the national income. By 1997 it had fallen to 17 percent, the smallest share of the gross national product (GNP) since the nineteenth century. *[By 2010 this had fallen to 11%.]*
- "In 1965, 31 percent of our labor force had manufacturing-equivalent jobs. By 1997 that figure was down to 15 percent, also the smallest share since the nineteenth century.
- "Since 1980 the United States has lost 2.6 million manufacturing jobs.
- "For the first time, as many Americans work in government as in manufacturing. In twenty-eight states, including California, New York, and Texas, government workers outnumber manufacturing workers.
- "Americans no longer make their own cameras, shoes, radios, TVs, toys. A fifth of our steel, a third of our autos, half our machine tools, and two-thirds of our textiles and clothes are made abroad.
- "However, jobs at Wal-Mart rose from just 21,000 in 1978 to 628,000 in 1996. *[2.1 Million in 2010.]*
- "Foreign interests own 17 percent of the U.S. federal debt. In 1996 foreign purchases of U.S. Treasury bills totaled $122 billion, more than the entire federal budget for all of 1997. *[We owed $13.7 trillion to foreign interests in 2010.]*
- "As of mid-1997, the Treasury's custody account held $628 billion worth of U.S. securities on behalf of foreign central banks, a near doubling since 1993. A hint by Japan's prime minister that Tokyo might sell its share dropped the Dow 192 points in one day.
- "Not since Colonial days has America been so vulnerable to foreign regimes. When Mexico threatened to default in 1994, we had to cobble together a $50 billion bailout, lest Mexico's default bring on a financial panic in the United states.

"While Millions of jobs have been created in retail sales to move the mountains of imports, the manufacturing jobs that enabled Americans with high school diplomas to live the American Dream have been shipped and created overseas.... In building their new world, our elites treat fellow Americans like obsolete equipment."

Perhaps it's time for the Nation to do what so many working-class Americans have been forced to do: declare bankruptcy. Declare all foreign debt and foreign ownership of strategic American property null and void. Let foreign creditors squabble over our relinquished foreign holdings and expel our military presence (a further saving for us), and start living within our means. What a concept! No more foreign credit? Good—that will prevent us from making the same mistakes again. And if they don't like it? Well, that's what our nuclear deterrent is for.

Smoke & Mirrors

If there's any single topic that unequivocally proves the real nature of *the Republicrat Junta*, it's the entire smoke-and-mirrors, slight of hand sold to the American Public under the banner of *free trade*. To hear the broad-based *bipartisan* support for this program, one would think they were giving away tickets for Noah's Ark.

Here's how *the government*, through the Department of Commerce's International Trade Administration (www.TRADE.gov), describes this absolutely wonderful, idyllic, beneficial program that will elevate the standards of living for all working Americans, solve the unemployment problem, and bring about world peace:

The International Trade Administration (ITA) strengthens the competitiveness of U.S. industry, promotes trade and investment, and ensures fair trade through the rigorous enforcement of our trade laws and agreements. ITA works to improve the global business environment and helps U.S. organizations compete at home and abroad. ITA supports President Obama's recovery agenda and the National Export Initiative to sustain economic growth and support American jobs.

Free trade agreements (FTAs) have proved to be one of the best ways to open up foreign markets to U.S. exporters. The defining purpose of the International Trade Administration (ITA) is helping to create economic opportunity for American workers and businesses. By promoting trade and investment we are promoting prosperity and a better world. To increase trade and investment, ITA helps U.S. companies navigate foreign markets. We help educate companies about how to tailor their activities to the specific market with respect to their product slate, financing, marketing, assembly and logistics. The International Trade Administration (ITA) consults with U.S. industry to assess the impact of proposed domestic and international regulatory policies that affect U.S. industry's competitiveness and the expansion of U.S. exports. ITA ensures that U.S. industry's commercial interests are represented in trade negotiations, bilateral and multilateral discussions, and the U.S. rulemaking process. ITA advances policies and strategies that stimulate innovation and investment, enhance economic growth, and support U.S. manufacturing and services industries.

Hey, what patriotic American could *possibly* be against *that*?

Nobody but a goddamned godless commie socialist, they assure us.

Details, you have the temerity to ask?

Don't worry about it, they reply. We're from the government. We're here to help....

(We don't have to show you no steenking details!)

Well, *here's* how it works, and I invite *any* politician to prove me wrong (as if the suffering of the American worker doesn't provide sufficient evidence):

Suppose I own a textile mill in Massachusetts. I've invested in state of the art computerized equipment, and the result is a highly efficient operation. I employ, say. 3000 workers in various capacities. I consume U.S. materials (cotton, wool, synthetics, etc.). I pay taxes on revenues generated. I pay property taxes that support my local community. My employees pay taxes on their incomes, and contribute to Social Security based on the competitive salaries I pay them. They spend their money, paying sales tax, contributing to the local economy, and supporting jobs for their neighbors.

Introduce these various 'free trade' laws.

The way the laws are set up, if I move that mill to China, I can reduce my production costs to pennies on the dollar. While the operation over there is less efficient—positively primitive, in fact—this is more than offset by the inexpensive (near slave) labor, so I don't *have* to be as efficient to still generate massively increased profits. In addition to just the lower hourly wage, I don't have to provide any of the benefits that those *greedy* American workers expect. As an employer (answering to single-minded stock holders), I don't want to *know* if those 'benefits' include safety and occupational hazards that would not be possible here, child labor, and so forth. In addition, I don't have to pay those inflated prices for overpriced American raw materials and supplies—cotton, steel, tools, paper, you name it—savings all around!

As an American company, my domestic profits *are* still taxable, but wait, they tell me: I can set my own prices when shipping components between my foreign and domestic divisions *(wink, wink; nudge nudge),* and with the help of some savvy lawyers and accountants, all of the profit remains offshore, so, like General Electric, who paid precisely $0.00 tax on their $14 billion in profits, I won't actually be paying those at all. In addition, there since there are no tariffs when I bring the manufactured goods back into this country for sale (that would be ...*[gasp]*...protectionism) , every penny of my swollen revenue stream is pure profit.

But, that doesn't tell the whole story, our politicians insist. Increased export will create more jobs for the American worker! Everyone will benefit. Let's all join hands and sing *Kumbia*!

Well, I have to concede this point. Free trade *has* created jobs.

Of course, if you consider a $25.27/hour manufacturing job to be interchangeable with the $8.23/hour Wal-Mart pays their 'valued associates', then yes, you *should* be celebrating this triumph for the working American. What do you *mean* you can't support your family on $17,118.40/year? That's not *our* fault! It's those damned greedy, lazy, gold-bricking *government workers*, and their unions! (Doesn't it piss you off that *they're* still making what you *used* to make?) Vote for *me* and we'll cut them down to size! We'll...*redistribute*...their wealth back to you in the form of...tax reduction! *Then* you'll be able to live the good life on that $17,118.40 annual salary.

Uh huh.

Indeed, 21,000 jobs at Wal-Mart in 1978 *have* become 2.1 million in 2010. Go team!

And the 4 million manufacturing jobs lost since 1979? The 42,000 U.S. factories closed?

Americans didn't want *those* crummy jobs anyway.

Hey! Wait a minute. Look over *there*: Mexican illegals are *stealing* the jobs Americans *really* want! And...***socialism***! And how about those damned unwed welfare moms, squirting out babies and driving to the supermarkets in their Cadillacs, dressed in fur coats, and buying fillet mignons? Look at *them*! (Don't look at us.) Socialism! Socialism! Socialism everywhere! "Pay no attention to man behind the curtain, Dorothy. I am *Oz*! The great and magnificent!"

Ever heard the term 'supply and demand'?

It's the basic principle underlying the economic theory known as 'Capitalism'.

Basically, it holds that when supply increases or demand decreases, prices fall.

This applies to labor as well as goods.

So, if we effectively double or triple the size of the workforce by including foreign workers (who, work for 1/10 of the pay, and don't demand those pesky perks, like a safe workplace, 8-hour day, no child labor, etc,), what do you *think* is going to happen to the price of labor?

Ixnay ethay ageway alktay!!! Americansway illway evernay oticenay ifway eway on'tday elltay emthay.[1]

They say that a picture equals a thousand words, so here are a few to ponder:

Figure 19

Figure 19 shows *The Emma Maersk*, part of a Danish shipping line. This breathtaking marvel transports goods across the Pacific in just 5 days! She is one of *three* ships presently in service, with another two ships commissioned to be completed in 2012. They hold an incredible 15,000 containers, and have a 207 foot deck beam! The full crew is just 13 people on a ship longer than a US Aircraft Carrier (which has a crew of 5,000) Talk about reducing labor costs!

1 Pig Latin. Translation: Nix the wage talk!!! Americans will never notice if we don't tell them.

Figure 20

With its 207' beam it is too big to fit through the Panama or Suez Canals. It is strictly transpacific. With a cruise speed is 31 knots, its cargo arrives 4 days before the typical container ship (18-20 knots) on a China–to–California run. The command bridge is higher than a 10-story building. It has 11 cargo crane rigs that can operate simultaneously, unloading the entire ship in less than two hours (**Figure 21**).

Figure 21

Cost of constructing these magnificent vessels? Over $145,000,000.00 each. Who could possibly afford to *build* such incredible ships? All three were commissioned by…Wal-Mart, who imports 91% of their products from China. Yes, *91%* of Wal-Mart products are made in China. This behemoth is so incredibly fast that even perishable goods can be imported from China, replacing those 'overpriced' alternatives supplied by American farmers.

Figure 22

Fully loaded, this behemoth carries 123,200 tons of cargo each west-to-east voyage. On the trip from America ***to*** China? Zero. Zilch. Nada. All of those containers are shipped back to China, ***empty***, ready to be refilled with more Wal-Mart products for Americans to buy. Yep, that's right. We send ***nothing*** back on these ships.

Well, that's not **quite** true. American ***jobs*** are on board for the return voyage, but as you can see by that elevated waterline, those don't weigh much, and have no intrinsic value whatsoever, at least to those who are purportedly protecting *your* interests in government.

Who supported the laws that make this a viable business model?

Bill Clinton, Ronald Reagan, Jimmy Carter, Newt Gingrich, Bob Dole, John F. Kennedy, Lyndon Johnson…in other words, virtually every Democrat and every Republican.

There remains, however, one last missing piece if this baffling puzzle is going to present a coherent picture:

Total 1989-2010 lobbying expenditures of top 140 donors: $1,949,094,924.00.

Wal-Mart?

In 2010 alone they spent $6,160,000.00 on lobbying, and $3,194,439.00 on political contributions, of which $1,330,050 went directly to individual politicians.

How much of *your* annual income did you manage to use for purchasing political influence? Maybe this is one of those 'rare' areas in which corporations *aren't* 'just like people'. As the saying goes: "you get what you pay for," and that includes freedom, liberty, and government protection.

I guess *this* is where you find bipartisan agreement—they ***ALL*** agree that ***your*** interests are worth less than zero, while those of the corporations who fill their pockets are inviolate.

But...but...***Newt Gingrich***[1] says: "The idea that a congressman would be tainted by accepting money from private industry or private sources is essentially a ***socialist*** argument."

*Socialism bad...**Republicrat** good....*

*Socialism bad...**Republicrat** good....*

Hey, Newt; you're a slimy amphibian, not Obi-Wan Kenobi, so you can skip the Jedi mind control trick. Americans *aren't* your Imperial Storm Troopers.

Okay, now a quiz on what we just learned. You are:

1. **Rich**
2. **Stupid**
3. **Outraged**

Pick one.

Question 2: Which part of 'getting sodomized' don't you understand?

Extra Credit: There is still ***ONE*** thing we still manufacture here in America. What might *that* be?

[1] Yes, that would be the same 'family values matter' Newt Gingrich who claims his marital infidelity was a matter of patriotic duty and national security.

Why...weapons, of course....

We build them. We sell them. We use them. ***LOTS* of them!**

So, whereas "world peace" may have been the original motivation for free trade, like so many other noble undertakings, it has been derailed and perverted by *the Republicrat Junta* into its exact opposite.

There's an old saying that says: when all you have is a nail, everything looks like a hammer. Well, when all you have to sell is a bomb, what else do you market but wars and violence?

We make wars because it's the only way we can still make money.

So, here we have a reprehensible institution that has garnered the unqualified support of those in our government who portray themselves as 'Socialists' (Democrats) and 'Capitalists' (Republicans). But what about real people of *integrity* who embrace these supposedly opposing ideologies? Well, this is one of numerous topics on which they, too, concur:

Noam Chomsky, the great American linguist, philosopher, cognitive scientist, and social activist, who describes himself as a "libertarian socialist," writes:

"One goal of NAFTA was to 'lock Mexico in' to the so-called reforms of the 1980s, which created billionaires at about the same rate as they enhanced poverty. These 'reforms' are the great benefit to the US owners, managers, and investors, though not to working people. NAFTA was one of those rare treaties that managed to harm the working populations in all countries participating: Canada, the US, and Mexico. The US labor movement had proposed alternatives that would have benefitted the workforce in all 3 countries. Similar proposals were developed by Congress's Office of Technology Assessment (since disbanded). The proposals were never entered to the political agenda, and were even barred from the media.... In brief, NAFTA, duly imposed by executive power, in opposition to the public will."[1]

"Nobody in the corporate world or government takes free trade seriously. The parts of the economy that are able to compete internationally are primarily the state-subsidized ones: capital-intensive agriculture, high-tech industry, etc. The government has the public pay for research and development and provides a state-guaranteed market for waste production. If something is marketable, the private sector takes it over. That system of public subsidy and private profit is what is called free enterprise."[2]

On the 'other side' of the political and philosophical spectrum, we have Pat Buchanan, whose conservative credentials require no defense. *His* thoughts on free trade?

[1] Noam Chomsky, *Hopes and Prospects*, Haymarket Books, 2010, pp. 35-36.
[2] Noam Chomsky, *What Uncle Sam Really Wants*, Odonian Press , 2002, p. 13.

"To [the] new corporate elite, putting America first betrays a lack of loyalty to the company. Some among our political elite share this view. Here is Strobe Talbott, Clinton's roommate at Oxford and architect of his Russian policy: 'All countries,' said Talbott in 1991, 'are basically social arrangements...No matter how permanent and even sacred they may seem at any one time, in fact they are all artificial and temporary...within the next hundred years...nationhood as we know it will be obsolete; all states will recognize a single, global authority'.... This is the transnational elite, our new Masters of the Universe.

"As you may have heard in my last campaign, I am called by many names. 'Protectionist' is one of the nicer ones; but it is inexact. I am an economic nationalist. To me, the country comes before the economy; and the economy exists for the people. I believe in free markets, but I do not worship them. In the proper hierarchy of things, it is the market that must be harnessed to work for man—and not the other way around.

"The second bill that [George] Washington signed into law was the Tariff Act of 1789. Madison saved the nation's infant industries from being buried by the dumping of British manufactures, with the first truly protective tariff, the Tariff Act of 1816. 'Give me a tariff and I will give you the greatest nation on earth,' said Lincoln. 'I thank God I am not a free trader,' Theodore Roosevelt wrote to Henry Cabot Lodge.

"Under economic nationalism, there was no income tax in the United States, except during the Civil War and Reconstruction. Tariffs produced fifty to ninety percent of federal revenue. And how did America prosper? From 1865 to 1913, U.S. growth averaged 4% a year. We began the era with half Britain's production, but ended with twice Britain's production."[1]

Parenthetically, as elaborated elsewhere, one of the founders of the entire 'free trade' concept was also the author of our nation's first income tax laws (the federal income tax laws of 1913 and 1916), and the inheritance tax of 1916, Cordell Hull.

So, is the only alternative 'protectionism', trade barriers, and isolationist policies? Not unless your primary interests are enriching the corrupt corporations that supply an endless stream of graft into your own pockets; and not unless your regard and concern for *the People* of the United States is lower than a snail's rectum.

A close friend, former colleague, and retired United States Air Force Lieutenant Colonel, proposes the following solution:

[1] Source: Pat Buchanan's Speech on Free Trade Given to C.F.R Address to the Chicago Council on Foreign Relations November 18, 1998.

"Fairly simple—we set up an amount of imports we're willing to take without matching exports. This will handle critical import categories such as oil, rare earth metals, etc. that aren't really available at the required quantity in this country. Every import above that must have a matching export credit. These are dollars paid to U.S. manufacturers, or service providers, that are used to offset the cost of the exports. Those wishing to import additional goods to the U.S. must buy these export credits from the product/service providers, thus driving down the cost of the exports and hence increasing the export volume. There's lots more details but that's the basic idea. Works like the energy cap and trade concept but for imports."

Isn't it astonishing what you can come up with if you're not driven by personal greed, corruption, and allegiance to special interests?

PART II

BASIC CONCEPTS

Language

Although, strictly speaking, it might be an exaggeration to say that language is what separates us from other animals, the complexity of our linguistic capabilities is certainly a substantive contributor to all of our advanced competencies. The Second Edition of the *Oxford English Dictionary* contains full entries for 171,476 words in current use, and 47,156 obsolete words. To this may be added around 9,500 derivative words included as subentries. The field of psycholinguistics is vast and nuanced, but it can be stated with little fear of contradiction that one of the great values of so extensive a lexicon is that it permits us to communicate highly complex concepts in a very concise manner.

As an analogy, consider the *language* of mathematics.

Without using any mathematics whatsoever, I can describe the situation in which a traveler traverses some distance, say, two miles, in a specific amount of time, let's say, one hour. We can discuss the concept of average velocity, and most people will easily understand that, in the aforementioned case, the traveler, having covered two miles in one hour, did so at an average speed of two miles per hour, written mathematically as *2m/h*. At this point, we have no information about the details of the trip. For example, if the traveler was strolling at a leisurely pace, he or she could have covered the entire distance at the nominal average speed, that is, they walked at two miles per hour for one hour, so, multiplying:

2 miles/hour ***times*** 1 hour ***equals*** 2 miles.

However, we can easily see how this wouldn't necessarily be the case. Perhaps they rode a bicycle at 4 miles an hour for fifteen minutes, stopped for a half hour to pick some flowers, then rode the remaining distance at 4 miles per hour.

Alternatively, they might have been in a car. Perhaps, this person was a mechanic, trying to diagnose a problem with the engine's timing. The owner reported hearing a 'pinging' sound under hard acceleration, so the mechanic takes the car to this remote 2-mile stretch of road, and alternatively stamps on the accelerator, listening for the reported sounds, then comes to a stop, repeating the process until the 2-mile length of the road is exhausted.

In each of these cases, the traveler's speed is more difficult to describe because it isn't steady; it changes over time. This change in velocity over time is known as acceleration. However, recall that velocity itself is described as the change in *position* over time, so acceleration is the change *in the change* in position over time.

One can easily appreciate how descriptions, and discussions, of complex mechanical situations could easily burgeon to the point where any in-depth analysis would become prohibitively unwieldy. Fortunately, mathematicians have invented a special language for dealing with these, and vastly more complex, systems. In the current discussion, we simply say that:

$$v=dx/dt,$$

$$a=dv/dt.$$

Any mathematician since the time of Isaac Newton, regardless of their primary language, regardless of where they studied, can look at these two statements, and immediately infer the entirety of the preceding 358 words.

The point of this brief mathematical digression is to demonstrate how a tiny symbol or two can invoke a huge amount of information, some of it clear and unambiguous, some merely suggestive, shadowy, or visceral. So, just to ensure that *we* are using language in a mutually consistent manner, I'm going to explicitly address what I mean when I use some critical verbiage.

Regardless of your political orientation, if you are reasonably intelligent, you should strongly resent being manipulated. Guileful scoundrels in business, government, and media smugly assume that *they* are smart, *you* are not, and that their transparent tricks will inevitably prevail.

Remember Pavlov and his famous canine? As any dog owner will attest, if your dog expects to receive an edible reward in response to an external event, he/she will begin to salivate in anticipation of the food. This is not a conscious act. It is completely subliminal. Words are the same kind of thing. We have been programmed, indoctrinated, conditioned to associate pleasant or repulsive reactions with certain words, often quite independent of the word's actual objective meaning. Freedom, democracy, dictatorship, anarchist, pedophile, terrorist, spiritual leader, religious charlatan, bigot, white supremacist, Nazi, fascist, police officer, storm trooper.... The source of trouble is *loaded words,* which can be used to manipulate your reactions, much like that salivating dog.

Stimulus…response. The propagandist will say something in a certain way, and the probability is overwhelming that the vast majority of the populace will react in a highly predictable manner, often in a way that is contrary to their own beliefs, values, and self-interest. (Do you *like* the idea that there are people who think of you as no more than a brainless wooden puppet, whose strings *they* can operate at will?)

Words are said to be 'loaded' to the extent that they carry with them surreptitious information in addition to their apparent meanings. Again, these nuances allow us to communicate in a highly compressed and efficient manner. However, this strength brings with it a corresponding danger. It is the misuse of this very formidable power that results in the phenomena known as *propaganda*.

Propaganda

Propaganda is defined as: *the deliberate and systematic propagation of information or ideas by an interested party, especially in a biased, distorted, or prejudiced way, in order to encourage or instill a particular attitude or response, or to further one's cause or to damage an opposing cause. (OED).*

Failure to be aware of these machinations renders one subject to manipulation. I don't know about you, but I like to believe that I can think for myself, analyze information, and draw my own conclusions, thank you very much. I resent *anyone*, whether I happen to agree with them or not, presuming that they can pull my strings and *trick* me into supporting their agenda as if I were some wooden-headed marionette.

Recall those scenes from *1984*, in which the brainwashed masses respond to blatant government lies with mindless chants of support? Keep this image in mind whenever you find yourself reacting viscerally to a *word, phrase, or abstraction.*

I am convinced that the vast majority of intelligent Americans want to think of themselves as open-minded, free thinking, individualists, not dull-witted pawns in someone else's nefarious agenda. Regardless of where your reasoning leads you, I can respect that destination, and will assume you reached it on the basis of well-considered logic, if you got there on your own. I can respect almost *any* point of view, providing it's not merely a result of programming or cynical manipulation by external forces.

Like all 'baby boomers', I passed my formative years in the era of the cold war. I remember the frequent nuclear attack drills, the funny little ditties and jokes about Nikita Khrushchev and his barbarous nation of baddies, the cartoons, comics, and earnest tales of our brutal and inhuman enemies.

Were some of these images accurate? I have little doubt they were. Were they *all* true? Incontrovertibly not.

I can recall my parents, teachers, clergymen, all preaching to me that there are always two sides to every story. Sage advice, except for the fact that it was always qualified with the unspoken understanding: 'except where America is concerned....' And this, my friends, brings us to the topic of *American Exceptionalism*.

Exceptionalism

Exceptionalism is the perception, theory, or assertion that something is exceptional in relation to others of the same kind; most commonly, that a country, society, institution, movement, or time period is *so* unusual or extraordinary in some critical way that it is exempted from the necessity of conforming to normal rules or general principles.

Espousing this philosophy accomplishes nothing, other than to make us look ignorant, stupid, naïve, deceitful, arrogant, gullible, or some reprehensible combination thereof. Nobody (at least nobody worth listening to) is saying that America is *all* evil. Nobody is saying America has not been a steadfast friend to many. Nevertheless, America is *not* perfect, and this is a reality that sometimes appears to be visible to everyone on earth *except* certain Americans. Inevitably, these are the very same ones who consider themselves to be *the only true Americans*. In fact, nothing could be further than the truth.

Moreover, from a purely practical perspective, if we persist in denying we have any faults at all—that we have ever made a single mistake—we preclude any possibility of improvement. As any ancient Roman might attest, the society that ceases to advance, must inevitably decline.

In the words of Pat Buchanan: "America should be loved by her patriotic sons and daughters not because she has a glorious mission to pursue or she is the 'world's last superpower' or 'the indispensable nation.' This is puerile braggadocio.... America should be loved for herself, for what she is: our country. As for the 'national greatness' crowd, they do not understand true patriotism."[1]

If we truly want to show the world that we are exceptional among all nations in history, how about holding ourselves to the same standards we demand of others. Now *that* would be unique!

[1] Patrick J. Buchanan, *A Republic, Not an Empire-Reclaiming America's Destiny,* Regency Publishing, 1999, p xxi.

The biggest lie, of course, is that we are always smart, good, and righteous, and that 'the other side' is depraved, evil, and stupid. This is a lie that is easy for us to believe, because it exonerates us from the necessity of continuously evaluating, reassessing, and testing our beliefs in the face of ever changing circumstances. It's so much simpler to just dismiss the alternatives as fallacious, especially when those who rule us are continuously assuring us that it is fitting and proper to do so.

*Terrorists are whomever we **say** they are.*

We do not negotiate with terrorists.

Therefore, we need not engage in diplomacy whenever the use of force better suits our purposes.

Those who buy into this blatant prevarication are about as perspicacious as one of those clever little bobble-heads, agreeably nodding their acquiescence to every ill-understood proposition placed before them.

In the words of the inimitable Noam Chomsky: "Everybody's worried about stopping terrorism. Well, there's a really easy way: stop participating in it."

Conservatism

One difficulty we face today is the fact that the *Republicrat* faction that portrays itself as 'conservative' is anything but. While the term 'neoconservative' has been used to differentiate these criminal posers from true Conservatives, the distinction is too frequently lost in the heat of contrived rhetorical battle.

When former Treasury Secretary Paul O'Neill tried to warn Vice President Dick Cheney that growing budget deficits, expected to top $500 billion, posed a threat to the economy. Cheney cut him off. "You know, Paul, Reagan proved deficits don't matter," Cheney replied. "We won the midterms [congressional elections]. This is our due."

Was this the philosophy of a *true* Conservative?

Would it have been the least bit surprising if it had come from the lips of Bill Clinton?

A month later, Cheney told the Treasury secretary he was fired.

Noam Chomsky observes that: "The political policies that are called conservative these days would appall any genuine conservative, if there were one around to be appalled. For example, the central policy of the Reagan Administration—which was supposed to be conservative—was to build up a powerful state. The state grew in power more under Reagan than in any peacetime period, even if you just measure it by state expenditures. The state intervention in the economy vastly increased. That's what the Pentagon system is, in fact; it's the creation of a state-guaranteed market and subsidy system for high-technology production.

There was a commitment under the Reagan Administration to protect this more powerful state from the public, which is regarded as the domestic enemy. Take the resort to clandestine operations in foreign policy: that means the creation of a powerful central state immune from public inspection. Or take the increased efforts at censorship and other forms of control. All of these are called 'conservatism,' but they're the very opposite of conservatism. Whatever the term means, it involves a concern for Enlightenment values of individual rights and freedoms against powerful external authorities such as the state, a dominant Church, and so on. That kind of conservatism no one even remembers anymore. (Interview by Adam Jones, February 20, 1990).

The traditional meaning of the word 'conservative' is: *"marked by moderation or caution...a cautious or discreet person" (Merriam Webster's 11th. Collegiate Dictionary).* A true conservative would thus be a person who always prefers to err on the side of caution. The conservative, in the words of William Shakespeare, would: "rather bear those ills we have, than fly to others that we know not of..." (*Hamlet*, Scene I). When I use the word in this generic sense, I will spell it with a lower-case 'c'. The other common meaning refers to a specific political party, movement, mindset, or orientation, the characteristic principle of which is the maintenance of existing *institutions*, political and ecclesiastical. In this latter instance, the word is capitalized. This distinction is crucial, as the two meanings are frequently diametrically opposed to one another. For example, let us consider the contentious issue commonly referred to as 'global warming'.

Global warming refers to the purported increase in the average temperature of Earth's near-surface air and oceans since the mid-20th century, and its projected continuation. According to the 2007 Fourth Assessment Report by the Intergovernmental Panel on Climate Change (IPCC), global surface temperature increased 0.74 ± 0.18 °C (1.33 ± 0.32 °F) during the twentieth century. The evidence for this change is conclusive, but contention exists as to whether any, all, or most of the observed temperature increase since the middle of the last century was caused by increasing concentrations of greenhouse gases resulting from human activity such as fossil fuel burning and deforestation. It has also been suggested that global dimming, a result of increasing concentrations of atmospheric aerosols that block sunlight from reaching the surface, has partially countered the effects of greenhouse gas induced warming. (By way of comparison, during the last ice age, the average global temperature was a mere three-degrees lower than today.)

Conservative (lower case) estimates show that for every 1-degree (Celsius) elevation in average temperature, world crop production will decrease by 10%, and at this juncture, there is no slack—we consume 100% of what we grow. You think we have a refugee (illegal alien) problem *now*? At present we have, perhaps, a half-million people each year illegally crossing our borders, many of them returning south after the harvest season is over. What about when we have ten times that number? Yes, we *can* close the border, but doing so entails the creation of a true iron curtain, and the willingness to kill people in massive numbers.

Think we have division among Americans *now*? What do you suppose we're going to have when the army starts killing men, women, and children wholesale (as they have already shown themselves to be perfectly willing to do)? For those who insist that America is founded on 'Christian values', is this a course of action of which Jesus would approve?

It was recently revealed that The Pentagon is seriously developing strategies to deal with the aftermath of global warming. Indeed, these plans were under way even while the George W. Bush administration was busily denying that climate change even existed. This should not be taken as any kind of admission of the reality of the effect or verification of its causes; it merely means that the military, prudently, takes a *conservative*, worst-case-scenario approach in order to be prepared for all eventualities.

Although this debate is frequently posed in terms of Liberal versus Conservative, with the Liberals portrayed as demanding the immediate cessation of all fossil fuel usage, regardless of the human, societal, economic, and strategic implications, while the Conservatives are painted as flatly denying the existence, severity, or importance of the effect, I submit that this demarcation is misleading, inappropriate, and indeed, contrived.

Few would characterize the great Theodore Roosevelt as a Liberal, but he was also one of the greatest environmentalists who ever lived, demonstrating the intimate linkage between the words 'Conservative' and 'conservation'. In 1916, he wrote the following:

"Defenders of the short-sighted men who in their greed and selfishness will, if permitted, rob our country of half its charm by their reckless extermination of all useful and beautiful wild things sometimes seek to champion them by saying 'the game belongs to the people.' So it does; and not merely to the people now alive, but to the unborn people. The 'greatest good for the greatest number' applies to the number within the womb of time, compared to which those now alive form but an insignificant fraction. Our duty to the whole, including the unborn generations, bids us restrain an unprincipled present-day minority from wasting the heritage of these unborn generations. The movement for the conservation of wild life and the larger movement for the conservation of all our natural resources are essentially democratic in spirit, purpose, and method."[1]

And this:

"To waste, to destroy our natural resources, to skin and exhaust the land instead of using it so as to increase its usefulness, will result in undermining in the days of our children the very prosperity which we ought by right to hand down to them amplified and developed."

And this:

[1] A *Book-Lover's Holidays in the Open*, 1916

"Here is your country. Cherish these natural wonders, cherish the natural resources, cherish the history and romance as a sacred heritage, for your children and your children's children. Do not let selfish men or greedy interests skin your country of its beauty, its riches or its romance."

Let's approach this matter dispassionately, with some degree of logical detachment.

I believe most people can agree that average temperatures *have* risen by the claimed amount, during the period under discussion. The areas of contention are:

1. Is the effect caused by human activity, or is it, rather, simply part of a cyclic pattern of natural origin?
2. Is the outcome as catastrophic as predicted, or, indeed, negative at all?
3. Regardless of the cause or effect, is there anything that can be *done* about it in either case?

These are critical and valid questions which have yet to be definitively answered to my satisfaction.

In such instances, where complete information is unavailable (which is more often than not the case), I tend to favor the *risk management* approach that has served me well in the management of large technology projects.

Risk management is the identification, assessment, and prioritization of risks (defined in ISO 31000 as the effect of uncertainty on objectives, whether positive or negative), followed by coordinated and economical application of resources to minimize, monitor, and control the probability and/or impact of unfortunate events.

Risk management can be quite rigorous and quantitative in nature, as is shown in the following mathematical example:

A *risk* is the total of each of the *hazards* that contribute to it. The risk of any particular hazard, **H**, can be defined as its probability, **p**, multiplied by its consequence, **c**. In layman's terms: how likely it is to happen and how bad it will be if it does happen?

$$\textit{Hazard} = \mathbf{p}_{\mathbf{H}} * \mathbf{c}_{\mathbf{H}}$$

Therefore the total risk, **R**, of an event, **e**, is the sum of the **n** potential hazards that would result in that event:

$$R_e = \sum_{i=0}^{n} H_i$$

The *consequences* can be defined as:

- **Catastrophic**—Multiple Deaths, extensive property loss, irreparable damage to the ability of the earth to sustain life.
- **Critical**—Extensive damage to the economy, widespread famine, social unrest, multiple deaths.
- **Marginal**—Slowing of the economy, some loss of wealth, loss of consumer confidence.
- **Negligible**—Inconvenience, discomfort, possible devaluation of some investments.

The Probability is identified as 'Certain', 'Likely', 'Possible', 'Unlikely' and 'Rare'

Whether or not this stringent, quantitative approach is appropriate under any particular circumstance is debatable. The real value, in my experience, is that it forces stakeholders to at least *consider* the possibility that inopportune events *might* transpire, and what might be done in such eventualities.

In his *Seventh Annual Message to Congress*, Theodore Roosevelt said: "Optimism is a good characteristic, but if carried to an excess, it becomes foolishness."

Spoken like a true and prudent conservative.

In project management, the counter-approach is to blindly blunder forward, hoping against all odds that every turn of events will favor the desired outcome. Sometimes people get lucky, but more often than not, the project fails.

The 'dot.com bubble' is a prime example. In the beginning, the sheer size of potential profits ensured that the few successes offset the many failures. The bubble continued to inflate. Inevitably, however, as more and more speculators, of ever decreasing talent, vision, and just plain luck jumped into the rush, the balance began to shift. Eventually, it reached the point where investors would throw money at anything that had 'dot.com' in its name, without even the most perfunctory attempts at due diligence. The balloon inflated, inflated…inflated… and then…***POP!***

So, a lot of people lost a lot of money…that's why they call it 'gambling'. Some innocent people were also affected when their pensions, invested in these risky technology issues, evaporated; and that was unfortunate. However, money may equate to life *style*, but it is not life itself, or survival of the species, or survival of life in general. Once again, I'm not concurring that this dire effect *is* inevitable, but when performing a risk analysis, one must consider *all* possibilities, analyze their danger, and consider timely mitigations. So, in the case of our climate change discussion:

Scenarios:

1. Global warming is real, and is caused by human activity,
2. Global warming is real, but is part of naturally occurring cycles
3. Global warming is nonexistent

Reactions:

1. Act immediately to decrease carbon output,
2. Wait while we do further studies,
3. Do nothing and ignore the issue.

This gives us a total of nine combinations:

1-1 Global warming is real, is caused by human activity, and we act immediately to decrease carbon output.

1-2 Global warming is real, is caused by human activity, and we study the problem further before making any commitment.

1-3 Global warming is real, is caused by human activity, and we do nothing and ignore the issue,

2-1 Global warming is real, but is part of naturally occurring cycles, and we act immediately to decrease carbon output.

2-2 Global warming is real, but is part of naturally occurring cycles, and we study the problem further before making any commitment.

2-3 Global warming is real, but is part of naturally occurring cycles, and we do nothing and ignore the issue,

3-1 Global warming is nonexistent, and we act immediately to decrease carbon output.

3-2 Global warming is nonexistent, and we study the problem further before making any commitment.

3-3 Global warming is nonexistent, and we do nothing and ignore the issue,

We can arrange these possibilities in a simple matrix in order to better understand the entire picture:

		Consequence			
		Marginal	*Severe*	*Critical*	*Catastrophic*
Probability	*Certain*				
	Likely				
	Possible				
	Unlikely				
	Rare				

Since completing this matrix would inevitably introduce irrelevant and distracting contention, I'll leave it to the individual reader to put the various scenarios wherever *they* feel they belong. Regardless of your particular belief system, priorities, and orientation, one conclusion is inescapable:

The worst case, even *if* the probability is low, incurs consequences *so* dire that failure to consider it seriously is not only imprudent, it is absolutely criminal.

Conversely, the next worst-case scenario, in which we jump in with both feet and direct significant resources toward an issue that turns out to be nonexistent, is at worst critical, and more likely, only marginal.

How do I reach these conclusions? Well, the doomsday scenarios predicted by the Global Warming proponents are well documented, and since we *are* asking for a worst-case scenario, must be taken at face value. Water levels rise, coastal cities are destroyed, weather patterns are altered, crops fail, widespread famine leads to countless deaths, wars break out, society collapses. Not a pretty projection. Sounds to me like rather high stakes, except in the case where the alternatives are equally severe, or worse. So let's consider *those* alternatives.

Second worst case: All of the research, development, alternative energy experiments and clean air initiatives are not only totally ineffective, but in addition, we learn absolutely nothing from the effort, *and* no relevant spin-off technology whatsoever emerges. This is not only unlikely, but absolutely unprecedented in the annals of recorded history. It would, in fact, be completely analogous to shutting down all technology and production, and putting every human being on earth to the task of counting the grains of sand on their nearest beach. Then, with decades of time and billions of dollars wasted, and absolutely nothing to show for it, major industries would fail, the economy would plummet, wars would erupt, and society would fail. In other words, the same things that are predicted by the worst-case scenario would come to pass, *except for the natural catastrophes*.

Moving one step back, to the *third* worst case (severe): we spin our wheels for several decades, only to find that Global Warming was an erroneous prediction; however, from that effort emerge several new technologies, industries, and benefits. For example, the finite nature of fossil fuels may be tangential to the utter destruction of the environment, however, it is nonetheless consequential, and the development of alternative energies will pay dividends of their own. Yes, many people will lose a great deal of wealth, however, if history is any indicator, others will profit correspondingly. Oil men may grumble, but the new 'green' multi-millionaires will not. Power structures may shift (and *that* is what most of those in government *really* care about), but society will persist.

So, to boil it down to the essence: If we listen to the 'Global Warming' folks, and they're wrong, some people will lose some money. If we listen to their opponents, and *they're* wrong, life as we know it will be irrevocably destroyed.

Well, I don't know about *you*, but to me, the *conservative* approach is to err on the side of caution. Alternatively, just *how greedy* must a person be who would rather risk all life on earth in order to be certain of retaining *their personal wealth*? I would submit that this is not merely greed, it is criminal psychosis of the highest order, and is well exemplified by the likes of Bernie Madoff, Ken Lay, and the host of others of their ilk.

Don't get me wrong, I have nothing against rich people. Someone like Bill Gates, who made his money through a combination of skill, luck, and yes, even cut-throat cunning, nonetheless, *produced* something. Like him or not, he's probably done more than any single individual to turn the computer into something most of our grandmothers own and use. He has advanced technology, employed countless people, and helped innumerable causes, foundations, and individuals. This is fundamentally different than someone who deliberately sets out to do nothing except indulge his or her own hedonistic appetites, indifferent to the damage done to innumerable victims. *These* individuals are in every sense worse people than most murderers. They are enemies of humanity, enemies of civilization, enemies of society. Murderers most often commit crimes out of passion. Terrorists kill for a *cause*, regardless of how twisted that cause may be. People like Madoff destroy others solely for their own personal gratification. So you tell me, who really is the *worst of the worst*?

As a final example, consider the debacle of the U.S. invasion of Iraq. All other considerations aside, by the reports of everyone who was actually there when the decision to go to war was being 'debated', nobody who attempted to identify the risks, or consider any but the *best-case* scenarios, was given any credence whatsoever. The only consensus the administration would *permit* to be reached was the one that assured we would be greeted with chocolates and flowers, and would be in and out quick order, with minimum expense or loss of life. That was...when?

March 19, 2003

Can you honestly believe the worst-case scenario was adequately and *conservatively* considered?

Conservative?

March 19, 2003: Bush launches Invasion of Iraq

"We know where [the weapons of mass destruction] are. They're in the area around Tikrit and Baghdad and east, west, south and north somewhat." (ABC This Week, 3/30/03)

Or Reckless?

Democracy

The very word brings tears to our eyes and makes us want to stand up, slap hand over heart, and recite the pledge whose words most of us have never bothered to analyze or understand. Democracy. It's synonymous with all that is good and right—liberty, justice, fair play, and the American way of life. Most of all, it is what America is, does, stands for, and fights for all over the world, right?

Well, that's what *they* would *like* us to believe, but does it stand up to close scrutiny and careful analysis? You can decide for yourself.

First, the definitions:

"A government in which the supreme power is vested in the people and exercised by them directly or indirectly through a system of representation usually involving periodically held free elections." (Merriam Webster **1b***)*

"The absence of hereditary or arbitrary class distinctions and privileges" (Merriam Webster **5***)*

"Government by the people; that form of government in which the sovereign power resides in the people as a whole, and is exercised either directly by them (as in the small republics of antiquity) or by officers elected by them. In modern use often more vaguely denoting a social state in which all have equal rights, without hereditary or arbitrary differences of rank or privilege." (OED)

Let's begin with an important, and often misunderstood fact: The United States of America, as defined in The Constitution thereof, is *not* a democracy, nor was it ever envisioned as such or intended to be one. America is a Federal Republic, and it's critical that we understand the distinction, the implications, and the reasons this is the case. This is not a matter of right versus wrong, or better and worse. The problem, as we shall see, is that the ruling *Republicrat Junta* has played fast and loose with these concepts, using one or the other when it suits their own interests and agendas, regardless of the legality, constitutionality, or impact on the governed.

These two forms of government: Democracy and Republic, are not only dissimilar but antithetical, reflecting the sharp contrast between (a) the Majority Unlimited, in a Democracy, lacking any legal safeguard for the rights of the Individual and The Minority, and (b) the Majority Limited, in a Republic under a written Constitution safeguarding the rights of the Individual and the Minority; as we shall now see.

The chief characteristic and distinguishing feature of a Democracy is: Rule by Omnipotent Majority. In a Democracy, the Individual, and any group of individuals composing any Minority, have no protection against the unlimited power of the Majority. It is a case of Majority-over-Man.

Hence, if 51% of the populace decides that Christian worship should be outlawed, *that* would be the law of the land. If the majority decides that the Thirteenth Amendment should be rescinded, and slavery reenacted, that's the way it would be.

In all variations of Democracy, the majority's rule is absolute. There is *no* limitation. If it is decided that everyone in the nation should have their feet measured, and all of those with a size 10-1/2 shoe should be taxed at a rate twice that of everyone else, well, tough luck—that's what a Democracy is all about.

This opens the door to unlimited Tyranny-by-Majority, and is what The Framers of the United States Constitution meant in 1787, during debates in the Federal (framing) Convention, when they condemned the "excesses of democracy" and abuses under any Democracy of the unalienable rights of the Individual by the Majority.

Democracy, as a form of government, is utterly repugnant to—is the very antithesis of—the traditional American system: that of a Republic, as expressed in essence in the Declaration of Independence. The underlying philosophy expressed by the Founding Fathers placed primary emphasis upon the People forming their government so as to permit them to possess only "just powers" (limited powers) in order to make and keep secure the God-given, unalienable rights of each and every Individual and therefore of all groups of Individuals. (So no, Bubbah, just because Lamar, and Bobby-Joe, and Jimmy-Lee, and all your white-hooded neighbors decide it's perfectly okay to drag a man to death behind your pickup truck, that doesn't make it lawful.)

A Republic has at its essence an entirely different purpose than a Democracy; that being to *control* the abuses of the Majority, primarily to protect the Individual's God-given, unalienable rights, and therefore, for the protection of the rights of the Minority, of all minorities, and the liberties of people in general.

The definition of a Republic is: a constitutionally limited government of the representative type, created by a written Constitution—adopted by the People and changeable (from its original meaning) by them *only by its amendment*—with its powers divided between three separate Branches: Executive, Legislative and Judicial. Here the term "the People" means, of course, the electorate.

Let's pause a moment here, and note that the above-emphasized phrase infers that *every* politician who has voted to enact a law that restricts individual rights without amending the constitution is, by definition, *a traitor*.

Again, as in a Democracy, the Republic is characterized by "The absence of hereditary or arbitrary class distinctions and privileges."

Just ask yourself: What rights do members of congress enjoy, as a result of their own legislations, compared with an 'ordinary citizen'? Have they not, in every sense, implemented a *de facto* aristocracy, populated by themselves and their cronies?

Nazism

This is another of those loaded words, like anti-Semite, that is too often used to squelch conversation by demonizing those holding opposing views (often views which have nothing whatsoever to do with Adolph Hitler). The actual definition of the term is: "*The political doctrines evolved and implemented by Adolf Hitler and his followers, esp. those relating to racial superiority, the all-powerful state, and the cult of the leader." (OED).* For the present discussion, there are three components in this definition that merit close scrutiny:

1. Racial superiority,
2. The all-powerful state,
3. The cult of the leader.

While many apologists, usually Liberals, are fond of belaboring the fact that this nation was built on a foundation of racial injustice, I see no point in revisiting this particular issue. Injustices were perpetrated, recognized, and rectified, so let's move on. I am far more concerned with what we *continue* to do today.

By now, even the most skeptical among us are aware of the *Tuskegee Syphilis Experiments,* in which poor Southern black citizens were allowed to die of the dread infection so that researchers could study the progression of the untreated disease. While it might be possible to dismiss this particular incident as an aberration, or an instance of a well-intentioned program gone wrong, a proliferation of similar callous, abusive, inhuman, and clearly racially-charged events renders this charitable interpretation impossible.

As recently as October, 2010, the United States government was forced to acknowledge, and apologize for, deliberately infecting over 1500 Guatemalans with Syphilis between 1946 and 1948 in a similar 'study'. U.S. scientists infected prostitutes with syphilis or gonorrhea and sent them to have unprotected sex with soldiers or prison inmates, later testing them for possible cures. When few became infected, scientists turned to patients at a mental health hospital, exposing them to infection by rubbing it on their genitals. None of the subjects were informed about the study or offered consent, U.S. officials said.

Try as I might, I can find no basic theory in the Christian dogma upon which this country was purportedly founded that supports the notion that foreign citizens, or poor people, are somehow less worthy of ethical treatment than rich, white Americans.

While, on the surface, we have made great strides in combating racism over the past fifty years or so, the fact of the matter is that the underlying notions of racial superiority remain, just beneath the surface at best. The veiled comments about welfare, entitlements, street crime, and a thousand other topics are often little more than code for the racial concepts that are actually at the core of the debates.

The second tenet of the above definition of Nazism, "the all-powerful state," scarcely requires comment or justification. The framers of the Constitution—the founders of this country—wisely realized that freedom meant that different people would want to live different kinds of lives, and any attempt to force-fit them into one common mould would not only be doomed to failure, but would incur a backlash that would serve to drive factions further apart, rather than bring them together.

The concept of States' rights has, of late, become cast as a metaphor for racism and separatism, but this not necessarily the case. As a signatory to The Constitution of the United States, every state has an obligation to adhere to the principles described therein. Period.

Let's come at this from a different angle, shall we?

Would the antagonism between, say, California on one end of the spectrum and Texas or Arizona on the other be anywhere near as acerbic if residents of either didn't fear that the attitudes, values, and preferences of the other weren't in imminent danger of being forced on *them*? Part of life, liberty, and that elusive pursuit of happiness means being able to live amongst people of your choice, who embrace values similar to your own—once again, within the limits outlined in the Constitution. If you don't like where you happen to be, you have every right to get up and go someplace where people are more like you. What you *don't* have is the right to force everyone else to conform to *your* expectations and sensibilities; and this comment is just as applicable to the Liberals as to anyone else. Sorry folks, but if 90% of the parents attending your high school's soccer tournament want to stand up before the game and recite a common prayer to their mutual deity, well, what of it? Sorry if it makes *you* feel uncomfortable to be amongst the 10% who remain seated, but so long as they don't turn around and beat you up, or burn you at the stake, your choices are to live with it, or move elsewhere. Life ain't perfect, this isn't Burger King, and you don't always get to have it *your way*.

On the other hand, if citizens of California want to allow adults to smoke a common, naturally growing plant substance without fear of persecution, or acknowledge same-sex unions with the word 'marriage', in what way does that impair *your* freedoms? Makes you uncomfortable to see two guys or two gals holding hands? I can understand that, but it doesn't mean that you have the right to insist that *your* sensibilities should impinge on *their* freedoms. Live with it, look the other way, or go somewhere else. *Those* are *your* choices.

Clearly, if the other guy wasn't looking to take away *your* freedoms, these alternative attitudes, lifestyles, and priorities might be no more than a source for good-natured jests, rather than the outright rage they have now become.

As we will prove later, this state of affairs is not mere chance or happenstance, but by way of a preview, ask yourself precisely who benefits by making everyone the same, and by fermenting antagonism between neighbors? The answer is the big businesses, who thrive on the economy of scale that only result from a homogeneous purchasing public, and the politicians whom they own, who, in turn, are motivated to maintain their personal power at the seat of an all-intrusive central seat of power.

The third tenet in the *OED* definition of Nazism is the establishment of a leadership cult.

By deifying our particular favored leaders, we preclude ourselves from considering their *actions* in a fair and balanced manner. Today, saying anything *positive* about Richard Nixon is as unacceptable in some circles as speaking ill of Ronald Reagan or John F. Kennedy. Why? Because doing so is interpreted as endorsing or opposing an entire canon of beliefs with which each has become inextricability, and unreasonably, connected.

Now, I believe Richard Nixon was an unpleasant, ill-mannered, heavy-handed, despot who abused his power and had no regard whatsoever for the rights of the American citizens. That said, I can still acknowledge that he *was* the one who got us out of Viet Nam, and opened a dialog with the Chinese.

I believe that Ronald Reagan was a decent, well-intentioned, sincere and honorable man. He did a lot of things that were good for the country, and for the rest of the world. He also did some things that were just plain wrong. Does that make him a demon? Hardly. Am I some kind of subversive for recognizing that he was an imperfect human being, who made some mistakes? I don't believe so.

This kind of hero worship has been promoted by politicians and their complicit media since the middle of the last century. Once you convince people that a particular public figure is more than human—is a shining beacon and icon of everything that his or her supporters hold sacred, questioning *any* of their actions or decisions automatically becomes sacrilege.

Just because Bill Clinton can blow some cool notes on his horn, and seems like the kind of guy you might like to hang with, doesn't mean he can't also be an unfaithful, lying profligate, whose basest instincts rule his better judgment. Just because those who accused him might, in your opinion, be puritanical prudes, or outright hypocrites, that doesn't change the fact that he lied under oath—something that would send most of us straight to jail.

Similarly, George W. Bush might come off just like the guys you work with at the machine shop, or fish with on weekends, or tailgate with after the NASCAR race, but that doesn't change the fact that he has admitted to decisions that many might argue constitute war crimes.

As I write this, Barak Obama, whom I *did* support, ordered American armed forces to attack Libya, in response to UN Resolution 1973. He did so without consulting congress—an action which, according to his own earlier legal writings, constitutes an impeachable offense. Democratic Senator Dennis Kucinich has joined Republicans in calling for an investigation, and in doing so, has shown himself to be a man of rare integrity; a statesman amongst the hordes of sleazy politicians who rule this country.

"Standing behind" a politician just because you voted for him or her does not make you patriotic, or loyal, or even smart—what it does make you is derelict in your responsibilities as a citizen.

Socialism

Socialism: *"A theory or policy of social organization which aims at or advocates the ownership and control of the means of production, capital, land, property, etc., by the community as a whole, and their administration or distribution in the interests of all" (OED).*

Like most other theories, there are degrees and nuances to Socialism that are neither good nor bad, but must be considered in terms of the situation, the circumstances, and most importantly, the integrity of the implementation. Judging the abstract theory of Socialism by a particular flawed implementation, for example, that of the former Soviet Socialist Republic, is as misguided and erroneous as judging Capitalism by the deeds of Bernie Madoff.

In our current political dialog/diatribe, the word 'socialism' has become an indictment of the reckless 'tax and spend' philosophies espoused by the Democratic Party over the past fifty years or so, but, like so much of the misleading propaganda employed to manipulate the American citizens, this bears little resemblance to the true meaning of the word.

The basis of society itself is that by combining resources for a common goal, economies of scale facilitate accomplishments that no sub-group could do alone. As Theodore Roosevelt acknowledged: "I am a strong individualist by personal habit, inheritance, and conviction; but it is a mere matter of common sense to recognize that the State, the community, the citizens acting together, can do a number of things better than if they were left to individual action."

In nature, the strong always exploit the weak. That's the way things work. Lions eat gazelles. If the Lion is slow, and the gazelle is fast, the lion starves to death. If not, the lion eats and the gazelle dies. Many who embrace the philosophy of rugged individualism, often quoting "who says life is fair?" point to this as justification for their particular (and peculiar) world view. Oddly, these are often the same folks who are so fond of pointing to their own European heritage as evidence of racial superiority. It apparently never occurs to them that the *reason* for this purportedly sublime cultural development was that these groups had learned to cooperate. Could Michelangelo have devoted his life to art if he was forced to hunt and/or gather his daily meals, make his own clothes, build his own shelters, and so forth?

For those who insist on extolling their rugged individualism, I suggest the following experiment: Get yourself a modest yacht, load it up with all the guns and munitions you can handle, and go sailing alone in the waters off Somalia. No *friends*, now, because *that* would be the beginnings of *socialism*. Just you versus those *organized* Somali pirates. Let me know how that works out for you….

If there is a shred of intellectual honesty in a person, then they must acknowledge that the only reason they *can* live this wonderful iconoclastic life is that someone else provides key elements they lack, be it the ability to forge steel, formulate gun powder, or manufacture those fancy compound archery bows.

All progress is contingent upon, and proportional to, a group's ability to cooperate. This holds for ants and termites, apes and elephants, as well as people. Socialism favors the advancement of the species over the advancement of the strongest and most selfish individual.

What about city services? Local police, state police, federal police, fire fighters, trash removal, municipal sewers and water, a standing army? What about the interstate highway system? How about the internet? Without suggesting any judgment, it's important to acknowledge that there have *always* been elements of socialism in our *society*. Some you may like, some you don't.

Taken to the extreme, as Noam Chomsky observes, we would be compelled to "eliminate highway taxes because they force you to pay for a road you may never drive on. As an alternative, they suggest that if you and I want to get somewhere, we should build a road there and charge people tolls on it. Just try generalizing that. Such a society couldn't survive, and even if it could, it would be so full of terror and hate that any human being would prefer to live in hell."[1]

Then, of course, there is the 'hidden' socialism, about which nobody has much to say. For example, as much as you might decry the inflated cost of just about every necessity for daily life, that food, the fuel used to cart it across the country or across the world, and just about everything else you buy is subsidized through government tax-breaks, incentives, and outright give-aways to the giant corporations that have all but driven smaller competitors into extinction. In *The Value of Nothing: Why Everything Costs So Much More Than We Think*, author Raj Patel shows, through a careful and detailed analysis, that in the absence of all subsidies, the price of a fast-food burger would be around $200! As I shall demonstrate later, the difference is actually shifted to subsequent generations, who will simply *perish* as a result of shortages arising from our current free-wheeling lifestyles.

[1] Noam Chomsky, *The Common Good*, Odonian Press, 2002.

Take a deep breath and at least *consider* the possibility that maybe the problem is not Socialism versus Capitalism, but rather, honest implementations of either, versus their misuse to exploit others.

We are urged to eschew extremism in all its forms, *except* in the case of grotesque distortions used by our rulers to manipulate our emotions and control our behavior.

Whether you consider yourself an environmentalist or not, if someone poisons the water table, have they not effectively *stolen* the value of *your property*? How about if your upstream cattle-baron neighbor dams your water supply so *your* livestock cannot drink? Don't you want some recourse, other than engaging in a range war (that *you* might lose, despite being in the right)?

The *problem* arises when the arbitrator upon whom all parties agree turns out to be on the other guy's payroll, or has an entirely different agenda of his own.

For example, we have an Environmental Protection Agency, whose job is *supposed* to be to protect *your* property, so your greedy neighbor can't, say, come by and dump a load of manure in your well in order to render your property worthless and then gobble it up for pennies on the dollar. What has actually happened is plain to see. The EPA has taken big payoffs from the most egregious polluters in return for ignoring their crimes. The results are places like the Love Canal in New York, and numerous other toxic dumps. People whose lives are ruined are bought off, if necessary, but most often just ignored until they run out of resources to continue the fight. To those on the sidelines, the explanation is posed in terms of progress, jobs created, and the overall benefit to 'the economy'. When all else fails, the opposition is portrayed as liberal, socialist, commie tree-huggers, and their objections summarily dismissed. Meanwhile, corrupt, deceitful politicians, of which Rick Perry is a current and highly visible example, seize upon this failure in implementation and pose it as a failure in concept, in order to remove any remaining restrictions on the polluting corporations that have purchased their complicity.

Of course, as the situation grows more and more egregious, the explanations become increasingly circuitous, the justifications increasingly complex, and the final truth all but unfathomable. It's like that old shell game, where the objective is to distract your attention from the fact that the pea has been removed and no longer resides beneath *any* of the three shells.

As a glaring example, let's examine the Social Security situation. As Republicans are fond of pointing out (*ad nauseam*), this is clearly a socialist institution, an assessment with which no reasonable person can argue. Where the misdirection has taken place is in the tacit assumption that the source of the problem is the fact that it *is* a Socialist institution, rather than the fact this it is an institution that has been criminally mishandled, and outright plundered by the shady gangsters from both political parties, over a span of decades.

Make no mistake about it—Democrats *and* Republicans have outright *embezzled* this retirement bank account into which you have been forced to save. This is *not* a matter of well-intentioned investments gone bad, or unforeseeable circumstances. It is theft, plain and simple. Why don't the Democrats, who, presumably, are the ones who favor socialist programs call the Republicans on this sleazy bit of sophistry? The answer is obvious: because *they* have been equally complicit in the crime. So long as the victims of this robbery are busy arguing over abstract (and irrelevant) ideologies, they totally ignore the fact that this *Republicrat Junta* has simply *taken* our money and spent it in the furtherance of their own self-serving agendas, just as surely as did Bernie Madoff.

Perhaps the proper reaction to this theft is *not* to re-elect the thieves, but instead, subject them to some good old-fashioned *Islamic*-style justice—chop off their hands!

Public education is a similar 'Socialist institution' that has become the object of misdirection from both corners.

The vast majority of Americans, I'm convinced, *want* their children to have greater opportunities than their parents, and most will concur that education is a critical part of this equation. We may have different ideas as to what constitutes a good education, but let's set that aside for a moment.

First let's ponder the inscrutable truth that other countries, some Capitalist, some Socialist, some Communist, have been managing to turn out highly educated students from their public education systems, while an increasing number of *ours* are, well, dummies. Is this because they're being taught evolution instead of creationism? Too many tests? Too few? Not enough emphasis on science? Too much emphasis on science? Not enough corporeal punishment? Crowded classrooms?

How about an entire infrastructure built on benefiting administrators, rather than the students? Teacher's unions are not at fault, *these particular* teacher's unions—which, are more interested in maintaining the power of union officials than in protecting good teachers—are the problem. Charter schools are not the answer—not unless we buy into the prevarication that business and profit interests automatically guarantee integrity. Laws like 'No child left behind' are not the answer, unless we think that these greedy, corrupt, self-serving politicians, who have proven their dishonesty in every other field, have suddenly changed their stripes.

What *is* the answer?

Well, a big part of the problem is that everyone, from the politicians, to the school administrators, right down to the parents themselves are so preoccupied with their own oh-so-important pursuits, that they can't be bothered with the effort of...thinking. Instead, they look for automated rules that can be applied without the expenditure of any effort whatsoever.

Forty percent failure rate? Teacher gets fired. Sixty percent failure rate? Shut down the school and deploy a for-profit charter school....

Does it occur to *anyone* that, by this logic, *Jesus* should be judged an abject failure based on the way some Christians choose to apply his teachings?

A completely natural and inevitable outcome of this 'zero-tolerance' mindset is the case of the child who was found in violation of a school's zero-tolerance weapons laws when he fastened a tiny plastic toy soldier to the brim of his hat for Veterans' Day. Similarly, a little girl was recently forced to throw her half-dollar-sized pet turtle in the trash because carrying it onto an airplane violated some statute or other. We are turning into a nation of rigid, mindless, rule-driven bureaucrats, incapable or unwilling to exercise any degree of common sense or compassion.

An alternative answer might entail...common sense, common decency, and a willingness to admit to the *possibility* that those who believe differently from you *might* be honest, even if they *are* wrong.

Give me *wrong* and *honest* any day!

When I was growing up, I was taught lots of stuff in school that my father thought was "bullshit," and he said so, and you know what? I believed *him*, not my teachers. Later, as an adult, I revisited many of these issues. Some, I reversed, others, I embraced. The point here is that I really don't *care* if my child is taught the creationist creed, or the Darwinian doctrine. I don't care if he or she pledges allegiance to one nation 'under God' or otherwise. If I am truly an engaged parent, then I will be fully capable of putting any and all of these teachings into perspective. If I am not, then I should be ready to accept the default and stop bitching about it. Just so long as he or she learns to add a column of figures, construct a comprehensible sentence, and, most importantly, think for him– or herself, and recognize blatant propaganda whenever it's encountered.

I've heard it claimed that nowhere in our Constitution is public education even mentioned, much less placed under the purview of the federal government. True enough. On the other hand, the right to equal opportunity *is* guaranteed by the Constitution, and what could be more important in today's world than a competitive education? Lest we forget, in earlier times the self-educated man—Lincoln for example—was capable of competing on a level playing field. Today it's the diploma that rules.

In the domain of education, we must also acknowledge that institutionalized education is not a result of one gifted individual—Socrates, Plato, or Aristotle—sharing their insights in return for appropriate remuneration. The codification of our most essential knowledge is predicated upon the work of thousands and thousands of individuals and institutions, many of them supported by publicly funded grants and endowments; and the knowledge they seek to transfer is often the result of tax-subsidized private-sector research. To turn around and claim that the resultant education is anything *but* a common right to all citizens who have contributed to that body of knowledge is not only disingenuous, it is deliberately manipulative and misleading.

For now, let's just say this: If *it* (creationism, evolution, or whatever) is important enough to you, then it is up to *you* to present it to your children in an manner that will make it more convincing than the alternatives. In the end, if the goal is to nurture adults capable if independent, critical thinking, they will make up their own minds, without the benefit of officially sanctioned government indoctrination.

In conclusion, despite the efforts of some to use the word 'Socialism' as some kind of rallying cry, it's important for every *reasonable* person to acknowledge that anything other than a solitary existence as a cave-dwelling hermit entails *some* degree of Socialism.

Communism

Communism is one of those words which, like *racist*, *anti-Semite*, *anarchist*, *Nazi*, *pedophile*, and so forth, is just *so* loaded with baggage that it's virtually impossible to utter it without generating deeply visceral reactions that have little to do with the actual meaning of the word. That meaning, as given by the unabridged *Oxford English Dictionary* is as follows:

1. a.1.a A theory which advocates a state of society in which there should be no private ownership, all property being vested in the community and labor organized for the common benefit of all members; the professed principle being that each should work according to his capacity, and receive according to his wants.

1. a.2.a Applied to any practice which carries out this theory in whole or part; e.g. that mentioned in Acts ii. 44 seq., as practiced in the church of Jerusalem, or that prevailing in monastic communities.

Hey! Wait a minute! Godless red communism in the *Bible*?

Well, here's the exact passage (King James version):

44 *And all that believed were together, and had all things common;*

45 *And sold their possessions and goods, and parted them to all men, as every man had need.*

46 *And they, continuing daily with one accord in the temple, and breaking bread from house to house, did eat their meat with gladness and singleness of heart.*

So, here we have a case where the government (which *has* been known to mislead citizens in furtherance of its own agenda), says one thing about communism, and the *Bible*, which some citizens, at least, consider the literal word of their God, says something quite different. I leave it to each reader to weight the respective sources in accordance with their individual convictions.

Witness, similarly, the Israeli kibbutz program, which is essentially communism/communalism in its purest form.

None of this is to suggest that the Soviet's *implementation* of Marxism, under despots such as Lenin, or Stalin, or Nikita Khrushchev, was anything *but* a brutal, oppressive, dictatorial, and inefficient establishment; it was. The issue is that we must always be cognizant of making inappropriate generalizations based on traits that are specific to an individual instantiation. In this day and age, *most* Americans would scarcely be inclined to reason that because some Italians are mafia, then all Italians are mafia; because some African-Americans are thugs, therefore all African-Americans are thugs; because some Fundamentalist Christians are revealed to be hypocrites, all people of faith are hypocrites….

Because *some* Communists are corrupt, we can no more conclude that *all* Communists are corrupt than to reason that because some Capitalists are honest, therefore Bernie Madoff is honest.

" Ye shall know them by their fruits." (Matt 7:16)

Liberalism

According to the unabridged *Oxford English Dictionary*, this word originally identified those pursuits that were considered 'worthy of a free man'. A meaning more relevant to political applications might be: "Free from narrow prejudice; open-minded, candid. Free from bigotry or unreasonable prejudice in favor of traditional opinions or established institutions; open to the reception of new ideas or proposals of reform."

Notice that no mention is made of disarming citizens, a welfare state, gay marriage, abortion rights, religious practice, evolution, creationism, illegal immigrants, the environment, animal rights, vegetarianism, or a host of other specific causes that are frequently, and erroneously, associated with liberalism. All it says is that the liberal is willing to *consider* new ideas with an *open mind.*

Of course, there is no shortage of rigid dogmatists who would proclaim themselves 'Liberal', but I would contend that they are as far from the true essence of liberalism as Ronald Reagan, Newt Gingrich, or Jerry Falwell.

I consider myself a Liberal in terms of methodology, in that I always want to hear and consider all possibilities, but lean toward the Conservative when it comes to a final determination, to the extent that I always tend to favor the least risky solutions.

Attempting to paint all Liberals (or any group, for that matter) with a single broad brush is not only an injustice to all concerned, including the painter, but also an exercise in futility.

Contrast, for example, former Saturday Night Live alumni, and current *Senator* Al Franken, whose mode of self expression is best characterized by the title of his book: *Rush Limbaugh is a Big Fat Idiot* (Dell; twentieth edition, January 12, 1999) with the thoughtful, balanced, and always erudite analyses of Noam Chomsky, or the impassioned but focused observations of Ralph Nader.

Indeed, the very word 'liberalism' derives from the Latin *liberalis*, meaning "of freedom").

Like Conservatives, Liberals espouse a vast array of views, depending on their understanding of the underlying principles of each philosophy. As shall be demonstrated throughout this book, true Liberals and true Conservatives actually agree on a number of critical issues, such as the importance of liberty and equal rights, constitutions, democracy, free and fair elections, human rights, Capitalism,[1] and the freedom of religion.

These ideas are widely accepted by most *honest* political groups, even those that do not openly profess a liberal ideological orientation, and can provide a basis for the consensus and coalition that will be critical for ousting the corrupt *Republicrat Junta* that has usurped our government.

Liberalism first became a powerful force in the Age of Enlightenment, rejecting several foundational assumptions that dominated most earlier theories of government, such as hereditary status, established religion, absolute monarchy, and the Divine Right of Kings. The early liberal thinker John Locke, who is often credited for the creation of Liberalism as a distinct philosophical tradition, employed the concept of natural rights and the social contract to argue that the *rule of law* should replace absolutism in government, that rulers were subject to the consent of the governed, and that private individuals had a *fundamental right to life, liberty, and property.*

The revolutionaries in the American Revolution and the French Revolution used liberal philosophy to justify the armed overthrow of tyrannical rule.

Obviously, these are aspects that those who hold power through coercion, bribery, and corruption do *not* want honest people of any persuasion to recognize or consider.

Perhaps we need to put aside these emotionally overburdened labels for a while, and simply identify ourselves as ***Anti-Republicrats.***

[1] As we shall demonstrate in the next chapter, there is a vast chasm between *true* Capitalism, and the *perversion* of Capitalism practiced by the *Republicrats*, which is often referred to as 'Crony Capitalism'.

Capitalism

Capitalism as a socioeconomic system developed incrementally from the 16th. century in Europe, although capitalist-like organizations existed in the ancient world, and early aspects of merchant capitalism flourished during the late Middle Ages. Capitalism became dominant in the Western world following the demise of feudalism, and gradually spread throughout Europe. (As I argue throughout this book, our current system has much in common with feudalism.)

There is no real consensus on the definition of capitalism, nor how it should be used as an analytical category, however there is little controversy that *private ownership* of the means of production, *creation of goods or services* for profit in a market, and *market-driven prices and wages* are central elements of capitalism. Economists usually put emphasis on the degree to which *government does not exercise control* over markets (*laissez faire*), and on *property rights*; whereas most political scientists emphasize *private property*, power relations, wages, labor, and class. There is a general agreement that capitalism encourages economic growth. The extent to which different markets are 'free', as well as the rules determining what may and may not be private property, is a matter of *politics and policy*, so in practice, what results is more accurately termed a 'mixed economy'. So, to summarize, the key factors of a *true* capitalist system are private ownership of the means of production, creation of goods or services, and property rights. To this we can add that the implicit backbone which supports the capitalist system is the abstraction known as the market. In a nutshell, this simply means that the value of any object or service is determined by its value, which in turn is quantified by how much someone is willing to pay for it.

For our current purposes, the most important aspect of capitalism regards the extent to which the *word* has been used to polarize public opinion, manipulate the populace, and generate contention and enmity between citizens. Hence, we need to carefully analyze the extent to which those who *portray* themselves as promoting capitalist ideals and policies are being truthful, versus the ways in which their practices actually *conflict* with true capitalist principles. Most critically, we must continually remind ourselves that just because proven liars and criminals have contrived to *label* their misdeeds as 'capitalism', doesn't necessarily make it so. Jim Jones was a Christian minister. The Grand Inquisitor of Spain was a Catholic authority. Do we denigrate Christianity on the basis of a few ignoble individuals sullying the name? Of course not.

Similarly, it would be absurd to condemn capitalism itself on the basis of its pathological misuse by deviants like Bernie Madoff, Jeffery Skilling, or the Koch Brothers. Rather, we acknowledge that these are perversions of a basically well-intentioned system. Nor do we seek to *excuse* the actions of these nefarious individuals in an misguided effort to defend capitalism itself, for to do so is to argue that these individuals are the *essence* of the system, rather than a pathological aberration.

Indeed, like 'patriotism', 'conservatism', 'freedom', and a host of others, nefarious prevaricators have deliberately co-opted our most cherished concepts in order to deceive us into supporting their diametric opposites. Hence, I must make it absolutely clear that while I *support* capitalism, I abhor the *perversion* of capitalism that has been inflicted upon the American People by greedy, self-serving enemies of all we hold sacred.

'Crony Capitalism' is a term that has gained some traction of late in describing some of the practices employed by unethical business and government conspirators, but I don't believe this label adequately addresses the full scope of our current perversion of what is basically a noble and productive system. Crony capitalism is defined as:

A misapplication of capitalism in which success in business depends not, as intended, on free market drivers, but rather, on close relationships between business people and government officials. It is characterized by favoritism in the distribution of legal permits, government grants, special tax breaks, passage of unjust laws, and so forth.

While these factors are certainly *components* of our current misuse of capitalist principles, they do not cover the entirety of the aberration represented by our current economic and social system. To differentiate these exploitative practices, I shall refer to them as *AmeriCapitalism.*

Proponents of *AmeriCapitalism* would have us believe that a free market system is the be-all and end-all, and *obviously* the *only* necessity for a self-regulating society; but is it really? According to this simplistic analysis, the guy who had the bright idea of running guns over to Africa, swapping them for black slaves, whom he then transported back for sale to the American plantation owners was the ideal capitalist. The *only* issue these people have with such a business model is that it was eliminated by "unnecessary, meddlesome government interference." In fact, I have little doubt that the vast majority of these self-serving wealth accumulators would be only too happy to finance slavery if there was a way to get around the regulations.

As we shall see when we examine the concept of *wage slavery*, they are doing precisely that, and it isn't difficult to demonstrate how this mentality permeates every area and every level of our society. What these amoral dynasty builders really want *is* slavery—but in a sanitized form, so they don't have to see the faces of the downtrodden; don't have to whip their own niggers.

(To the committed racist, who's probably thinking: "Yeah, so? What's the problem?" I can only point out that, historically, slavery has not been the sole domain of white enslavement of blacks, and regardless of where *your* ancestors originated, there were probably some groups that would have been more than happy to enslave *them*.)

As Noam Chomsky astutely observed: "[C]apitalism is basically a system where everything is for sale, and the more money you have, the more you can get. And, in particular, that's true of freedom. Freedom is one of the commodities that is for sale, and if you are affluent, you can have a lot of it. It shows up in all sorts of ways. It shows up if you get in trouble with the law [...] what you're going to find is that the defense of free institutions will largely be in the hands of those who benefit from them, namely the wealthy, and the powerful."[1]

We shall explore these concepts further when we discuss *entitlements*, but essentially, proponents of this anything-goes interpretation contend that one is entitled to anything their money can facilitate. The ultimate extension of this attitude is the basis of the 2005 movie *Hostel*, in which attractive young travelers are lured to a remote compound where rich patrons pay for the privilege of torturing them to death as a form of entertainment. Indeed, that particular movie was based on *true* events: In certain Thai villages, organized crime syndicates rule, and poverty forces residents to part with family members for excessive amounts of money. These people are then transported to cities where some rich subhumans gamble to see how long their victims survive being tortured, while others pay exorbitant amounts of money to do the torturing and killing.

(I can almost hear some of these people saying: "Yeah? So? What's your point? Sounds like a win-win, market-driven model to *me*....")

The most important, and most repugnant aspect of *AmeriCapitalism* is the selective manner in which it is manipulated in order to benefit those who can afford to purchase their agendas with their corrupt cronies who pass the laws.

In 2009, a controversy briefly erupted, now conveniently forgotten, about toxic Chinese drywall being used in the construction of homes in the United States. The specifics of the problem are irrelevant to the current discussion. What *is* significant should be obvious to anyone who has ever

[1] Noam Chomsky, *Language and Politics*, Polity , 1999.

had occasion to actually install, or even handle this material: the stuff is *heavy*. How is it even remotely economical to ship such weighty, and relatively inexpensive building components halfway around the world?

The answer is that government subsidies allow greedy multinationals to squander a critical, and rapidly diminishing resource—oil—by moving low-value materials from point to point, in order to make a quick profit, a portion of which is funneled back to those who create this absurdly wasteful business environment. In an analogous business model, West-coast business criminals ship chickens from California to China to be plucked, then ship the processed carcasses back across the Pacific Ocean for sale here. Thus, taxpayer dollars are being used to create an artificial cost-value relationship in which it is cheaper to squander oil than to allow an American worker to earn a living. Nor can one reasonably argue that the problem arises from workers not wanting to do such unpleasant labor. If *that* were the issue, then it would make far more sense to import guest workers from Mexico, legally and temporarily, and require them to pay taxes on the income earned.

No, the sole motivation is to allow a few cunning, greedy individuals to reap massive and undeserved profits at the expense of the taxpayers, and of future generations.

We must continually remind ourselves that oil is used for far more critical applications than driving container ships, or even powering our snowmobiles, ATVs, motor homes, and jet-skis. Oil is essential for plastics, medicines, and, of course, fuel applications more essential than merely filling the bloated pockets of a few swinish individuals. Their opulent lifestyles come at the expense of your children's *lives*; and, moreover, *you're* being made to *subsidize* it!

Look at it this way: If Capitalist principles were really being allowed to work; if all the outsourcing of jobs being made economically feasible by the subsidization of oil were kept here; then consumers would easily be able to afford even $10/gallon gasoline, we would drastically reduce our reliance on foreign oil, and greenhouse emissions would be significantly reduced. Of course, honest, working Americans don't funnel billions of dollars in bribes to politicians, so *their* wellbeing is of little concern to those enacting the laws.

***Which* is John Galt?**

To understand the *ideals* of capitalism, one need only analyze the characters created by one of its most widely-read proponents: Ayn Rand.

Rand's political views, reflected in both her fiction and nonfiction work, emphasize individual rights (including property rights) and *laissez-faire* capitalism, enforced by a constitutionally limited government. Her two most famous novels, *The Fountainhead*, and *Atlas Shrugged*, illustrate core tenets of Rand's philosophy of *Objectivism,* and express her emphasis on human achievement. Although widely misquoted and inappropriately identified with *AmeriCapitalism*, careful analysis of Rand's characters illustrate the critical differences between *real* capitalism and our current aberration thereof:

Atlas Shrugged takes place in a dystopian United States, when the most creative industrialists, scientists, and artists go on strike and retreat to a mountainous hideaway where they build an independent free economy. The novel's hero and leader of the strike, John Galt, describes the strike as "stopping the motor of the world" by withdrawing the minds of the individuals most contributing to the nation's wealth and achievement.

Rand's heroes must continually fight against 'parasites', 'looters', and 'moochers' who demand the benefits of the heroes' labor. These are compelling and recognizable archetypes, capable of generating righteous indignation and powerful emotional reactions in most people.

Unfortunately, unscrupulous propagandists misuse these images by projecting the most provocative aspects in glaring detail, whilst slyly shuffling the real-world relationships, so that those whom they seek to manipulate associate the critical icons with real-world entities embodying precisely the *opposite* traits.

For example, in *Atlas Shrugged*, Hank Rearden is an brilliant, committed industrialist, who has steadfastly dedicated ten years of his life to the development of a revolutionary new alloy called *Rearden Metal*. It is stronger but cheaper than steel, and will outlast any other metal in existence. Rearden is an honest, direct, straight-talking hero of the Gary Cooper cast, beset by shifty, double-dealing, parasites from within his family, his company, and, of course, the government. Those who produce nothing want not only to profit from the inventor's creation, but indeed, to simultaneously deprive *him* of the fruits of his own labor. They are utterly despicable, worthless…scumbags.

It is certainly appropriate that normal, righteous people should despise such lowlifes. The shell-game aspect comes into play when we stop to analyze and identify which real-life entities we have been directed to associate with each character in this acerbic morality play.

Who, today, are the innovators, and who are the parasites?"

" *Ye shall know them by their fruits.* " (Matt 7:16).

Sam Walton, the founder of Wal-Mart, *was* a true innovator and entrepreneur. He had a vision, along with the drive, tenacity, and resourcefulness to instantiate it. He pioneered supply-chain coordination that brought levels of efficiency hitherto unimagined. He perceived a market need, and filled that need perfectly, creating jobs for many, and delivering value to many more. Sam Walton *earned* his success. Whether or not you agree with his vision, it's difficult to ignore his achievement.

Now, however, comes the bait-and-switch....

Who *is* Wal-Mart today? A consortium of parasitic Walton progenies who never worked a day in their lives, armies of slimy slugs in three-piece-suits with Harvard MBAs, chomping their cigars and conniving on golf courses how best to exploit overseas workers while evading corporate taxes and raking in billions of dollars in government hand-outs; and an infection of 'investors', totally disinterested in the operation or effect of the corporation, and focused solely on their unearned income with the same spirit as one might purchase a weekly lottery ticket.

Who *are* the innovators and who are the parasites in today's economy?

Is it in any way patriotic to export your country's strategic steel industry, for example, in the interest of quick profits? Is it productive to gobble up rival companies, rather than honestly competing with them, then shut them down, lay off their employees, and ship their jobs overseas? Who is profiting? Certainly not those who have lost their jobs. Not even those across the ocean who *get* those jobs, because they are invariably exploited, abused, and often all but enslaved. In every case, the beneficiaries are those who *produce nothing, give nothing back, and make nothing except unscrupulous deals.*

No, that's not quite true. They *do* make *policy*, and they do so through the politicians they all but purchase, from the freshman congressmen right up through the Supreme Court and the President of the nation. And once you have infiltrated the law-making structures of government, what's the first thing you do? Pass even *more* laws to expand and further entrench your power base. Like a nuclear meltdown, once a certain critical mass is attained, reversing the disaster is nearly impossible.

The latest, most visible, most egregious, and for the present discussion, most relevant event would have to be the *Citizens United* case upon which the Supreme Court recently ruled.

Once you strip away all the legalese smoke and mirrors, it boils down to a core kernel of transparent corruption that any American can easily digest (or, more appropriately, regurgitate):

We, the corrupt, completely compromised, government thugs, do hereby rule and decree that those who have been bribing us all along, may continue to do so, without limitation, and may use their great wealth and unanswerable power to usurp the will of the people in any election whatsoever. So let it be written. So let it be done.

Which *is* John Galt?

What makes this a particularly interesting event to scrutinize is the fact that it was something that *almost* brought all Americans together. Like a pail of ice water to the face, everyone suddenly shook their heads, opened there eyes, and said: "Hey! Wait a minute! That just ain't right…!"

And then?

Quick! Distract them! Divide and conquer!

Hey! Look over there! Socialists everywhere!

Quick! Look at those Tea Party maniacs! They're going to end civilization as we know it!

Illegal immigrants stealing American jobs!

No more right to choose!

Gay rights!

Medicinal marijuana!

Unemployment!

Terrorist threat!

Bombing in Libya...

•••

*Forget the fact that we just legalized graft and executed a takeover of the United States Government…we're betting you'll just move on with your life and never even notice…Step right up, ladies and gentlemen…a winner every time… Hit a balloon and win a kewpie doll…**SUCKER!***

Anyone who rules in this way should be wearing a white shroud, not a black robe.

To listen to our huckster politicians, everyone in Washington is concerned with "the small business owner."

"We want to encourage small business...."
"This law will hurt small business...."
"...small business...."
"...small business...."

That's what they *say*, but everything they *do* directly benefits big, *big*, ***BIG*** businesses—the kinds of corporations that eat small businesses for breakfast, just to get them out of the way—the kinds of corporations that have the resources to provide some *serious* bribes, not the little campaign contributions that an honest startup can afford.

Bait and switch.

Example? General Electric, one of America's largest corporations, made $14,200,000,000 in profits in 2010 and paid $0 in taxes—that's right, fourteen ***BILLION*** dollars in profits, ***zero dollars in taxes***. Jeffrey Immelt, GE's CEO, doubled his own compensation package, and at the same time, is asking 15,000 of their unionized workers to make major concessions in wages and benefits.

Oh yes, by the way... Mr. Immelt is chair of President Obama's Council on Jobs and Competitiveness.

Surprised?

How much did GE contribute to government criminals?

Spent on lobbying: $39,290,000 (2010).
Number of Lobbyists: 12,982 (2010).
Political contributions: $2,696,141 (2010).
Contributions to *individual* politicians: $6,723,281 (2010).
Total contributions 1990 to 2010: $19,725,132.00.
Party Breakdown: 52% to Democrats, 48% to Republicans

Here are some of the big winners in 2010:

Name	Office	Total Contributions
Portman, Rob (ROH)	Senate	$61,910
Himes, Jim (DCT)	House	$56,550
Dodd, Chris (DCT)	Senate	$40,700
Shelby, Richard C (RAL)	Senate	$40,500
Driehaus, Steve (DOH)	House	$36,850
Neal, Richard E (DMA)	House	$34,500
Clyburn, James E (DSC)	House	$31,500
Hatch, Orrin G (RUT)	Senate	$27,000
Larson, John B (DCT)	House	$27,000
Blumenthal, Richard (DCT)	Senate	$26,075
Blunt, Roy (RMO)	House	$25,900
Lincoln, Blanche (DAR)	Senate	$24,000
Gillibrand, Kirsten (DNY)	Senate	$21,700

Name	Office	Total Contributions
Camp, Dave (RMI)	House	$21,500
McCain, John (RAZ)	Senate	$20,400
Coakley, Martha (DMA)	Senate	$18,300
Berman, Howard L (DCA)	House	$18,050
Murphy, Scott (DNY)	House	$17,250
Murphy, Chris (DCT)	House	$16,950
Graham, Lindsey (RSC)	Senate	$16,900
Schumer, Charles E (DNY)	Senate	$16,300
Boehner, John (ROH)	House	$16,200
Stabenow, Debbie (DMI)	Senate	$16,000
Leahy, Patrick (DVT)	Senate	$15,250
Yarmuth, John A (DKY)	House	$15,000
Isakson, Johnny (RGA)	Senate	$14,900
Carney, John (DDE)	House	$14,300
Brown, Scott P (RMA)	Senate	$13,750
Dahlkemper, Kathleen (DPA)	House	$13,250
Bennet, Michael F (DCO)	Senate	$12,100
Spratt, John M Jr (DSC)	House	$12,000
Tonko, Paul (DNY)	House	$11,500
Bono Mack, Mary (RCA)	House	$10,900
Vitter, David (RLA)	Senate	$10,400
Feinstein, Dianne (DCA)	Senate	$10,200
Bean, Melissa (DIL)	House	$10,000
Cantor, Eric (RVA)	House	$10,000
Crapo, Mike (RID)	Senate	$10,000
Dicks, Norm (DWA)	House	$10,000
Frelinghuysen, Rodney (RNJ)	House	$10,000
Hoyer, Steny H (DMD)	House	$10,000
Pelosi, Nancy (DCA)	House	$10,000
Skelton, Ike (DMO)	House	$10,000
Smith, Adam (DWA)	House	$10,000
Peters, Gary (DMI)	House	$9,800
Burr, Richard (RNC)	Senate	$9,500
Davis, Geoff (RKY)	House	$9,500
Thune, John (RSD)	Senate	$9,500
Dreier, David (RCA)	House	$9,150
Fudge, Marcia L (DOH)	House	$9,000
Grassley, Chuck (RIA)	Senate	$9,000
Levin, Sander (DMI)	House	$9,000
Pomeroy, Earl (DND)	House	$9,000
Chandler, Ben (DKY)	House	$8,900

Name	Office	Total Contributions
Feingold, Russ (DWI)	Senate	$8,500
Inglis, Bob (RSC)	House	$8,500
McKeon, Howard P (RCA)	House	$8,500
Crowley, Joseph (DNY)	House	$8,000
Dingell, John D (DMI)	House	$8,000
Edwards, Chet (DTX)	House	$8,000
Inouye, Daniel K (DHI)	Senate	$8,000
Lewis, Jerry (RCA)	House	$8,000
McIntyre, Mike (DNC)	House	$8,000
Roskam, Peter (RIL)	House	$8,000
Arcuri, Michael (DNY)	House	$7,500
Bishop, Sanford D Jr (DGA)	House	$7,500
Blackburn, Marsha (RTN)	House	$7,500
Larsen, Rick (DWA)	House	$7,500
Murtha, John P (DPA)	House	$7,500
Sanchez, Loretta (DCA)	House	$7,500
Shimkus, John M (RIL)	House	$7,500
Waxman, Henry A (DCA)	House	$7,500
Turner, Michael R (ROH)	House	$7,450
Kosmas, Suzanne (DFL)	House	$7,385
Reid, Harry (DNV)	Senate	$7,150
Murkowski, Lisa (IAK)	Senate	$7,050
Becerra, Xavier (DCA)	House	$7,000
Boucher, Rick (DVA)	House	$7,000
Childers, Travis W (DMS)	House	$7,000
Israel, Steve (DNY)	House	$7,000
Marshall, Jim (DGA)	House	$7,000
Ryan, Tim (DOH)	House	$7,000
Schiff, Adam (DCA)	House	$7,000
Schultz, Debbie W. (DFL)	House	$7,000
Space, Zachary T (DOH)	House	$7,000
Taylor, Gene (DMS)	House	$7,000
Young, C W Bill (RFL)	House	$7,000
Giffords, Gabrielle (DAZ)	House	$6,900
Garamendi, John (DCA)	House	$6,800
Teague, Harry (DNM)	House	$6,800
Murphy, Patrick J (DPA)	House	$6,750
Sowers, Tommy (DMO)	House	$6,550
Conyers, John Jr (DMI)	House	$6,500
Frank, Barney (DMA)	House	$6,500
Kilpatrick, CarolynC. (DMI)	House	$6,500

Name	Office	Total Contributions
Mica, John L (RFL)	House	$6,500
Whitfield, Ed (RKY)	House	$6,500
Barrow, John (DGA)	House	$6,400
Halvorson, Deborah (DIL)	House	$6,300
Ryan, Paul (RWI)	House	$6,200

Money well spent, it would appear. (Rather telling that neither Ron Paul nor Dennis Kucinich were recipients of GE's bribery.)

Now, stop and remind yourself that these figures represent money given by just *one company*. Multiply that by, say, the Fortune 500, and then ask yourself whose interests these politicians are going to serve? Yours? Mine?

If it looks like a bribe, and smells like a bribe....

Either GE knows and loves an awful lot of politicians, or else it's just spreading cash around so *all* of them are in the thrall of GE. End result? GE pays ***no*** taxes. ***None. Zero. Zip. Nada.***

How about *you*? How many politicians do *you* own?

What percentage of *your* income goes to paying taxes?

Think there might be some connection?

Now, let's compare what GE pays in, ahem, political contributions with what they would likely have paid in taxes if the law was applied honestly:

Well, average federal corporate tax rates are 15%–35%. Let's give GE the benefit of the doubt and assume that, *if* they were honest, they would qualify for the lowest rate. That means their 2010 tax liability *would have been* $2,130,000,000.

So, let's understand this. In 2010, GE spent $40 Million lobbying, and $2.5 Million in direct political contributions, and in return, they were permitted to *evade* a bit over **$2 billion** in taxes.

That works out to an $15 for every honest taxpayer in the United States. Again, multiply this by the Fortune 500, and it's easy to see that *you pay taxes so they can evade them.* Keep this in mind the next time one of our scumbag politicians tells us how 'we all' have to tighten our belts.

I may not be an economist or a mathematician, but my calculations indicate a net savings of $2,088,017,859. Feel free to check my arithmetic.

How much of those savings are they passing on to you (or other Americans who *work* for a living, for that matter)?

How many *domestic* jobs did they generate as that big tax break 'trickles down' to the American citizen?

Follow the money and all becomes clear!

So, in effect, the working people are being asked to tighten their belts, while the corrupt politicians reap some healthy payoffs, GE maximizes their profits, paying massive dividends to greedy, parasitic investors who produce nothing, and at the same time, GE cuts benefits to their workers—those whose jobs they haven't managed to outsource.

Now, take a deep breath, and remind yourself once again that GE is *one* company. Scale these numbers up by the total cash flow of the Fortune 500, or the Global 2000, and it's pretty easy to see that our financial house is not in disorder because the *unionized workers* are living the high life. It's because this *Republicrat Junta* has created ***the most corrupt, unanswerable, greedy system in the history of civilization,*** and, they are working night and day to convince you that the guy down the street (not you, of course), is responsible; and their primary tactic is to ensure that Liberals are so angry at Conservatives, and Conservatives are so disgusted with Liberals, that neither one pays any close scrutiny to the *real* scoundrels who are busy betraying both. If this isn't a triumph of Madison Avenue marketing, I can't imagine what *would* be.

Ayn Rand's heroic figures accurately embody the essential positive traits of *true* Capitalism. Specifically, they *create* things—they work, invent, produce, innovate, and take risks with their own resources. In so doing, they create jobs, here, where the production is accomplished, and hence, their revenue does in fact 'trickle down' to those around them. Of course, they expect financial rewards, but this is not their primary motivation; creative people create because it is the only way the know to live. *It is what they **are**.*

The children's story *Never Worked and Never Will*, by Margaret Wise Brown, illustrates this in a highly relevant and utterly charming way:

Never Worked and Never Will

by Margaret Wise Brown

Once upon a time, in a time we are now living, there was an old man who made things out of wood. He had a shop on a street in a small town where all day long he carved wooden ducks and wild geese for weather vanes and hunters' decoys and, also, for people to buy and hang in their houses like pictures—flocks of wild, black geese flying across a white wall. All his life the old man had loved to carve wood. And so that was what he did. All his life he had sat in his shop with a knife in one hand and a block of wood in the other hand, carving wild geese. He would paint them the green and black colors of wild ducks and the wonderful colors of wild geese and hang them in the windows of his shop where people passing by could see them.

People from all over would come to his shop to buy the things he made and talk to the old man, because he was a happy old man.

But there was one thing people from all over the world could not understand. Over the woodcarver's door was a large sign with the old man's name on it:

"How," said the people from all over, "can Jim Bailey carve wood all day and paint it and sell it and then say he 'NEVER WORKED AND NEVER WILL'?"

"Why," said the people from all over, "he works all day, and he has worked all his life carving wood, and he will work tomorrow. What does he mean?"

So the people from all over said, "Jim Bailey, what does your sign mean?"

NEVER WORKED AND NEVER WILL

"It means," said Jim Bailey, "that I never worked a day in my life and I never will."

"But you work from eight in the morning until eight at night, every day, carving the wild geese out of wood. What do you mean?"

"If you don't know, I can't tell you," said the old man. "I never worked and I never will."

And then the old man laughed because the people were so puzzled and he laughed some more because he was a happy man.

Then the people from all over the world went away with the wooden ducks and the weather vanes they had bought, shaking their heads. "We don't know what he means. He works harder than any of us, yet he says, 'I never worked a day in my life and I never will.'"

Then the lazy children from all around came to the old man's shop to watch him carve the wooden ducks out of blocks of wood. When they saw his sign, NEVER WORKED AND NEVER WILL, they thought, "Here is a man like us. He doesn't work either."

But when the lazy children saw him carving wild geese out of wood from eight in the morning till eight at night, they said, "Jim Bailey, you do work. You work harder than we do."

But the old man shook his head and said, "Go away, lazy children. You don't know what I mean, but still I say, 'I NEVER WORKED A DAY IN MY LIFE AND I NEVER WILL.' And you wouldn't have to work either, if you knew my secret."

But the lazy children from all around were too lazy to guess his secret, so they went off shaking their heads. They said. "The old man is crazy. We don't know what he means. The old man is crazy, he works all day."

Then the other children from all around came to the old man and watched him carve the wild geese out of wood and then paint his wooden geese the wonderful wild bird colors. It made them happy to see what the old man was doing, and sometimes he let them help him paint the lovely, wild bird colors.

But they never asked the old man what his sign meant, because they were so delighted with what he was doing that they never thought of it as work. And that was how they knew the old man's secret.

The End

This classic children's story exemplifies the underlying philosophy of *true* Capitalism: that most people will do useful work because they are fulfilled by doing so, and should be rewarded for what they produce.

AmeriCapitalism, conversely, appeals to an entirely different mindset.

The lure of *AmeriCapitalism* is predicated upon a nebulous promise that if you participate in this shell game, you may hit it big, make a wad of dough, and be able to spend the remainder of your life lying beside your swimming pool, doing nothing whatsoever. Hence, the rewards of capitalism are presented in much the same way as hitting the lottery: a windfall that will allow players to abandon even the pretense of useful work.

Thus, *AmeriCapitalism* has as its central tenet, the exhalation of sloth and greed as unquestioned virtues.

A key assumption of the canon of (true) capitalism is that it encourages hard work and productivity as people are motivated to 'get ahead'. Unfortunately, like much of the *Republicrat* house of cards, this structure collapses at the slightest breath of truth. Just look at the people who are most motivated by material gain, versus those who are not:

The image of teachers, research scientists, missionaries, saints—indeed, all of the people we most admire (for the right reasons), are those who dedicate their lives to a noble task, indifferent to the monetary remuneration. (*Never Worked and Never Will.*) On the flip side, who do we see? Greedy politicians, rapacious industrialists, amoral attorneys, gangsters, mercenaries who will kill innocent women and children for the highest bidder, brutal right-wing dictators, hypocrite televangelists.

But these are only the most obvious. The ones upon whom they prey are those who do as little as possible for as much compensation as they can get, either playing the lottery (lower caste), or the stock market (middle caste), in the hopes of getting something for nothing so they can stop even pretending to do anything resembling work at all. Just watch some early morning infomercials for getting rich in real estate, or whatnot, and what is the invariable pitch? Some fat slob laying near his swimming pool, in front of his mansion, luxury cars in the background, surrounded by bikini-clad bimbos, boasting how he makes a six-figure salary by working only 3-hours a week….

This is the audience of *AmeriCapitalism*—no wonder it's so popular. It represents the world's most pervasive game of chance, for people too ignorant to realize that the odds against them hitting the big one are infinitesimal.

Consider Bernie Madoff, Jeffrey Skilling (Enron), and Kenneth Lay (Enron), three of the worst swindlers in history, whose unmitigated greed deprived thousands of their life savings, and pilfered the old-age security of those whose only crime was trust. Together, these three steaming heaps of excrement defrauded their friends, families, neighbors, and anyone who made the mistake of trusting and believing them, of almost seventy billion dollars, That's ***$70,000,000,000.00.***

It's difficult for the ordinary person to even wrap their mind around this kind of number, so here are a couple of comparisons to help understand the sheer scope of these people's greed and crimes:

- Seventy billion dollars is enough to pay the average salaries of 1,305,678 qualified high school teachers for one year.
- A person working for a $7.25/hour minimum wage would have to work 4,641,909 (that's over four and a half million) **years** to earn what these three criminals stole.
- Poverty level in the contiguous United States for a family of four, as of 2011, is $22,350.00. This means these three criminals stole enough money to support 3,131,991 families of 4 for a year.
- Remember, we're *not* comparing successful entrepreneurs who *earned* their riches to some nebulous welfare abusers living off entitlements. We're contrasting *thieves* who happen to call their crimes 'capitalism' with honest, hard working people, trying to earn a living for their families.
- Most people will agree that a family with an income of $100,000/year, while by no means *rich*, are certainly capable of living a comfortable and secure existence. This is the kind of salary a well-trained engineer or other professional can expect to earn after accumulating, perhaps, a decade of experience under his or her belt. Well, these three scoundrels stole enough to sustain almost three quarter of a million families at that level.
- The monetary cost of the American Civil War, adjusted to year-2000 dollars, was only $62 billion.
- These three rogue capitalists cost their victims more than half of the total cost of the Viet Nam War!
- The 2011 earthquake, tsunami, and nuclear disaster in Japan, which also took some 18,000 lives, is expected to have a final financial cost of $310 billion, so this deadly act of nature was only 4.4 times as costly as the damage incurred by these three enterprising 'businessmen'.
- Finally, this works out to $500 for *every* taxpayer in the US.

When our smiling politicians in their 350-dollar haircuts mutter the term 'class warfare', and oppose taxing the rich, these are the scoundrels whom the are really protecting.

Although not as stunning in terms of the sheer numbers, no less egregious is the case of Stewart Parnell, who deliberately connived to circumvent health codes in order to distribute salmonella–tainted peanuts to unsuspecting consumers. Several lives were lost, and many more suffered severe illness. Under the tenets of *AmeriCapitalism*, this is simply a well-justified business decision.

Finally, consider the so-called 'Cash for Kids' case:

Seventeen -year-old Hillary Transue, a stellar student who had never been in trouble, was brought before Judge Mark Ciavarella Jr. as a result of mocking her school's assistant principal on her *MySpace* page (the posting was clearly identified as a joke). Instead of a simple lecture or reprimand, she and her parents were stunned when she was taken away in handcuffs, sentenced to three months at a juvenile detention center on a charge of harassment.

"I felt like I had been thrown into some surreal sort of nightmare," said Hillary. "All I wanted to know was how this could be fair and why the judge would do such a thing."

Why indeed?

The answer became crystal clear when it was later revealed that Ciavarella, and fellow judge Michael Conahan, in cahoots with Western PA Child Care, a privately-operated juvenile incarceration facility owned by friends, had been sentencing virtually *every* child brought before them to prison time, in return for massive cash kickbacks.

Hillary Transue, however, was far more fortunate than Ed Fonzo of Wilkes-Barre, whose life was snuffed out by these money-hungry scumbags just as surely as if they had pulled the trigger themselves.

Ed had been a star wrestler at Coughlin High School in 2003 when he was caught at an underage drinking party, and charged with possession of drug paraphernalia. It was his first offense, so the seventeen-year-old expected he would get a fine and be released. Instead he was sent away to Western PA Child Care.

Ed Fonzo subsequently committed suicide.

All told, these criminals in black robes had sentenced *thousands* of youthful offenders, many innocent or guilty of minor infractions, to prison time for the sole purpose of lining their own greedy pockets.

As a final insult to injury, in a blatant display of all-too-typical old-boy cronyism, Judge Edwin Kosik made light of the whole sordid case by joking as he released Ciavarella "to the custody of his pregnant daughter," pending sentencing!

While all civilized societies must abhor vigilantism, if ever there were circumstances in which frontier justice is warranted, this is it. Mark Ciavarella shouldn't be enjoying the company of his family, he, along with Michael Conahan, should be rotting carrion, hanging from gibbets as a warning to others of their ilk.

If I've belabored this issue, I believe the attention is merited. Saying these scoundrels are representative of capitalism is akin to holding up Jim Jones as representative of Protestant Christianity, Bin Laden as the norm for Islam, or pedophile priests as the essence of Catholicism. No rational, sane, and morally grounded human being could possibly defend or excuse these greedy, self-serving psychopaths, but, as we shall see, this is precisely what is routinely done by our politicians, and even Supreme Court Judges, all of whom rely on this very stripe of criminal for their continued personal enrichment. People who question these nefarious prevaricators are accused of being socialists, or anti-capitalist, in much the same manner that critics of Israel are dismissed as being anti-Semite, or anyone questioning the deeds of a person of color is accused of racism; simple, loaded, propagandistic labels used to silence opposition while evading the relevant issues.

And that relevant issue is: These few high-visibility examples simply represent a handful who happened to get caught, and whose sloppiness ensured that they couldn't be ignored by the media, or swept under some rug by complicit politicians. As egregious as the deeds of these greedy individuals were, the toll on human life was relatively minimal compared, for example, to the crimes perpetrated by Union Carbide at Bhopal, by Massey Energy, British Petroleum, and scores of others. Nor are we just talking about so-called 'accidents', caused by the deliberate circumvention of safety procedures. What about the outright *murder* of those seen as impediments to profit, both at home and abroad?

In a quintessential example, Shell Oil conspired with the government of Nigeria to hang nine activists for speaking out against the extreme, irreparable environmental devastation to Ogoniland being caused by Shell exploitation. In order to avoid the prospect of a high-visibility trial, shell paid $15.5 million to settle the resulting lawsuits.

Both Shell and the Nigerian government admit that Shell contributes to the funding of the military in the Delta region. Under the auspices of 'protecting' Shell from peaceful demonstrators in the village of Umeuchem (10 miles from Ogoni), the police killed 80 people and destroyed houses and vital crops in 1990. Shell conceded that it twice paid the military for going to specific villages. Although it disputes that the purpose of these excursions was to quiet dissent, each of the military missions paid for by Shell resulted in Ogoni fatalities. Shell has also admitted purchasing weapons for the police force that guards its facilities, and there is growing suspicion that Shell funds a much greater portion of the military than previously admitted. In 1994, the military sent permanent security forces into Ogoniland, occupying the once peaceful land. It is believed that Shell is responsible for the murder of at least 2000 people.

In recent years, various (*Republicrat*) administrations have made much of America's 'duty' to 'build democracies' in various parts of the globe. Ignoring, for the moment, that *nowhere* in our Constitution is *any* branch of government empowered to exercise such influence over any foreign country, the reality of our foreign entanglements reveals the abject hypocrisy of this claim.

Although it might be argued that supporting brutal right-wing dictators might be appropriate in cases where the end result is to counter military threats represented by their opposition, in the vast majority of cases, the demonstrable objective is to further the profits of American corporate interests.

Haiti offers another representative example.

Jean-Bertrand Aristide was the first democratically elected president of the first black republic in the world; following the fall of the brutal dictatorships of François 'Papa Doc' and Jean-Claude 'Baby Doc' Duvalier.

Coming of age under these dynastic dictatorships, Aristide was deeply moved by the abject misery endured by Haiti's poor, and became an outspoken critic of the brutal regime. After completing his post graduate studies, he was ordained as a Catholic Priest 1982, and was appointed curate of a small parish in Port-au-Prince.

Following a popular uprising against the dictatorial rulers, Aristide was elected president with over 67% of the vote. During Aristide's short-lived first period in office, he attempted to carry out substantial reforms, which brought passionate opposition from Haiti's business and military elite. He sought to bring the military under civilian control, and initiated investigations of human rights violations.

He was ousted by a military coup, led by high ranking members of the Haitian National Intelligence Service (S.I.N.), which had been set up and financed in the '80s by the Central Intelligence Agency as part of the 'war on drugs', and were reportedly still receiving funding and training from the C.I.A. for 'intelligence-gathering activities' at the time of the coup,

Although the military junta was denounced by the United Nations, which imposed a trade embargo, President George H.W. Bush granted an exemption from the embargo to Texaco and many other U.S. companies doing business in Haiti. President Bill Clinton extended and expanded these exemptions.

A campaign of terror against Aristide supporters was started by Emmanuel Constant after Aristide was forced out. In 1993, Constant, who had been on the C.I.A.'s payroll as an informant since 1992, organized the FRAPH, which targeted and murdered Aristide supporters.

Despite having actively supported the military Junta, President Bill Clinton was compelled by United Nations Security Council Resolution 940 to make a show of supporting Aristide's return. Accordingly, Clinton deployed troops to Haiti in 1994, but forced Aristide to accept programs that removed all import barriers. This forced Haiti to import rice and other agricultural commodities from giant U.S. agribusinesses, which receive massive state subsidies, and against which Haitian rice farmers could not compete. This, in turn, further increased poverty in Haiti, while funneling money to the American corporations which ultimately control U.S. policy.

Aristide's first term ended in February 1996, but he was reelected in 2000, and subsequently toppled by a coup in 2004, which Aristide claimed was orchestrated by the United States. It was later revealed that the U.S. Embassy in Haiti's chief of staff came to Aristide's house to say he "and a lot of Haitians would be killed" if he refused to leave immediately. He was spirited out of the country on a U.S. Military flight, and taken to exile in South Africa.

When asked for his response to these allegations, Colin Powell (whose mendacity has since been conclusively established) said that "it might have been better for members of Congress who have heard these stories to ask us about the stories before going public with them so we don't make a difficult situation that much more difficult" and he alleged that Aristide "did not democratically govern or govern well."

Well then, *that* logic justifies the thesis of this book, and the call to depose the illegal *Republicrat Junta*!

CARICOM, an organization of Caribbean countries that includes Haiti, called for a United Nations investigation into Aristide's removal, but were reportedly pressured by the US and France to drop their request. Some observers suggest the rebellion and removal of Aristide were covertly orchestrated by these two countries. In a 2006 interview, Aristide said the U.S. went back on their word regarding compromises he made with them over privatization of enterprises to ensure that part of the profits would go to the Haitian people and then "relied on a disinformation campaign" to discredit him.

Recent leaked documents *prove* that the United States has continually worked to prevent this popular figure from returning to his home country, diplomatically punishing any country that attempted to help Aristide, including threatening to block a UN security council seat for South Africa. Even as late as 2011, President Barack Obama attempted to pressure South African President Jacob Zuma to prevent Aristide's return to Haiti. To his credit, Zuma refused to bow to this coercion, and allowed Aristide, by far the most popular figure in Haiti today, to return home.

Whatever the motivations or convoluted machinations behind U.S. involvement in Haiti, one thing is manifestly clear: this tiny, poverty-stricken Caribbean nation posed no military threat, and our continued meddling was driven by one thing and one thing only: the financial interests of the greedy multinational corporations that actually dictate 'our' country's domestic and international policies.

This was only the latest in nearly a century of blatant interventionism in, and exploitation of, the Caribbean and South and Central America, all motivated solely by corporate avarice.

Once again, we need to continually remind ourselves of how we (*the People*) are faring now, as compared to the past. The government, when finally caught red-handed, inevitably attempts to paint the benefit to American *corporations* as a benefit to the American people, but a simple reality check exposes their blatant deception. This is about a very few very rich, very greedy individuals getting ever richer, at the expense of human misery and suffering throughout the world, and using these ill-gotten gains to increase their power over a corrupt government, and further erode the influence of 'we the People'.

So brazen and high-handed have these corrupt criminals become that they have *dared* to rule that these corporations can openly exert their influence on government with the blessing of our so-called 'Supreme Court'. Make no mistake—this is not merely a difference of opinion. What it is, is *treason*, and the perpetrators, in every branch of government, are as much an illegal ruling junta as any CIA-backed coup in any third-world nation.

Inevitably, their first line of defense is to engage the usual propaganda machinery, painting anyone who questions these policies as anti-business, and therefore, a socialist, or (gasp!) communist plotter. Lest my position be similarly distorted, allow me to provide some counterexamples of businesses that have been operated by ethical, moral individuals, who still managed to make a fair profit without exploiting others, and as such, embody what capitalism is *supposed* to be all about:

First, however, consider what Theodore Roosevelt had to say on this topic:

"Our aim is not to do away with corporations; on the contrary, these big aggregations are an inevitable development of modern industrialism, and the effort to destroy them would be futile unless accomplished in ways that would work the utmost mischief to the entire body politic. We can do nothing of good in the way of regulating and supervising these corporations until we fix clearly in our minds that we are not attacking the corporations, but endeavoring to do away with any evil in them. We are not hostile to them; we are merely determined that they shall be so handled as to subserve the public good. We draw the line against misconduct, not against wealth."

Malden Mills

In late 1995, a fire destroyed Malden Mills in Lawrence, Massachusetts. The 90-year-old manufacturer employed a loyal and productive workforce of 3,000 who could scarcely afford to lose their jobs, especially coming as it did just two weeks before Christmas.

At a time when offshore manufacturing had became standard procedure in American business, Malden Mills' CEO Aaron Fuerustein opted to stay put and to rebuild his factory on the very site where his family had made textiles since the turn of the century.

Using his own money, Fuerustein announced plans to pay his employees their full wages for 30 days. He subsequently extended that offer to 90 days for the paychecks and 180 days for benefits. Total cost to Feuerstein: $25 million.

While many considered this business madness, Fuerustein responded saying: "I think it was a wise business decision, but that isn't why I did it. I did it because it was the right thing to do."

Right and wrong? What a concept!

It took years, but Malden rebuilt in Lawrence and eventually hired back all the displaced workers. The workforce repaid Fuerustein with cooperation and productivity. Fuerustein's commitment to employees drove significant bottom-line outcomes:

- Business grew 40% from pre-fire levels.
- Customer and employee retention reached 95%.
- Off-quality products dropped from 6-7% pre-fire to just 2%.
- Production increased from 130,000 to 200,000 yards per week.

Compare this to what has since become the norm in large corporate environments: Even successful companies are punished by greedy shareholders if their profits exceed projections, but don't *exceed* projections by as *much* as investors had hoped. The inevitable result? Domestic layoffs of the workers who did *their* jobs, and outsourcing to places where worker exploitation can be expanded in order to direct more and more money into the pockets of those who produce *nothing*—except, perhaps, misery.

Is this wealth 'trickling down'? If so, it's trickling down to similarly greedy, exploitive criminals in places like India and China.

Sadly, Fuerustein's principles, decency, and humanity were rewarded, as is too often the case, with perfidy: In 2004, Fuerustein was ousted as president because... "there's no line on the balance sheet for 'loyalty' or 'ethics'." Malden Mills, Aaron Fuerustein's family business, still operates in Lawrence, Massachusetts, it's name changed to *Polartec,* after its flagship brand, but it now employees a mere 1,000 workers, most of them overseas.

Ask yourself who has benefited from this change. The workers in Lawrence, Massachusetts? Workers in India or China? You? Me? Or a handful of greedy investors who consider *their* bottom line more important that the livelihood of 3,000 of their fellow Americans?

Digital Equipment Corporation (DEC)

When I was in college, I took a Business Administration course that focused on "the best run companies in America." DEC was one of the most illustrious examples, and by the time I completed that course there was no doubt in my mind that *this* was where I wanted to work upon graduation.

In fact, I went to work for DEC *before* graduation, earning extra money as a part-time security officer at their New Hampshire facilities, and was subsequently hired as a computer engineer at their Advanced Semiconductor Development laboratory in Hudson, Massachusetts.

I first met the late Ken Olsen, DEC's founder and President, when, in my capacity as a mobile security officer, I was dispatched to let him into their Merrimac, NH building late one Saturday evening. I expected him to arrive by helicopter or limousine, but he rolled up driving his own Ford Fairlane, dressed in simple chinos and a madras shirt. He was friendly, amicable, and solicitous of my thoughts and opinions about the company (all of which were sincerely positive). Later, I discovered that my impression of him was echoed by virtually everyone who'd had the good fortune to make his acquaintance.

Formed in 1957, DEC became a leading vendor of computer systems, software, and peripherals from the 1960s to the 1990s. Its PDP and VAX products were arguably the most popular and innovative minicomputers for the scientific and engineering communities from the 1970s thru the 1990s. Their PDP-8 series is widely regarded as the first minicomputer, and the PDP-11 was among the best platforms for real-time data acquisition, instrument control, and telemetry ever built. DEC's VAX-11 series were the first 32-bit minicomputers to achieve broad acceptance, often competing with the much larger, and more expensive, IBM-360/370 mainframes. The DEC Alpha (the project in which I was involved through most of my years at DEC), was a highly-innovative, 64-bit processor that was, at the time of its introduction and throughout most of its lifetime, the fastest microprocessor in the world.

Technology aside, DEC was highly regarded as a company that valued its employees, and treated them accordingly. Nor was this appreciative attitude limited to the techies. Everyone, from the secretaries to the custodians to the security guards, were never made to feel as if they were less than essential contributors to a great, cooperative effort.

Ken Olsen actively fostered a culture that valued innovation and excellence above all else. Engineers were encouraged to take risks in pursuit of advancing the state of technology. For example, the project in which I was involved entailed the investigation of quantum effects that were, at the time, believed to impose an upper limit on the speed of computer processors. The result was the DEC Alpha, which operated at clock speeds hitherto believed to be impossible.

Obviously, mistakes were made, sometimes costly ones, but the successes invariably pushed the envelope of technology. *This*, my friends, is how capitalism is *supposed* to operate—not merely striving for the accumulation of nebulous wealth for a few greedy cut-throats. In the words of Henry Ford: "A business that makes nothing but money is a poor business."

At a time when engineers could easily make two– or three–times the salary at the many downtown high-tech startups, very few did. Up until the early 1990s, DEC was a company justifiably proud of the fact that it never had a general layoff. At its height, DEC was the second largest employer in Massachusetts, second only to the State Government.

This all changed in June of 1992, when Ken Olsen retired, and was replaced as President by Robert Palmer.

Palmer had joined DEC in 1985, as head of the Semiconductor Engineering group—the division I joined at about the same time as a junior engineer, so I had a good opportunity to observe his rise, from the beginning right through his ultimate destruction of the company that had been Ken Olsen's life work.

Whereas Olsen had fostered a culture of informal competence and innovation, Palmer believed that these laid-back engineering types were a bunch of prima donnas, hopelessly out of step with modern business realities. His attitude was: why design and build, when you can buy, repackage, rebrand, and mark-up? And if you're not innovating, why do you need engineers at all?

When I had begun to move into more management-oriented positions, one prerequisite was attendance of a week-long management seminar, specially tailored to the Olsen-era DEC culture. The manager's job, we were taught, was to absorb as much of the unpleasant but necessary business aspects of the operation, shielding the technical folks, who were the backbone of the company, from distraction. The rule at DEC was: "Delegate everything you would love to do yourself, and do yourself everything you wish you could delegate."

Indeed, through all of my front-line engineering days, I never once had to write any kind of formal progress report. My group met once a week, we discussed our projects, and then we went back to work. Unbeknownst to me at the time, my supervisor then compiled all this information, checked any necessary details, and fed the information upward, in increasingly distilled and polished formats.

Over the ten or so years of my own tenure there, I watched as the really brilliant innovators became rarer by the month, replaced by a new hoard of MBAs in 3-piece suits. The problem, they decided, was a shortage of written reports. Everybody had to write regular reports. Weekly, monthly roll-ups, sometimes daily briefs. Strict formats were enforced, these often changing on a week-to-week basis, and woe to the engineer who mistakenly submitted *this* week's status report using *last* week's template!

At the same time, layoffs became regular events as the company continually downsized in an effort to stay afloat. Nobody seemed to make any connection to the fact that, with all the innovators gone, the company's product offerings had become no more than proprietary packaging of off-the-shelf components that customers could buy and configure in-house at a fraction of the cost. As a result, these status reports quickly became nothing more than desperate exercises in trying to justify one's own job, overflowing with hyperbole and totally devoid of substance.

Upon ascending to Ken Olsen's throne, Palmer's first act was to have himself crowned chief executive officer ("CEO"); a title that had never been used during Digital's 35-year existence. Where Olsen had been a down-to-earth, compassionate, engineer, Palmer was a strutting, self-important, ego-swollen despot who never left any doubt that *he* occupied one strata, and everyone *else*, several tiers beneath him.

Following his self-coronation, Palmer's next order of business was to... design a more modern *logo* for the company....

As profits continued to plummet, Palmer attempted to restore profitability by eradicating the established DEC business culture, mainly by hiring additional levels of management and outside executives who more closely resembled his own kind. The resulting culture could best be described as the ruthless leading the clueless.

His next line of attack was to sell off what he considered DEC's ***'non-core'*** business units.

Such as?

- Well, ever hear of the *Oracle* database product? Well, until Palmer came along, that innovative product—the first viable relational database system—had been known as *VAX-Rdb*.
- INTEL'S *Pentium* series of microprocessors? Well, Palmer unloaded the ALPHA technologies, and indeed, the entire semiconductor development group, to INTEL.
- Familiar with object-oriented technology and client/server architectures? Well, one of the cornerstones of this technology, CORBA (Common Object Request Broker Architecture), and its sophisticated messaging software, *MessageQ*, were sold to BEA Systems, Inc.
- Ever heard the term ***'ethernet'***? Yup, that originated at DEC, whose world-class networking business was unloaded to Cabletron Systems.
- The group that created DEC's state-of-the-art voice production and recognition technologies, DECtalk and DECvoice, were spun off, ultimately becoming Fonix.
- Dec's printer business unit was sold in 1997 to GENICOM.
- Tape technologies, more important then than now, went to Quantum Corporation.
- The company's highly-respected worldwide training group was spun off as Global Knowledge Network.

•

What was left, one might well wonder?

What indeed?

Naught save hoards of scurrying bean counters in three-piece-suites, with ever fewer beans to count—in other words, nothing of any worth to anyone.

Ultimately, the once mighty, innovative company was purchased, for a fraction of its earlier worth, by COMPAQ, which subsequently merged with Hewlett Packard. DEC was a thing of the past; an anachronism of innovation in a culture that values making deals, rather than making goods. Yes, Robert Palmer was a man ahead of his time—a preview of the greedy, naveish, self-serving, talentless *scumbags* who would one day destroy our entire economy.

The Huckster Mentality

A natural outgrowth of *AmeriCapitalism* is the Huckster Mentality.

Sure, there have always been unscrupulous individuals who would take advantage of others in their quest for a quick buck, but in today's society, it has been elevated to the level of unquestioned dogma.

In a normal, healthy implementation of capitalism, the businessman seeks to make a profit as a result of his ability to deliver value to some segment of the populace. By treating them fairly, he tries to ensure that they will have loyalty to him, and will continue to use his service or buy his products.

"The development of capitalism consists in everyone's having the right to serve the customer better and/or more cheaply. And this method, this principle, has, within a comparatively short time, transformed the whole world."[1]

In our *perversion* of the Capitalist dogma, *cheating* the customer is considered good business, because, in the minds of these 'entrepreneurs', everyone else is a mark, a rube, an idiot incapable of recognizing when they're being cheated.

Remember when Folgers started packaging their coffee in 12-ounce cans, instead of the traditional 16-ounce containers? It wasn't as if they had advertised: "new, more convenient size...." They simply slipped it by, assuming nobody would notice, and by the time they did, Folgers would have raked in millions of dollars by unfairly competing with more honest producers because their prices would *seem* so much lower.

More recently, I brought home my usual brand of bathroom tissue, and noticed something odd: the rolls seemed rather narrow compared to the holder in my bathroom. Some quick measurements confirmed that indeed, these cunning connivers had shaved a half inch off of each roll. Nowhere on the package was there any notification that they had done this. There was no campaign to tell us that it was more eco-friendly, and would save so many trees, while remaining just as serviceable. No, some greedy little pipsqueak came up with the idea that his company could save a bunch of dough by ripping off their customers.

[1] Ludwig von Mises, *Economic Policy*, p5

A friend of mine related his experience of getting ripped off through the same online ticket vendor scam that was brought to light during the 2009 Bruce Springsteen concerts. To reiterate, a matter of *minutes* after the tickets went on sale, they were showing up as sold out, but visitors were directed to 'another' ticket supplier who 'might' have some available. This 'other' vendor did, but at a hefty markup. It was later determined that the original ticket seller actually *owned* this alternative scalper site.

This is egregious at so many levels, but it is typical of the "new American business 'ethic'."

Much as I detest the big-time Wall Street rip-offs, for the most part, they're preying on other greedy scumbags looking to build their security by wheeling and dealing instead of actually *producing* anything of value. In this case, however, they're ripping off the working stiffs who are trying to get out and see a show, be it Springsteen or Ringling Brothers. It's an insidious brand of entitlement (which we'll discuss in detail shortly) that says just because you know how to manipulate the technology, you can use it to scam whomever you want. It's also, sadly, representative of about 90% of the 'business entrepreneurs' I've had the misfortune to encounter through most of my career. The credo is to screw the other guy at every opportunity, with nary a thought devoted to creating value. The fact that one scumbag could suggest such a business model, and nobody shot his ass down for it, speaks volumes about the overall climate of American business since WW-II. These are not a few iconoclastic robber barons, or a small cabal of conspirators. It's the majority; and of the rest, virtually all are collaborators.

Price Gouging Versus Supply and Demand

Supply and demand is an economic model of price determination in a market. In 1890, English economist Alfred Marshall published his work, *Principles of Economics*, which was one of the first to analyze how supply and demand interacted to determine price. He concluded that in a competitive market, the unit price for a particular good will vary until it settles at a point where the quantity demanded by consumers (at current price) will equal the quantity supplied by producers (at current price), resulting in an economic equilibrium of price and quantity.

There are two key concepts in this definition that merit close consideration:

- 'In a competitive market', and
- 'equilibrium'.

If six local dairy farmers produce milk for sale in a certain geographical area, and a certain number of citizens consume dairy products, both of these critical elements are in play, and the principle of supply and demand operates as envisioned and intended. The farmer who produces the superior product, or delivers at a lower price, or both, will prevail. If one farmer's cows fall ill, the supply is decreased while the demand remains steady, and prices will rise. If people move away, and demand decreases, prices will drop.

This balance can be altered in numerous ways.

In the old days, all the farmers might get together and agree to charge the same, inflated price. Presumably, each would then enjoy approximately the same market share, but would greatly increase their profits. This was a rather obvious, and pretty fragile arrangement, and today, 'price fixing' is prohibited in most situations.

One method in common usage in today's anything-goes environment is for one farmer to reduce his prices below his, and his competitors', actual cost; in other words, he begins selling at a loss. This sustained loss is supported either by investing his own capital or by going into debt. The normal mechanisms of supply-demand seek to establish a new equilibrium; in this case, one in which the selling price is such that no *honest* farmer can possibly compete. In time, the rest of the farmers go out of business. Then, with no competition, the remaining farmer can raise his prices to many times what they were originally, quickly recovering his 'investment', and raking in obscene profits from consumers who no longer have any choice but to buy from him. This is an approach favored by companies like *Amazon.com,* which, financed by greedy investors with long-term goals and deep pockets, could afford to operate at a loss for as long as it took to drive competitors out of business.

Another favored approach for manipulating supply and demand is for all of the farmers to get together, pool their resources, and buy themselves some politicians (polite term: lobbying). Politicians are bribed to introduce legislation that compensates the farmers for producing *less* milk, perhaps by butchering half of their cows. Prices rise due to decreased supply. Profit margins rise because the farmers are making more money from fewer cattle. (Perhaps some of the politicians had the foresight to 'invest' in milk futures.) In any case, they are assured of continued 'political support' if those farmers want to maintain their subsidies. Everybody wins…except, of course, the consumer, who now has to pay a greater portion of their (stationary) income for their required milk. In addition to subsidies, the farmers may negotiate for tax incentives, the resultant budget shortfall being filled by cutting services to citizens, and/or raising their taxes.

I remember hearing how, during Hurricane Camille (1969), people in Florida, desperate to board up their homes, were being charged ten or more times the normal price for plywood. Similar gouging was taking place for other staples: milk, bread, toilet paper; anything that might be considered essential. In recent years, laws have been passed to prevent such unscrupulous price gouging…at least on the part of those who cannot buy their agendas with those who pass the laws.

What do I mean by *that*?

Well, consider what happens to the price of heating oil when temperatures unexpectedly drop. Here in the Northeast, I've seen oil prices spike by as much as a dollar a gallon over the span of a week or less. Now, stop and remind yourself that this is oil that the providers have already drilled, pumped, refined, and stockpiled. Their cost and overhead is exactly the same today as it was a week ago. Why is doubling the price of plywood in response to a hurricane any more reprehensible than jacking up the price of oil in response to a blizzard? Three words: ***The Oil Lobby.***

Criminal oil executives buy protection from criminal politicians, just the way Al Capone used to buy protection from the local corrupt cops, judges, and politicians. Now, as then, *you* are the one at the bottom of the pyramid who ultimately bears the weight of the entire reprobate structure.

But wait, it gets even better:

Remember our earlier scenario in which farmers conspired to fix the price of milk at an artificially high price? When dealing with essentials—things people can't simply do without—all of the participating business-criminals are assured of maximizing their profits through this simple act of cooperation/conspiracy. Is it not amazing how *every* oil supplier, regardless of whether they get their crude from the U.S., or Canada, Alaska or Venezuela, Saudi Arabia or the North Sea, *all* react to fluctuations in demand at precisely the same time, and find it necessary to fix their final prices within pennies of each other? Amazing indeed! One might suspect some kind of collusion is afoot.

Of course, what makes this level of blatant corruption feasible is the fact that greedy business criminals need only buy their agendas in two places: The Democratic Party and the Republican Party. Take a moment and look back to page 135, where we examined the political spending of General Electric: 52% to the Democrats, 48% to the Republicans; with the resultant total a mere fraction of the taxes from which the 'two' parties they purchased have agreed to exempt them.

Of course, what *seems* to differentiate *this* brand of bribery from simply slipping a wad of cash into Boss Tweed's pocket is that bribes given to the parties are exposed to far less scrutiny than those given to individual candidates. The theory would seem to be that this practice makes it less akin to *quid quo pro*, but even the most cursory analysis of party machinations reveals that this distinction is merely illusory.

Consider how this financial value proposition would shift if the political scene were not monopolized by just these two complicit parties.

In the first place, the necessity of bribing six or seven parties instead of just two, multiplies the cost of admission accordingly. More importantly, however, is the existence of more eyes suspiciously cast upon one another. When multiple, viable parties compete for power, results inevitably depend on the formation of shifting coalitions focusing on various issues, rather than permanent, cozy alliances.

Cozy? How can I even *suggest* such a thing in light of the loud, adversarial, vehement tension between the two supposedly opposing parties?

The situation is in every respect identical to a professional wrestling match. Some players are bad guys to one group, some are good guys to another group. They do, indeed, inflict some minor bumps and bruises in the course of staging their entertainment, but at the end of the day, they all put on their street clothes, enjoy a beer together, and share a hearty laugh at the expense of the rubes who support their lavish lifestyles.

Although at least *some* politicians may start out with independent ideas and honest intentions, the structure of the party is such that only those who assimilate into the inner culture are ever permitted to rise though the ranks. The controlling mechanism? Money, of course. Big corporations, like GE, funnel massive amounts of capital at both parties, secure in the understanding that those in control of disbursing campaign funds 'know the score', and see to it that support only goes to those willing to 'play ball'. To have any chance of mounting serious campaigns, ambitions politicians learn to relax their ethical standards.

So who *cares* which side wins? Those who control the purse strings in 'both' parties, have the same vested interest in keeping the same 'customer' satisfied. All the other stuff is just part of the show. The real *business* of government is making corporations bigger and richer so they can send ever increasing mountains of money to the same 'made men' in Washington.

Of course, every now and then, an independent-minded outsider slips through the sieve, and finds him– or her–self swimming in the scum-covered pond with all the in-crowd sharks. In these rare instances, the insiders simply close ranks, conspiring to marginalize that individual in the eyes of an easily manipulated electorate. Dennis Kucinich and Ron Paul come to mind, as does Pat Buchanan. In the first cases, notice how even their so-called Democratic and Republican colleagues distance themselves from their more 'controversial' (honest) positions, shooting a knowing wink and nod when backs are turned. Similarly, Republicans were only too happy to allow democrats to paint Pat Buchanan as a anti-Semitic, racist, extremist, none of which is accurate or deserved.[1] Proof? Check back on pages 139-142, and

[1] I strongly disagree with many of Buchanan's social theories, however, I have seen no evidence that they are racially, ethnically, or religiously motivated, and in terms of accurately grasping the nuances of foreign affairs, I can think of nobody who is better qualified. In addition, I strongly believe that he is completely sincere, which puts him far beyond most of the ethically bankrupt scoundrels currently running our government.

notice that neither Ron Paul nor Dennis Kucinich are recipients of GE's 'generosity'.

There is one final insidious element worth noting in this incestuous relationship: The vast majority of all politicians are members of the same secret organization—the lawyer's cartel—also known as The American Bar Association. This topic was explored in depth in the section entitled *Serfs and Elites*. Now, however, we need to revisit its significance in terms of the interaction between corrupt businesses and corrupt politicians. As examples that typify this unholy alliance, consider the cases of numerous farmers whose crops were polluted by chemical giant *Monsanto*:

Monsanto is a massive corporation whose goals, among others, is to corner the market on agriculture by creating genetically-modified plants that are incapable of reproducing on their own, requiring farmers to continually buy new seed from…Monsanto. The fact that a single blight could, as a result, destroy every trace of the resultant non-diverse, non-reproductive food crop, leading to global famine, is of absolutely no interest or concern in their single-minded quest for profits. Fully 75% of the genetically-manipulated crops worldwide originate from Monsanto, who also brought us such environmentally-friendly products as DDT, PCP, and Agent Orange.

Percy Schmeiser is a farmer who took great pride in his natural, environmentally friendly farming methods, particularly of a nutritious grain known as Canola. David Runyon and his wife Dawn put a lifetime of work into their 900-acre Indiana soybean farm. 74-year-old Mo Parr is a seed cleaner; he is hired by farmers to separate debris from the seed to be replanted. Marc Loiselle, an organic farmer, was far more motivated by the preservation of pure, unsullied, natural seed stock than bottom-line profits. All four found themselves under attack in Monsanto's relentless war for agricultural hegemony.

The three farmers discovered their carefully-nurtured seed stocks had been *contaminated* by Monsanto's 'frankencrops'. Rather than compensation, or even an apology, what they got were lawsuits for patent infringement. Mo Parr, the 74-year-old seed cleaner, was prosecuted for 'aiding and abetting'. Monsanto's position was that it didn't matter whether or not farmers knew that their fields were *polluted* with Monsanto's unwanted technology, or whether or not they benefitted or suffered damages as a result.

Now, it doesn't take a law degree to comprehend the merits of these cases. One needn't be a new-age 'tree-hugger', or even *care* about organic foods to recognize the injustice involved when someone dumps something unpleasant, and unrequested on *your private property*, then not only demands payment, but paints you as a criminal besides. And one certainly doesn't need to be an accountant to understand how trying to defend yourself against armies of lawyers in the employ of a giant corporation can lead to financial ruin, regardless of the merits of your position.

As an aside, let's take a moment to remember that Abe Lincoln practiced law without the benefit of a law school degree, and nowhere in the Bible is it asserted that Solomon, whose judicial wisdom is legendary, was a member of any Bar Association. Those of us who have spent our entire lives under this system, take it for granted that there is no other way, but this is not the case. The job of attorneys is not to *facilitate* the law or ensure justice; their job is to manipulate, obfuscate, and in many cases, *pervert* the law in service to the highest bidder.

In the situation under examination, any reasonable citizen, particularly any farmers constituting a legitimate jury of peers, could easily comprehend the merits of the case and reach a just decision. However, after being 'instructed' by a politically motivated judge, to a level of detail and complexity that virtually compels their verdict, the result is anything *but* an open-and-shut case. Moreover, the lawyers—often in teams of a hundred or more—all being compensated with three-figure *hourly* fees, are only too happy to ensure that the case continues for months, years, or even decades. For companies like Monsanto, lawyers, like politicians, are a normal, expected, and highly efficient business expense.

The point here isn't the outcome of these particular legal skirmishes, but rather, the fact that our legal system has been deliberately skewed so that those with the deepest pockets have 'purchased all the justice for themselves', leaving nothing for *the People*. Therefore, your situation is in every respect identical to those of the feudal serfs who labored on the lands of their elite lords. They permit you the *illusion* of property and ownership, but these can be taken from you at the whim of many levels of lords, from business 'or' government (the distinction being largely illusory itself).

I'm reminded of a scene in the classic 1940 film, *My Little Chickadee,* in which W.C. Fields engages a sucker in a poker game:

Sucker: "Is this a game of chance?"
Fields: "Not the way I play it, no."

The relevant variation here might be:

Citizen: Is this *justice?*
Politician: "Not the way *we* do it, no."

If you think it's too great a stretch to imagine that we're living in a feudal society, read on.

Feudalism

"The system of political organization prevailing in Europe from the 9th to about the 15th centuries having as its basis the relation of lord to vassal with all land held in fee and as chief characteristics homage, the service of tenants under arms and in court, wardship, and forfeiture" (Merriam Webster).

Three primary elements characterized feudalism: lords, vassals, and fiefs; the structure of feudalism can be seen in how these three elements fit together. A lord granted land (a fief) to his vassals. In exchange for the fief, the vassal would provide services to the lord. The obligations and relations between lord, vassal and fief form the basis of feudalism.

For use of this land, the vassal incurred certain formal obligations to support the lord in various capacities: military services, financial support, a certain amount of his farm's output, and so forth. The vassal was also sometimes required to grind his own wheat and bake his own bread in the mills and ovens owned and taxed by his lord. Fiefs could be withdrawn at the whim of the lord.

What about the *serfs*?

Oh yeah, the serfs were part of the fief; they, along with the tools, implements, and livestock were part of what the lord bequeathed to the vassals.

Now, before you dismiss this model as archaic and irrelevant, consider closely the nature of your relationship with what you nominally consider '*your* property'.

Let's start with the most obvious: taxes. We are taxed on:

1. What we earn (income tax).
2. What we spend (sales tax)
3. What we own (property tax).
4. What we do (license fees, tolls, 'right-to-work' fees).
5. How we prosper (capital gains tax).

6. Our bad habits ('sin' taxes, such as that on tobacco products).
7. Just because they CAN (excise tax, such as that on gasoline).
8. Even what we ***are*** (In Missouri, single men between the ages of twenty-one and fifty must pay an annual tax of one dollar.).

The most obvious threat to property that is purportedly yours is property tax.

In my own case, I live in a 50-year-old, 1500-square-foot ranch home on a half-acre plot of land in a semi-rural area. My roads are plowed and maintained, and that's about the only public services I receive. I must maintain my own septic system, pump my own water, and pay a private company for trash removal. There is no public transportation, and the nearest store is about ten miles away. One of my children did attend our mediocre public high school for two years, but both of my children are running up unimaginable debt putting themselves through supposedly 'public' colleges. My property taxes are almost exactly 5% of what I paid for the house in 1993, and in the current housing market, I probably couldn't get a dime more than that now. So, in effect, I have to re-purchase the same property every twenty years. If I fail to pay this extortion, 'my' property will be taken away. So, is this property truly *mine*? Not by any accurate definition of ownership. (And, for the record, this is by no means some bloated McMansion that I couldn't afford in the first place. The house cost me $55k when I bought it, and I've probably put half again that amount into essential repairs.)

Perhaps I should be comforted by the prospect that when I shuffle off this mortal coil, my heirs might benefit by whatever miniscule equity may have accumulated, after inheritance tax, of course, but what might that amount to? Like many Americans, I have been forced to re-finance my residence for such 'extravagances' as dental co-payments, a new roof, a new septic system, and replacing a fifty year old well pump.... As noted earlier, home equity has fallen steadily over the past half century, in many cases for similar reasons.

While I personally eschew credit cards, most Americans have been encouraged—by government, by media, even by their religious leaders—to live beyond their means. Debt has even been portrayed as a patriotic imperative: This is precisely what happened when the Fed dramatically lowered interest rates and the rallying call everywhere turned to: 'spend, spend, spend or the terrorists win'.

Today, many people must use credit to meet their day-to-day expenses. Indeed, a recent article in the Scranton Times-Tribune about "property tax day" described how elderly people were flocking onto the local courthouse and using their credit cards to pay their delinquent property taxes in order to avoid seizure. Well . . . so what if they subsequently can't afford their medications, or food, or heat? So what if the reason they're in such dire straits is because conniving bankers have destroyed their savings and investments, or have reneged on their pension funds? Moreover, when I had the temerity to protest the upbeat tone of this article, brain-dead readers responded by labeling me a 'socialist', and inviting me to move northward . . . to Montreal.... Now, correct me if I'm wrong, but it seems to me that taking money from unwilling citizens to pay for services they don't receive IS socialism. Of course, reality, rationality, and logic are foreign concepts to those who are so thoroughly indoctrinated.

What is the ultimate result? The big corporations are, in effect, buying up all private property. The rich pass their wealth on to their children. The working people die in debt, and their property has to be sold off, inevitably purchased by the rich and the corporations, to be turned into rental property for those who can no longer afford to own.

Consider in this context the idea of a 'reverse mortgage', which kindly old folks like James Garner encourage the elderly to investigate.

What precisely is a reverse mortgage?

Well, the concept is simple enough. Back in the old days, the home was a working family's wealth; their dynasty. All their lives, they paid off a mortgage, some of the money going to interest (usury), some building equity in their house. After twenty or thirty years, they actually owned the property. Assuming they could manage the property taxes, they had some assurance of a roof over their heads in their 'golden years', and when the inevitable transpired, the equity inherent in that property would pass on to their heirs—nothing lavish, but maybe something to help them ensure some stability in *their* older years.

Today, however, as we've seen, people have less and less equity. In addition, most have accumulated considerable additional debt. When they wish to retire, or are forced by failing health to do so, compromised pensions, pillaged investments, and a failing economy mean that they simply do not have the income to support themselves.

Enter the ever-magnanimous bankers.

"A reverse mortgage," James Garner explains, "means that *we'll* pay *you* money, every month! And you don't have to make any payments at all!"

Gee, where do I sign?

So basically, the bank starts buying back equity on the old folks' family farm, at pennies on the dollar, of course. Now, when the owners die, guess what? No more equity. The bank owns the family farm. Kids get nothing, unless, of course, they want to buy or rent it back from the bank…at a substantial profit, of course. Net result, more ownership by the few, less by the many.

As in the aforementioned feudal system, the royalty owns the land, the serfs work it.

Which do you anticipate *your* children are going to be?

No property.

Couldn't afford an education.

Have to work at whatever job they can get, under whatever terms are dictated to them.

No unions to fight for a fair shake—did away with those long ago.

Can't afford to live, other than on credit....

Who *bequeaths* the credit?

The banks.

The *same* banks who own the house they rent. The ones who own the businesses where they work. The ones who buy the politicians who make the laws.

How long will it be before laws are passed that allow your grandchildren to be *born* into debt?

Mission accomplished: *A Nation of Serfs and Elites.*

Okay, so we're going off a bit into the realm of conjecture, but read the previous lines again, and ask yourself precisely *where* we morph into a scenario that you can't imagine happening?

Moreover, is it not a scenario that would be totally consistent with the way we've already seen these banks, businesses, and their complicit politicians are inclined to operate? To scheme? To plot?

Indeed, it was recently revealed that the Koch Brothers, those stalwart bastions of freedom and fair play, have been warning all of their employees that if they do not vote the way they are told, their jobs and livelihood *might* be in jeopardy.

Call me a starry-eyed optimist, but I simply can't believe that *this* is what *any* decent, hard-working, patriotic American wants, regardless of their position on the entire gamut of social, economic, and international issues.

Debt and tax delinquency, however, are not the only threat to the property ownership that purportedly identifies us as a democratic, capitalist system, as opposed to an indentured feudal one.

As we've already seen, the Supreme Court has already ruled that even if you are a tax-paying, law-abiding citizen in good standing, any branch of federal, state, or local government can confiscate your property and turn it over to a complicit crony, simply by applying this federally-sanctioned perversion of the concept of *Eminent Domain*. So, is that property *yours*, or are you being permitted to temporarily occupy it, at the whim of a feudal power structure?

Then, of course, we have an ever enlarging array of increasingly egregious property-seizure 'laws'.

A few preparatory observations aimed at the intelligent, open-minded, reader of a conservative persuasion:

Some common threads through much conservative discourse, with which I wholeheartedly concur, involve individual freedoms, respect for the Constitution and the intent of the authors thereof, and government restraint. Naturally, there arise circumstances, unforeseen by the Founding Fathers, that embody *such* great potential peril that new laws are rightly drafted to address the common danger involved. Allowing citizens to construct their own personal nuclear reactors, or manufacturing and stockpiling nerve gas for 'personal defense', are obvious examples.

The so-called 'War on Drugs' is a more complex case. Obviously, there are some substances that are so dangerous, both to individuals and to society at large, that valid arguments can be made for control of their proliferation. Such an argument can scarcely be made, however, for a natural, unprocessed, unrefined, botanical that the good Lord saw fit to plant on this earth. I refer, of course, to the much demonized cannabis plant.

There are several ways to approach this argument that should resonate, in particular, with Conservatives, and which should serve, if any internal honesty, integrity, and consistency are permitted to prevail, to counter the insidious propaganda that has been employed to manipulate this segment of the population.

First, let's talk about the purported 'dangers', *vis-a-vis* the rightly abhorred notion of the 'nanny state'.

Cigarettes are dangerous to one's own health, and also to others exposed to second-hand smoke. Nicotine, the active ingredient in tobacco, has been proven to not only be harmful (it's used in insecticides, by the way), but also to be one of the most addictive chemicals known to man. While Liberals would like nothing better than to outlaw smoking altogether, Conservatives argue that care of one's own health is a matter of personal responsibility and personal choice.

Bravo! (Of course, cigarettes *have* been taxed to the point where they are now over $5/pack, but that's another issue.)

Excessive alcohol consumption is not only dangerous to the health of the consumer, but is responsible for, or related to, a large percentage of traffic deaths, property destruction, domestic violence, industrial accidents, and so forth. Attempts were made to ban all alcohol, and not only was that effort an abject failure, but it actually resulted in the creation of vast organized criminal empires that vex us to this day. (At least in *that* case, the enemies of freedom had enough respect for the Constitution to actually go through the *legally prescribed* process of amending it.)

The propensity of firearms, a favorite target of *some* Liberals, to cause injury is not merely some undesired side-effect, but indeed, the core intent of all weapons. The central argument of Second-Amendment supporters (of which I am one), is that the problem is not with the tool itself, but its misuse by evildoers, and that control should be aimed at the criminal, not the tool itself.

Bravo once again —common sense (and the Constitution) prevails (so far).

Let's come at this from a slightly different direction:

If the counter clerk at a convenience store sells tobacco products to an underage customer, both the clerk, and the owner of the store, will receive a stiff fine. If a liquor store owner sells to a minor, he/she will likely lose their license, and if you buy alcohol *for* a minor, you will be prosecuted. If you sell firearms illegally, the penalties are quite severe (just ask Randy Weaver).

However, if you simply grow a few marijuana plants on your own 'private' property, for personal consumption, with no attempt whatsoever to transfer any of it to any other individual, you can automatically be stripped of anything resembling due process, as if you were a foreign terrorist, have your property confiscated by the state, and can be sentenced to a lengthy jail sentence, with no possibility of parole. (Ever heard the term 'cruel and unusual punishment'?)

Now, if you're one of those people who believe that my preference for smoking a joint after a hard day's work, in the privacy of my home, somehow makes me less deserving of Constitutional protection than the guy who partakes of a Miller, or a couple of martinis, then *you*, my friend, are the one whose credentials as a 'real American' need to be questioned.

What can we make of the situation in which, indifferent to both the will of the people and the government's instructions to stop persecuting medical marijuana dispensaries, rogue agents continue their personal wars on drugs? Is there any *other* way to interpret this than a situation in which their personal agendas take precedence over the rule of law? Is this violation of States' Rights any less egregious than one in which citizens are prevented from erecting 'religious displays' on municipal property during Christmas season? (Either you're in favor of government overruling the will of the People or you're not—you can't have it *both* ways!) Indeed, both represent a clear case of *taxation without representation*.

In fact, on May 16, 2011, the Supreme Court further trampled on the Constitution's Fourth Amendment protection against unreasonable search and seizure by ruling that police can kick down your door without an warrant if they "hear what they think is the sound of evidence being destroyed." What does that mean? If past experience is any indication, it can mean whatever the police *say* it means. In other words, according to these traitorous usurpers of the Rule of Law, search warrants are a thing of the past.

Let's examine a slightly different scenario. Suppose an ultra-left Supreme Court were to rule that the 2nd Amendment does not apply to individuals, and a complicit congress passes a law calling for the confiscation of all firearms. How many of our police will consider their oath to uphold the Constitution and refuse? How many will be perfectly willing to kick in your door, and, if you resist, kill you and your family members in cold blood, as they have done on so many other occasions in the past?

Does it matter to you that for some people, myself included, the right to "the pursuit of happiness" is every bit as important as the right to keep and bear arms?

I would advance the hypothesis that, to a significant extent, the persistence of these prejudices is a direct result of the ever strengthening central government, and the homogenization of America engineered to increase corporate profit and its attendant flow into the pockets of political power centers. Suffice it to say that, when one of those 'magic words' is involved—'war on drugs', 'white supremacist', 'militiaman', 'terrorist', 'anti-government extremist', and so forth—due process goes out the window. Again, just ask Randy Weaver.

To those on the left, the ruling junta has gone to considerable pains to represent those on the right as crazies in camouflage paint, rallying around a burning cross, blowing up children in federal buildings, stockpiling weapons in eager anticipation of a coming revolution.

To those on the right, 'the enemy' has been portrayed as a rich drug-dealing pimp, driving a fur-lined Cadillac, wearing diamond rings, big feathered hats, and snorting cocaine as he drives from schoolyard to schoolyard, blatantly getting innocent children addicted, and then using his ill-gotten gains to hire fat, sleazy, Liberal lawyers to abuse the court system over the helpless objections of honest, hard-working police and prosecutors. So of *course* we have to seize all their assets in order to preclude such a blatant miscarriage of 'justice'!

The point I'm trying to drive home is that what you *think* of as your private property, and your inalienable rights, as defined in *the Constitution of the United States*, are far more fragile than you might imagine, and, more importantly, when you allow yourself to be manipulated into abrogating those rights for someone you *don't* agree with, those same manipulations are inevitably being used, or plotted, against *you*! Once again, if you have any doubt whatsoever, just examine the credentials of those who are telling you what you're supposed to believe.

So, returning to our original definition of feudalism, it's not at all hyperbole to suggest that we live under a system in which any lord or vassal can take away your property for any reason they choose, or for no reason at all.

Fascism

“*A political philosophy, movement, or regime that exalts nation and often race above the individual, and that stands for centralized autocratic government headed by a dictatorial leader, severe economic and social regimentation, and forcible suppression of opposition” (Merriam Webster).*

According to most scholars of fascism, there are both left and right influences on fascism as a social movement, and fascism, especially once in power, has historically attacked communism, conservatism and parliamentary liberalism, attracting support primarily from the ‘far right’ or ‘extreme right’. Fascists seek to organize a nation on ***corporatist perspectives; values; and systems*** such as the political system and the economy.

As the saying goes, if it walks like a duck, and quacks like a duck....

Franklin D. Roosevelt wrote: “The first truth is that the liberty of a democracy is not safe if the people tolerate the growth of private power to a point where it becomes stronger than their democratic state itself. That, in its essence, is fascism—ownership of government by an individual, by a group, or by any other controlling private power.”

Thomas Jefferson, one of the founders of the United States system of government, wrote in 1816: “I hope we shall crush...in its birth the aristocracy of our moneyed corporations, which dare already to challenge our government to a trial of strength and bid defiance to the laws of our country”.

And, according to Theodore Roosevelt: “Behind the ostensible government sits enthroned an invisible government owing no allegiance and acknowledging no responsibility to the people. To destroy this invisible government, to befoul the unholy alliance between corrupt business and corrupt politics is the first task of the statesmanship of today.”

There can be little doubt that the stronger those in power have gotten, the more emboldened they have become with respect to the suppression of opposition. The really scary part is how successful they have been in indoctrinating the populace into believing that *some* fascism (i.e., that directed against those with whom they disagree) is perfectly okay.

Randy Weaver? Hell, he was a white separatist, for goodness sake! Sure, mistakes were made, but if the FBI murdered his innocent wife and child, well, he brought it on himself by…getting involved with guns, and the wrong sort of people...

And what *if* tax dollars are being spent to infiltrate non-violent peace groups and environmentalists? They're just a step away from being dangerous subversives….

Listen, folks—these people, and thousands and thousands of others, have but *one* thing in common: they question the authority of those whose reaction to these non-violent challenges represents the most conclusive proof that they are, indeed, the abusers of power their critics suspect.

"Justice Department thinking is illuminated by a confidential plan leaked to the Center for Public Integrity, entitled 'Domestic Security Enhancement Act of 2003.' This 'new assault on our civil liberties' vastly expands state power, Yale Law professor Jack Balkin writes. It undermines constitutional rights by granting the state the authority to rescind citizenship on the charge of providing 'material support' to an organization on the attorney general's blacklist even if the accused has no idea that the organization has been blacklisted. 'Give a few dollars to a Muslim charity Ashcroft thinks is a terrorist organization,' Balkin writes, 'and you could be on the next plane out of this country.' The plan states that 'an intent to relinquish nationality need not be manifested in words, but can be inferred from conduct;' inferred by the attorney general, whose judgment we must honor, on faith. Analogies have been drawn to the darkest days of McCarthyism, but these new proposals are more extreme. The plan also extends powers of surveillance without court authorization, permits secret arrests, and further protects the state from the scrutiny of citizens, a matter of great significance to the reactionary statists of the Bush II regime. 'There is no civil right—not even the precious right of citizenship—that this Administration will not abuse to secure ever greater control over American life,' Balkin concludes. President Bush is said to have on his desk a bust of Winston Churchill, a gift from his friend Tony Blair. Churchill had a few things to say on these topics: 'The power of the executive to cast a man into prison without formulating any charge known to the law, and particularly to deny him the judgment of his peers, is in the highest degree odious, and the foundation of all totalitarian government whether Nazi or Communist'."[1]

[1] Noam Chomsky, *Hegemony or Survival: America's Quest for Global Dominance*, Metropolitan Books, 2003, p21.

Is *THIS* Patriotic?

Want to squelch dissent? Accuse the dissenters of being *unpatriotic* and all of their neighbors, even those who may have known that person all their lives, will immediately treat them as enemies and outsiders. Hitler ordered the Germans to turn on their Jewish neighbors and hand them over for interment. Those who questioned these orders were deemed unpatriotic. Americans marched their own citizens into concentration camps and stole their property, on the basis that they *looked like* someone whom we considered an enemy. If you opposed the internment of Japanese citizens, you were *unpatriotic*.

"Patriotism is the conviction that your country is superior to all others because you were born in it." (George Bernard Shaw).

"The character or passion of a patriot; love of or zealous devotion to one's country. Sometimes ironically...." (OED)

This is another of those tricky terms/concepts that is often used by those in power to compel citizens to act in a way that is diametrically opposed to the principles they *believe* they are defending.

For me, *real* patriotism involves loyalty to the *principles* of the United States, not because of hero worship, not because I was told to do so, but because I have analyzed them and believe them to be good, just, and worthy of defending. Patriotism involves loyalty to my friends, neighbors, and countrymen, to the extent that we share this common set of principles. It does *not* mean standing behind every decision some self-serving despot *tells* me I should support, and it certainly doesn't mean turning a blind eye to actions I know to be unjust.

Here's an easy test: Whenever someone in government does something that makes you wonder, do a little research and ask yourself if this is something of which Washington, Jefferson, Madison, or Roosevelt (Teddy, not FDR) would have approved. Or, if you prefer, is it something *Jesus* would recommend? If the answer is negative, then those in power are probably not your leaders, but your *rulers*; usurpers of the government you *thought* you were supporting.

"Love it or Leave it!"

There exists a certain mythos about America as 'the shining nation on the hill'—the ultimate example of freedom, human dignity, hope, charity, and overall wonderfulness—that permeates our cultural identities and underlies our perception of all aspects of life. Unfortunately, even the most perfunctory assessment of historical fact reveals a yawing chasm between reality and this sublime illusion.

If we truly were the exceptional, 'city on the hill' society we like to claim, then our focus would be on *helping* the weak, rather than *exploiting* them, but all too often, precisely the opposite is true. I fervently hope, and truly believe, that these iniquities reflect the principles of a few greedy, self-serving criminals, and *not* the morality of the American People.

When confronted with undeniable atrocities such as the deliberate genocide perpetrated against the indigenous peoples of this continent, the kidnapping and enslavement of millions of African people, the obliteration of multitudinous helpless civilians using the most fearsome weapon ever conceived, deadly experimentation on our own citizens, and many others of this nature, apologists are fond of saying: "Sure, everyone makes mistakes, but that was in the past…." Unfortunately, as recent events reveal, the denial of human rights and dignities, the abuses of power, the abrogation of our own citizens' Constitutional rights, are very much a part of our *present* as well. Indeed, as this book illustrates, the real history of the United States under the *Republicrat Junta* represents an unbroken succession of deceptions, abuses, and atrocities; all of which begs the question: what does it *really* mean to be an American?

The basis of the problem is our very human propensity for self-deception when reality is too distasteful for us to accept. If our government tells us: "'They' hate us for our freedoms," we're only too happy to nod dully and say: "Yeah, *that's* it," because it would be too difficult for us to admit that our history of supporting brutal right-wing dictators, of toppling democratically elected leaders who (gasp) favored the interests of their citizens rather than those of exploitative U.S. corporations, of training and assisting torturers and murderers of millions of dissident voices, has painted us as unmitigated hypocrites in the eyes of many throughout the world.

But don't take my word for it. Here's what Pat Buchanan wrote in *A Republic, Not an Empire*:

"*'Why do they hate us?'* When some Americans raised this valid question about September 11, they were accused of giving aid and comfort to the enemy, as if exploring the motives of those who attacked us was the same as justifying their heinous actions. Hard analyses were evaded. Instead, we were instructed to believe that we were attacked because of our virtues.... the simple truth is: We are not hated for who we are or what we believe; we are hated for what we do.... We Americans have been behaving like the Roman Empire. Between 1989 and 1999, we invaded Panama, smashed Iraq, intervened in Somalia, invaded Haiti, launched air strikes on Bosnia, fired missiles at Baghdad, Sudan, and Afghanistan, and destroyed Serbia. We imposed embargoes and blockades on Libya, Iran, Iraq, and dozens of other states. The Iraqi sanctions may have caused the deaths of 500,000 children. When Madeleine Albright, secretary of state under President Clinton, was asked if all this horrific toll of Iraqi children was justified, she replied, 'We believe the price is worth it.'[...] Why did Osama bin Laden target America? Not because we are a democracy, but, by his own testimony, because he wanted the American infidels off the sacred soil of Saudi Arabia that is home to Islam's holiest shrines. The terrorists are over here because we are over there.[...] Now millions see the United States as an arrogant empire that flaunts its power, props up corrupt dictatorships, and spreads its ungodly culture among their young. How can we call a policy that reaps such a harvest of hatred a success?"[1]

Are these the words of some rabid, right-wing ideologue, as Mr. Buchanan is so often and unjustly portrayed?

Indeed, when Republican presidential hopeful Ron Paul professed a similar dose of reality, he was booed by the audience of self-professed 'conservative' Tea-Party supporters. Listen, folks: Refusing to acknowledge a reality that every thinking human being on the planet recognizes does not make your conservative, nor does it make you patriotic. All it does is show others that you are a dimwit, an idiot, a dolt.

A similar dose of reality is provided by Noam Chomsky when he writes: "George Kennan, in this case, briefing US ambassadors in Latin America on the need to be guided by a pragmatic concern for 'the protection of our raw materials'—ours, wherever they happen to be located, to which we must preserve our inherent 'right of access,' by conquest if necessary, in accord with the ancient law of nations.... It requires a heavy dose of intentional ignorance and loyalty to power to delete from memory the human consequences of instituting and sustaining 'strong regimes.' The same talents are needed to sustain faith in the appeal to national security invoked to justify the use of force, a pretext that can rarely be upheld for any state, on inspection of the historical and documentary record. As these few examples illustrate, even the harshest and most shameful measures are regularly accompanied by profession of noble intent. An honest look would only generalize

[1] Patrick J. Buchanan, A Republic, Not an Empire-Reclaiming America's Destiny, Regency Publishing, 1999, p x-xii.

Thomas Jefferson's observation on the world situation of his day: 'We believe no more in Bonaparte's fighting merely for the liberties of the seas, than in Great Britain's fighting for the liberties of mankind. The object is the same, to draw to themselves the power, the wealth, and the resources of other nations.'" [1]

The propensity of many Americans to simply stick their heads into the sand when faced with the truth is more than mere evasion, it represents a criminal dereliction of their duty as citizens in a government "of the people, by the people and for the people." Conversely, if your philosophy is that America should behave like Genghis Khan, or Attila the Hun, or the Roman Empire, or Nazi Germany; simply taking whatever it wants by force of arms, then just say so, rather than heaping hypocrisy on top of savagery by trying to justify such actions with patent absurdities.

Since so much has been said about *abstractions*, such as socialism, communism, and so forth, how about we learn to distinguish the difference between the *abstraction* of the United States of America, as described in both our Constitution, as well as the mythos of our culture, and what *certain individuals*, some good, some not so good; some competent, some otherwise; *have done* in the name of that country?

Theodore Roosevelt, one of the greatest American Presidents, said: "The President is merely the most important among a large number of public servants. He should be supported or opposed exactly to the degree which is warranted by his good conduct or bad conduct, his efficiency or inefficiency in rendering loyal, able, and disinterested service to the Nation as a whole. Therefore it is absolutely necessary that there should be full liberty to tell the truth about his acts, and this means that it is exactly necessary to blame him when he does wrong as to praise him when he does right. Any other attitude in an American citizen is both base and servile. To announce that there must be no criticism of the President, or that we are to stand by the President, right or wrong, is not only unpatriotic and servile, but is morally treasonable to the American public. Nothing but the truth should be spoken about him or any one else. But it is even more important to tell the truth, pleasant or unpleasant, about him than about any one else."

Spoken like a *true* patriot. Compare this to Richard M. Nixon's assertion that: "it isn't illegal when the President does it..."

Thus, when Ralph Nader states that: "This administration is not sympathetic to corporations, it is indentured to corporations," and Noam Chomsky observes that: "There's basically two principles that define the Bush Administration policies: stuff the pockets of your rich friends with dollars, and increase your control over the world," both are engaging in the most noble tradition of American Patriotism.

[1] Noam Chomsky, *Hegemony or Survival: America's Quest for Global Dominance*, Metropolitan Books, 2003, p21.

Let's consider one concrete historical event: *The Sand Creek Massacre.*

Much has been written about treaties broken and trusts betrayed, but these generalities really add no value in the current discussion. The specifics of *this* particular engagement, on the other hand, are well documented and clearly defined.

The 1851 Treaty of Fort Laramie between the United States and seven Indian nations, granted to the Cheyenne and Arapaho territory encompassing the lands between the North Platte River and Arkansas River and eastward from the Rocky Mountains to western Kansas. In November 1858, however, the discovery of gold on this land prompted federal authorities to renegotiate the extent of Indian lands in the territory.

On February 18, 1861, six chiefs of the Southern Cheyenne and four of the Arapaho, anxious to avoid confrontation, signed the Treaty of Fort Wise with A.B. Greenwood, Commissioner of Indian Affairs, a duly authorized representative of the United States Government. By this new treaty, they ceded most of the lands designated to them by the Fort Laramie treaty, agreeing to all the government's demands. The new reservation, less than *one-thirteenth* the size of the 1851 reserve, was located in eastern Colorado, between the Arkansas River and Sand Creek. In recognition of this unconditional acquiescence, Chief White Antelope was presented with a large American Flag, and was instructed to display it outside his lodge, so that all white men would see it and know these were peaceful Indians who enjoyed the full protection of the United States Government.

He took the *politician* at his word. (Always a big mistake.)

On November 29, 1864, U.S. Army Colonel John Chivington, despite being informed that these were peaceful Indians, ordered his 800 troops of the First Colorado Cavalry (who had spent the previous night in heavy drinking) to attack. Chief White Antelope, secure in the sanctity of the peace treaty, had sent most of the able-bodied men out to hunt food, leaving mainly women, children, and the elderly in the camp. Seeing the approach of the soldiers, he rode out to greet them, bearing his cherished American flag. He was shot and wounded before he could utter a word, after which, according to witness Stan Hoig, the soldiers scalped him, then cut off his nose, ears, and genitals. They then swept down upon the village, killing and mutilating an estimated 133 Indians, 105 of whom were women and children.

In his testimony before congress, witness John S. Smith reported: "I saw the bodies of those lying there cut all to pieces, worse mutilated than any I ever saw before; the women cut all to pieces….with knives; scalped; their brains knocked out; children two or three months old; all ages lying there, from sucking infants up to warriors…. By whom were they mutilated? By the United States troops…."

Legendary frontiersman and Indian fighter Kit Carson later wrote: "Jis to think of that dog Chivington and his dirty hounds, up thar at Sand Creek. His men shot down squaws, and blew the brains out of little innocent children. You call sich soldiers Christians, do ye? And Indians savages? What der yer 'spose our Heavenly Father, who made both them and us, thinks of these things? I tell you what, I don't like a hostile red skin any more than you do. And when they are hostile, I've fought 'em, hard as any man. But I never yet drew a bead on a squaw or papoose, and I despise the man who would."

Initially, the Sand Creek engagement was reported as a victory against a brave opponent. Within weeks, however, witnesses and survivors revealed the true nature of the massacre.

An interpreter living in the village testified, "They were scalped, their brains knocked out; the men used their knives, ripped open women, clubbed little children, knocked them in the head with their rifle butts, beat their brains out, mutilated their bodies in every sense of the word."

John S. Smith later testified that he witnessed, as did helpless Indian mothers and fathers, young children having their sex organs cut away. U.S. soldiers mutilated Native American women, cutting away their breasts and removing all other sex organs. After the Massacre, soldiers displayed the women's severed body parts on their hats and stretched them over their saddle-bows while riding in the ranks. The sex organs of every male were removed in the most grotesque manner. One soldier boasted that he would make a tobacco pouch from the severed scrotum of White Antelope, while another displayed the body parts of a woman on a stick. The fingers of Indians were cut off to get at the rings on them.

Lieutenant James Connor remembered a baby only a few months old who had been hidden in the feed box of a wagon for protection. When the soldiers discovered the baby some time later, the baby was thrown onto the frozen ground to die. Another witness, Robert Bent, reported seeing a pregnant woman who had been cut open and disemboweled. Her unborn child lay mutilated almost beyond human recognition beside her. In going over the site the next day, it was noted that every corpse was mutilated in some way, and scalped.

Several investigations were conducted – two by the military, and one by the Joint Committee on the Conduct of the War. The panel declared:

"As to Colonel Chivington, your committee can hardly find fitting terms to describe his conduct. Wearing the uniform of the United States, which should be the emblem of justice and humanity; holding the important position of commander of a military district, and therefore having the honor of the government to that extent in his keeping, he deliberately planned and executed a foul and dastardly massacre which would have disgraced the verist [sic] savage among those who were the victims of his cruelty. Having full knowledge of their friendly character, having himself been instrumental to some extent in placing them in their position of fancied security, he took advantage of their in-apprehension and defenceless [sic] condition to gratify the worst passions that ever cursed the heart of man."

While the Sand Creek Massacre outraged easterners, it seemed to please many people in Colorado Territory. Chivington later appeared on a Denver stage where he regularly delighted audiences with his war stories and displayed 100 Indian scalps, including the flayed off pubic areas of women.

As an uninvolved American citizen, your options upon being presented with such evidence are clear.

1. You can deplore the actions of these aggressors, on the basis that they do not represent the nature of the American sensibility, or your own sympathies,
2. You can support their actions, and try to present justifications as to why it is fitting and proper to mutilate old men, women and children,
3. You can indulge in denial, and refuse to accept irrefutable evidence, and hence, display yourself as disingenuous to all honest people.

The first choice is the way of the true patriot. The other two are consistent with the philosophy of "my country, right or wrong." When you parrot that mantra—My country, right or wrong—you are making a clear and unambiguous statement.

You are making a statement about your parents and your upbringing.

You are making a statement about your religion and its teachings

You are making a statement about your personal values and your humanity.

If your statement is: "I think it's just fine to cut off an old man's genitals or a women's breasts; okay to scalp infants and smash out their brains; acceptable to murder innocent Afghani civilians, cut off their body parts as trophies, and plant incriminating evidence on them; righteous to torture naked prisoners at Abu Grebe…," then by all means: stand up proudly and let the world know what you are, but please don't portray that as being the essence of *my* country. Don't present yourself as being an American. You are not!

However, if you love the same country that I love, then it's your duty to recognize those who besmirch its image in this way *not* as its representatives, but as its enemies.

If, where relevant, I report on offensive events perpetrated by certain groups and individuals acting under the color of the law, it is emphatically *not* my intention to besmirch *America* by doing so. It is not a matter, as those of the lowest mentality are so fond of phrasing it: "blame America first...". On the contrary, my point is to underscore the danger of allowing nefarious groups and individuals to go unchecked, committing what can only be characterized as atrocities in the name of *our* country. These individuals are *not* America. They do not *represent* American values. They are, in fact, the antithesis of what this country stands for. They are the enemies of America. They are criminals and traitors in every sense of the word.

The purpose of this book is not to disparage the *ideal* of 'truth, justice, and the American Way'. Quite the contrary. The point here is that the abstraction of the American ideal is a wonderfully noble one, but only through uncompromising candor will we ever be able to convert that abstraction into a reality. We need to continually remind ourselves that integrity and self-honesty are the very cornerstones of this cherished self-image.

As a more contemporary example, consider William Moyer, a sheriff's deputy from Shenandoah, PA, accused of obstruction of justice for covering up evidence in the murder of twenty-five year-old Luis Ramirez, an illegal immigrant. One of the perpetrators? The son of a local fire chief. The response of the community? A succession of fund-raising events supporting "Billy" (the deputy): bake sales, rallies, etc. Purportedly, these hundreds of people all seemed to have known and loved this rogue cop, which sounds pretty farfetched. One can only wonder—would their support have been so unequivocal if he had covered up the murder *of* the Fire Chief's brat *by* an illegal immigrant?

Regardless of your feelings about illegal immigration; regardless of what *other* illegal immigrants might have done—be it drug dealing, or keeping the price of your produce low—it's tough for anyone claiming to embrace 'Christian values' to argue that this *particular* individual deserved to be beaten to death simply for walking down *our* street.

The real core of the matter is that human history is an unbroken succession of provocations, counter provocations, accusations, and distortions between countless groups; each of which has always been 100% convinced of their own righteousness, the nobility of their cause, the reprehensible nature of their opponents, and the conviction of the 'fact' that the 'other side' is, for one reason or another, undeserving of humane treatment, and is, in fact, subhuman.

The one thing they all have in common? A predilection to say: "Yeah, but it's different with *us*." One side inevitably prevails, and hence, *their* interpretation becomes canon; the undeniable mythos of exceptionality. The bottom line is: Our Founding Fathers *intended* America to be exceptional, they provided its citizens with the basic guidelines to make that possible, but it is up to *us* to make it a *reality*.

The question has often been posed: how did the people of Nazi Germany allow the atrocities that took place right under their very noses? If they were not all of a mind in supporting the utter destruction of six million of their fellow human beings, if they did not share Hitler's single-minded hatred, if they did not believe in the suspension of due process, the seizure of private property, and the abrogation of the most basic laws of humanity, how is it that they stood by and permitted this to happen? Here we have the answer:

My country, right or wrong.

Love it or leave it....

No, I'm not trying to say that America is *not* admirable in many respects. I won't even say that it might not be the best there is, as *I* have not had an opportunity to experience all of the alternatives. All I'm saying is that by parroting these kinds of jingoistic platitudes, we accomplish nothing but to make ourselves ridiculous, and serve the interests of those to whom we are nothing more than puppets to be manipulated to their own ends.

I believe that there *is* a great deal to love and admire about the United States of America, but, as a nation run by fallible human beings, it has been involved in errors, mistakes, and even iniquities. If we cannot recognize this fact, we will never be able to ensure that these mistakes are not repeated.

In Stanley Kramer's 1961 movie masterpiece, *Judgment at Nuremburg*, Chief Judge Dan Haywood (played by Spencer Tracy), prefaces the pronouncement of sentence by observing that:

"There are those in our own country, too, who today speak of the protection of country, of survival. A decision must be made in the life of every nation at the very moment when the grasp of the enemy is at its throat. Then it seems that the only way to survive is to use the means of the enemy, to rest survival upon what is expedient, to look the other way. The answer to that is: Survival as what? A country isn't a rock. It's not an extension of one's self. It's what it *stands* for. It's what it stands for when standing for something is the most difficult. Before the people of the world, let it now be noted that here in our decision, this is what *we* stand for: Justice, truth, and the value of a single human being."

In a similar vein, Benjamin Franklin wrote: "They who can give up essential liberty to obtain a little temporary safety, deserve neither liberty nor safety." To this I would add: *and will inevitably lose both.*

In recent years, in the name of 'patriotism', we have seen citizens denied due process, suspension of the writ of *habeas corpus*, defense of torture, abrogation of privacy, extraordinary renditions, secret spying on Americans by the CIA—an agency specifically prohibited from such domestic activities—and the wholesale infiltration of citizen organizations, both on the right and the left, solely on the basis of their being critical of the ruling *Republicrat Junta*. The cynical naming of this seditious legislation as 'The Patriot Act', is *so* Orwellian as to merit no further comment, other than to observe that its sole aim can be none other than the repression of true patriotism in all of its manifestations. Again, consider the recent seditious ruling of our so-called 'Supreme Court', blatantly annulling a key tenet of the *Bill of Rights*. Obviously, according to these 'made men', corporations who pay them off *have* rights, citizens have *none*.

To quote Theodore Roosevelt once again: "No man is justified in doing evil on the ground of expediency."

Stated differently, and paraphrasing Spencer Tracy's rousing soliloquy: to the extent that we accept and even embrace these measures, the country we are purportedly protecting is no longer The United States of America.

For me, a true icon of modern patriotism has to be Johnny Cash.

Yes, he *did* say:

"I thank God for freedoms we've got in this country. I cherish them and treasure them—even the right to burn the flag. We also got the right to bear arms, and if you burn my flag, I'll shoot you."

Nevertheless, he respected everyone, and stood up for the rights of the downtrodden, free of the racist attitudes that permeated much of the country music scene of his day. He was a close friend of Bob Dylan, and guests on his TV show included Neil Young, Joni Mitchell, Stevie Wonder, Creedence Clearwater, and others with whom most country artists of that era would never associate themselves.

When invited to perform at the White House for the first time in 1972, Richard Nixon requested that he play "Okie from Muskogee" (a *satirical* Merle Haggard (Footnote: Just for the record, Merl Haggard himself, a patriotic American, did smoke pot, and had even dropped acid on at least one occasion.
) song about people who despised youthful drug users and war protesters) and "Welfare Cadillac" (a Guy Drake song which impugns the integrity of welfare recipients). Cash declined to play either and instead selected other songs, including "The Ballad of Ira Hayes" (about a brave Native-American World War II veteran, one of the men who raised the flag at Iwo Jima, who faced discrimination and disdain upon his return to Arizona), and his own anti-war compositions, "What is Truth?" and "Man in Black."

So, Johnny Cash was a man who defended the flag, opposed the Viet Nam war, was on friendly terms with Richard Nixon and Jimmy Carter, cherished traditional values, admired Bob Dylan, and hobnobbed with people from every social strata, political persuasion, and ethnic heritage. In other words, he was a real American and fine man. There was something more, however: he was a man who acknowledged his shortcomings, rather than attempting to excuse them away or hide them from view, as so many lesser people have done. Finally, he was a man who always gave back far in excess of what he received.

Regardless of your belief system, it's pretty hard not to admire a man like Johnny Cash. Was he utterly unique in human history? I doubt it. So why is it that we can't give the other guy the benefit of the doubt, even if he can't perform as well as The Man in Black, and assume that maybe, just maybe, he *might* be a good guy as well?

The answer to that question, as I demonstrate throughout these pages, is that we are being deliberately manipulated to fear, distrust, denigrate, and abhor huge segments of our neighbors. We are being deliberately polarized for one carefully, cunningly-engineered, nefarious purpose: to prevent us from uniting in order to purge this great land of a perfidious canker that has usurped the government that was *supposed* to be of the people, by the people, and for the people; and there's *nothing* patriotic about *that*!

Terrorism

The *Oxford English Dictionary* defines terrorism as: *1.1 Government by intimidation as directed and carried out by the party in power in France during the Revolution of 1789–94; the system of the 'Terror' (1793–4): 2.2 gen. A policy intended to strike with terror those against whom it is adopted; the employment of methods of intimidation; the fact of terrorizing or condition of being terrorized.*

At the time of the American Revolution against Great Britain, war had 'evolved' into a strictly codified system of mutually-respected guidelines controlling the methods, scope, and tactics of engagement. Officers were recruited from the educated gentry, with the assumption that their basic decency would prevent the fighting forces they controlled from degenerating into rape and pillaging. Bright uniforms ensured that one could easily identify the enemy, and would never mistake civilians for combatants. Indeed, it was not unusual for civilians to picnic on nearby hills where they could enjoy the spectacle of a battle in total safety.

When most of us were taught American History, the British soldiers were portrayed as stupid, stuffy, arrogant, popinjays, strutting into battle in absurd uniforms and formations while our brave freedom fighters picked them off like targets at a turkey shoot.

The reality, however, is that this custom of warfare was in every way equivalent to our current Geneva Accord, intended to bring some degree of civility to military encounters, protect civilians, and ensure at least a modicum of humanity. Inherent in this attempt was the underlying notion that, even though we may be on opposing sides of *this* issue, yet we may respect each other as human beings, and behave toward each other with some amount of restraint.

Those who flaunted these conventions were…terrorists. Of course, when the terrorists *win*, they write the history and sing the legends of their heroes, so that future generations never even question their methods, which brings us to the basic point I've been developing here: The whole basis of what constitutes a legitimate combatant, and whose behavior brands them otherwise, is a rather malleable one; so much so that the word is practically meaningless.

This becomes particularly troublesome when that *meaningless* word becomes a powerful legal precept, capable of being redefined and reinterpreted at the convenience of those whose primary goal is the maintenance of personal power. In other words, the more the word 'terrorist' becomes identical with 'political opposition', the more *every* American should start worrying about it.

Example: In 2000, Jeff Luers was convicted of 'eco-terrorism' for damaging three SUVs at the Romania Chevrolet dealership in Eugene, Oregon. He was sentenced to 22 years in prison for causing about $50,000 worth of property damage in a fire that took about 20 minutes to contain, and injured nobody.

Perhaps you find this behavior annoying, maybe even reprehensible; but are you in actually in *terror* for the safety of your Chevy Blazer? Indeed, if there *is* terrorism involved here, it's the blatant effort of the *Republicrat Junta* to strike terror into any who dare oppose their corporate-backed agendas.

Before the current 'Tea Party' movement, there was the original—the *Boston* Tea Party. Remember those legendary figures from our canonical folklore? *Those* guys (ohmygod!) destroyed *property* in order to make a political point. Do we denounce them as terrorists, or venerate them as heroes? No doubt back then there were lots of nice conservative colonists who denounced this action, saying something like: "King George should lock them up and throw away the key!"

For the sake of perspective, consider the following crimes and sentences:

- Michael Hunter, the police officer convicted of murdering two unarmed civilians in cold blood and injuring four others after Hurricane Katrina, and a subsequent cover-up, was sentenced to eight years in prison.
- Johannes Mehserle, a transit cop convicted of shooting an unarmed civilian, received a two-year sentence, and was subsequently released after serving just half of that.
- Salinas Police Officer Christopher Swanson was sentenced to 90 days in jail and 3 years on probation for firing at an unarmed couple during a traffic stop.
- Jon Burge, whose name in Chicago is synonymous with police brutality and racism, received a 4½-year sentence for torturing suspects (several of whom were subsequently proven innocent) into confessions.
- In 1997, Abner Louima , who was guilty of nothing more than standing outside a Brooklyn nightclub, was abducted by 5 on-duty New York City police officers, and taken to a police station storage room where he was assaulted, brutalized and forcibly sodomized with the handle of a bathroom plunger. The five police officers? One received 30 years in prison, a second served a 5-year sentence, and the other three served no time at all.

How much time did the Massey Energy Company officials who ordered safety equipment to be bypassed receive for their part in the death of 29 workers at their Upper Big Branch Mine in 2010? How about the BP officials whose profit-maximizing measures led to the death of 11, not to mention billions of dollars in damage to the ecology,in the Deepwater Horizon disaster of 2010? How about the mass murderers from Union Carbide, whose peculiar interpretation of capitalism killed over *twenty thousand,* and injured a half million more at Bhopal in 1984?

For a more direct comparison, on March 24, 2011, 22-year-old Army Specialist Jeremy Morlock, after pleading guilty to the deliberate, premeditated slaughter of three innocent, unarmed Afghani civilians for the simple sport of it, was sentenced to 24 years, with a possibility of parole after a mere seven. Morlock was part of a 'Kill Team', of military psychos who routinely murdered civilians, harvested their body parts for gristly trophies, then planted evidence to appear as if the victims were combatants.

"The plan was to kill people," Morlock told the hearing. Military prosecutor Andre Leblanc described the crimes as being of "unspeakable cruelty," and accused the soldiers of killing out of "pure bloodlust." On Friday, September 30, 2011, Private Andrew Holmes was sentenced to seven years in prison, as part of a plea deal, for shooting an innocent Afghani civilian in the same savage rampage. Holmes also pleaded guilty to one count each of possessing a finger bone of the victim and using marijuana. Others participating in the atrocities received even lighter sentences, and some were even allowed to remain in the military.

While the Army has been quick to condemn these atrocities, and repeatedly claim that they represent the actions of a few rogue soldiers and not the policy of the United States military, the facts argue otherwise. Indeed, part of Morlock's confession admits that these 'rogue outlaws' beat up a fellow soldier who "*complained to superior officers*."

Would these be the superior officers that the Army claims were *unaware* of the problem?

In fact, the evidence is clear that a culture of murder was not only tolerated, but encouraged; with promotions being directly linked to 'kill counts'. Historically, American soldiers who commit war crimes are acquitted or receive light sentences. Rarer still are convictions of commanding officers who turn blind eyes or even encourage atrocities. Indeed, the official reaction is as follows: "The United States and NATO are concerned that reactions could be intense to the publication of images documenting killings committed by US soldiers in Afghanistan."

Not concerned about the misery they have caused; not concerned about the betrayal of American principles and standards; like any other common criminals, they're simply sorry they got *caught*.

A final Orwellian twist on this story is the fact that these soldiers were supposedly carrying out the American strategy of counterinsurgency, or COIN, which called for *protecting and befriending* the Afghan population in the dangerous region around Kandahar. Perhaps they merely misinterpreted "winning hearts and minds" with "cut out their hearts and take their heads as trophies"?

These men are also accused of taking drugs while on duty. Is it not our own government that has repeatedly tried to connect the 'war on drugs' and 'the war on terror', painting drug dealers as supporting terrorism? Where are the additional harsh sentences for *these* criminals, who are not only using drugs that send ordinary civilians to jail, and result in the unconstitutional and unreasonable seizure of their property, but they are doing it while *on the payroll of the American citizens*? Is not 'drug use' routinely used as an aggravating factor in virtually all violent crimes?

I would be very interested to hear precisely *how* this situation differs from some drugged-up gang banger in East LA killing innocent civilians as part of their ongoing turf wars.

So, not only do we have simple, first-degree, premeditated murder, but conspiracy, gang-related crimes, racketeering, and probably treason as well.

Twenty four years for murdering three helpless human beings, twenty *two* years for *wounding* three pickup trucks. And *we* have the unmitigated gall to condemn Middle-Eastern theocrats for their harsh systems of 'justice'?

Okay, I *know* how tempting it is to take that typical "kill 'em all and let God sort 'em out," bravado attitude, but it's important to take a deep breath, step back, and realize that *this* is not what we're all about, is it? You think *John Wayne* would have sat still for the guys in *his* company doing that sort of thing? Or would he have slapped them around and straightened them out? Same goes for Gary Cooper, or Chuck Norris, and all the others we've grown up admiring as embodiments the American spirit of decency and fair play.

No, I don't like terrorists either—whether they wear rags around their heads, or Kevlar helmets, or three-piece suits and Rolex watches. And here's something *else* to consider: If someone gave the order, these are the same kinds of guys who would be just as happy to take *your* head as a trophy, or have a little fun with your wife, or your daughter. Thugs are thugs, regardless of whether you dress them up in khaki uniforms or street-gang colors. The difference, however, is that *your* taxes are being used to support these heinous activities, and *your* support of these policies, or even mere acquiesce, makes your complicit in the eyes of those who already consider us enemies; and by any objective standards, makes every American citizen a legitimate military target.

In an official statement, Colonel Thomas Collins said that the actions depicted in the photos are "*repugnant to us as human beings and contrary to the standards and values of the United States.*" So, if you're one of those gung-ho types rooting for these thugs, please don't add hypocrisy to stupidity by depicting yourself as a patriotic American. You're *not*.

The recent events in the Middle East pose some interesting questions. In Egypt, a brutal dictatorship was overthrown when the military *refused* orders to fire on peaceful demonstrators. Conversely, in Libya, the soldiers were only too happy to 'just follow orders', not only firing on the crowds, but deliberately murdering people with precision sniper fire. How do you suppose *American* troops would react to such an order? Before you answer, consider carefully the lessons of recent history: Kent State, Ruby Ridge, Waco, Hurricane Katrina....

Helter Skelter

When the horrific crimes perpetrated by Charles Manson's 'family' reached the public awareness in late 1969, the title of this hitherto innocuous song by The Beatles took on a grim new meaning. Indeed, the twisted strategy formulated by these deranged miscreants was, if anything, more dastardly than the murderous rampage that represented its first tactical salvo.

Manson, convinced of the inevitability of a race war in the United States, contrived to hasten its advent by committing brutal, senseless crimes which, he anticipated, would be blamed on black militants. The resultant conflict, which he called *Helter Skelter,* would decimate society, clearing the path for Manson and his followers to seize power in the aftermath.

While his tactics were obviously demented, was the underlying strategy sound? If we are to judge by the all but identical goals of those who have seized control of the United States Government, the answer must be a resounding affirmative. The similarities, however, go far beyond the obvious goal of inciting conflict in the interest of personal advantage.

Following the three days of peace and music at the Woodstock Festival in Bethel, New York, even the hitherto conservative, suspicious, and straight-laced upstate NY police officers had begun to admit that these hippie types were actually decent, likable people. (In fact, many attendees who came for the festival are now respected citizens of that Catskill region.) Then, suddenly, the peace and love of a half million people were overshadowed by the savagery of a few psychopaths. The government missed no opportunity to hammer home their message that *Manson*, not *Woodstock* was the face of the 'counter culture'. None of this is to argue that the hippies of that period, amongst which I counted myself, weren't flighty, irresponsible, or prone to excess—we were. However, my strong suspicion is that drug-addled flower children were responsible for

for far fewer grotesque massacres than, for example, good, clean-cut Americans, such as…Lieutenant William Calley.

In fact, perhaps the timing was merely propitious (from the perspective of the *Republicrats* in power), but this was just about the time when the details of the My Lai Massacre had escaped containment, and many mainstream Americans were beginning to question whether these 'long haired hippies' might not be on to something when they claimed that our activities in Viet Nam were not only immoral, but were, in fact, criminal.

Since the government always works hard to obscure memory of its worst atrocities, a brief synopsis is in order:

On March 16, 1968, three platoons of an Eleventh Infantry Brigade company under the command of Captain Ernest Medina, perpetrated the mass murder of between 347 and 505 unarmed civilians, most of them women, children (including infants), and elderly people. Many of the victims were raped, beaten, tortured, and some of the bodies were found mutilated. (Sound familiar?)

Typically, the army tried to describe the events at My Lai as a military victory that had resulted in the deaths of 128 enemy combatants.

When news about the high number of civilians killed at My Lai reached Brigadier General George H. Young, the assistant division commander, he instructed Colonel Oran Henderson to investigate. Henderson interviewed the men in Charlie Company, uncritically accepting their denials of any killing and dismissing the statements of those who reported otherwise. Henderson's report said that 20 civilians had been killed through bombardment and crossfire and that no one had been intentionally shot. He dismissed claims about a massacre as propaganda.

Lieutenant Colonel Frank Barker—in charge of the task force of which Charlie Company was a part on 16 March—also wrote a report about that day in My Lai. Like Henderson, he described a battle in which 128 enemy were killed, elaborating the story with such fictitious details as small-arms fire received from the enemy.

Despite efforts (led by a 31-year-old Army Major named Colin Powell) to cover up the event, too many American soldiers who had witnessed the event and testified to what had really happened; including Warrant Officer Hugh Thompson, Jr., a helicopter pilot from an aero-scout team, who had witnessed the large number of dead and dying civilians—all of them infants, children, women and old men, with no signs of draft-age men or weapons anywheres—as he began flying over the village.

Once the My Lai story became public, a different set of prevarications were concocted. Army Secretary Resor told a Senate Armed Services Committee investigation that, "... what apparently occurred at My Lai is wholly unrepresentative of the manner in which our forces conduct military operations in Vietnam." In what might have been the same script used during the trial of Army Specialist Jeremy Morlock for the slaughter of innocent civilians in Afghanistan, My Lai was blamed on the unauthorized actions of 'a few bad apples'. As a result, although all evidence indicates that this was a deliberate massacre, carried out under orders from above, only 26 US soldiers were initially charged with criminal offenses, and only one, Lieutenant William Calley was actually convicted of killing 22 villagers. He was initially sentenced to life in prison. Two days later, however, President Richard Nixon ordered Calley released from prison, pending appeal of his sentence. Calley's sentence was later 'adjusted' so that he would eventually serve four and one-half months in a military prison at Fort Benning.

When the incident became public knowledge in 1969, it prompted widespread outrage around the world, and also increased domestic opposition to the US involvement in the Vietnam War. Three US servicemen who had made an effort to halt the massacre and protect the wounded were later denounced by (*Republicrat*) US Congressmen. They received hate mail, death threats and found mutilated animals on their doorsteps. It would take 30 years before they were honored for their efforts.

So, the Manson murders came at a most convenient time for the *Republicrat* government. Suddenly, all those dead *gooks* were old news. These were young, attractive, *white* people, and they were killed not by American soldiers following orders, but by drug-crazed, long-haired hippies!

The similarities, however, go far beyond this most visible level.

While even the most ostensibly 'conservative' of *Republicrats* take pains to distance themselves from overt racism, both sides actually fuel the fire of racial divisiveness at every opportunity. Their reason for doing so is not difficult to understand, and can be seen clearly by referring, once again, to Viet Nam, and other wars as well.

In combat situations, brave white soldiers from Alabama and Mississippi stand shoulder to shoulder with black men from the ghettos of Detroit and Hispanics from East Los Angeles, each implicitly trusting each other to protect their lives against a common foe. While it would be hyperbole to claim that there is *no* prejudice in the trenches of battle, it can be stated with certainty that it is far less prevalent, and far less vehement than in many domestic scenarios.

Although we don't hear Trent Lott shouting "hang all niggers," or Al Sharpton counseling his constituents to "kill whitey," their subtle manipulations deliver similar messages, albeit it in a more subtle and insidious fashion.

To those on of a liberal sensibility, what is presented as the very embodiment of reprehensible, right-wing excess? Why, 'white-supremacist, neo-Nazis', of course. After all, what reasonable American could possibly find common ground with such abhorrent cretins? Like 'terrorists',' militant Islamists', or 'inner-city gang bangers', these simplistic archetypes serve several purposes. First, they exonerate one from the necessity of truly analyzing their positions, grievances, or motivations; as if understanding someone's reasoning is the same as endorsing their conclusions or their actions. By painting a group as universally one-dimensional: evil, stupid, violent, and hateful—we justify simply dismissing them as sub-human. The White Supremacist, neo-Nazi groups, such as Arian Nation, the KKK, and so forth are a perfect example. After all, what modern, intelligent, educated American would be willing to even suggest that these people could possibly have any basis for such patently reprehensible philosophies?

Although I emphatically disagree with their conclusions, their rhetoric, and their mode of expression, I nevertheless find it difficult to believe that every last one of them is the stupid, evil, vile, hateful, sub-human brute that many insist they are.

Is it not possible that at least *some* of these are simply *people*? People angry at seeing their jobs and livelihood stolen, deprived of the simple dignity of a basic lifestyle they were promised, and lashing out in rage? And whom do they blame? A 'foreign' phantom enemy they neither know nor understand, but one which, their trusted 'leaders' *tell* them, are responsible. True, these leaders are crafty enough not to use the explicit word, but they all know the code and what it means: Lazy ghetto dwellers, living on welfare hand-outs, driving Cadillacs.... A distant, shadowy enemy who can be easily demonized with no evidence to the contrary.

And on the other side? The man who cannot get an education because he is poor; cannot get a job because he has no education; and cannot escape poverty because he has no job. What is he told by *his* 'leaders'? Through the same sly code-speak, *he's* led to understand that 'the man'—the self same ones who dragged his ancestors from peaceful villages in chains; the same ones who broke up families, sold off children, and forced his people to work like animals—still conspires to keep him down. Just look at them! Rich, greedy, swinish criminals like Bernie Madoff, or Ken Lay, all the good old 'massahs' looking out for each other's interests.

Why is this so critical to the ruling junta? Because they know that the moment the People realize that their common enemies are not 'the blacks', and are not 'the whites', but the men in thousand dollar suits; in black robes of office; men with leather brief cases, fancy haircuts, and Rolex watches; men protected by blue uniforms and gold badges; no security force on earth will be sufficient to protect them from the righteous wrath of those whom they have conspired to exploit.

I don't know about *you*, but if some mercenary force wearing black masks, jack-boots, and Kevlar vests are grouping to attack *my* domicile, I take all the help I can get, from any of my fellow downtrodden Americans, regardless of their complexions, where their ancestors hailed from, what churches they attend, or any other superfluous details…just so long as they can shoot straight and hit hard. *That*, my friend, is what the Founding Fathers meant by 'the militia'; and that is the meaning of 'brothers in arms'. It is also *precisely* the scenario they had in mind when they wrote that Second Amendment into the Bill of Rights, and it's the mindset we're going to have to embrace if we're ever going to take back *our* country! The enemy isn't the black man or the white man, the Christian or the Jew, the white-collar or the blue-collar; it's the illegal junta in Washington, and the uniformed mercenaries who do their bidding.

Debts Deferred

A recurring lament amongst many Americans is that the spending of our burgeoning federal government is generating an obscene debt that will be passed on to our progeny. While this is, indeed, a valid concern, there are even more pressing debts being incurred for our children, which the *Republicrats* would rather we all ignore.

Consider the squandering of limited petroleum supplies, in the sole service of maximizing corporate profits. Recall the examples of chickens from California being shipped to China to be plucked, then shipped back to be sold in the United States, or the importing of drywall from halfway around the globe. Here we are not merely exploiting the near-slave labor in China, but squandering precious petroleum with no other justification than maximizing quick profits for rapacious investors. Will our children be burning worthless, devalued American currency for heat when oil can't be had for *any* price? As we stuff our bloated faces with those $200 greaseburgers, subsidized down so they fit conveniently on the 99¢ menu, will our progeny pick up the difference on a planet that can no longer sustain life at all?

More generally, under the guise of 'free trade', we not only deprive local workers and exploit foreign ones, but subsidize the differential through artificially cheap petroleum that makes it more attractive to move goods half way around the planet rather than manufacture them locally. Who actually *benefits* from these policies? Is it 'the consumer', as the *Republicrat Junta* would like us to believe? As Noam Chomsky observed: "If you mean by 'consumers' rich ones, yes. Rich consumers will gain. People who have lost their jobs, for example—and that will be true both in the rich countries and the poor—obviously are not going to be better consumers."

Wow! You *think?*

Who is *really* benefiting? The Chinese factory worker who must live in company housing, buy company food, at prices engineered to result in what amounts to slavery? The consumer, who would rather buy quality goods, but can afford only Wal-Mart junk because they are employed at sub-standard wages, as a result of competing for jobs with the foreign factory slaves? The citizens of the future, who will live without oil because we are squandering it in order to further engorge the appetites of these enemies of humanity? Or is it those few, whose monumental gluttony exceeds the most ludicrous caricature of comic-book villains—those who are selling out every living creature on their planet for all of eternity in order to satisfy their pathological acquisitiveness?

These people should not be permitted to profit their crimes; they should be tried and executed for the worst and most blatant crimes—against not only humanity, but life itself—in the history of this planet.

Contrast this wasteful, irresponsible, and unfair business model with the philosophy espoused by Theodore Roosevelt:

"We wish to control big business so as to secure among other things good wages for the wage-workers and reasonable prices for the consumers. Wherever in any business the prosperity of the businessman is obtained by lowering the wages of his workmen and charging an excessive price to the consumers we wish to interfere and stop such practices. We will not submit to that kind of prosperity any more than we will submit to prosperity obtained by swindling investors or getting unfair advantages over business rivals."

One might actually think that Roosevelt, like Nostradamus, was somehow blessed with a direct channel to his future, our present!

In addition to this blatant squandering of a precious, finite, irreplaceable resource in service to malignant rapacity, this short-sighted business model incurs a plethora of secondary, equally negative side effects; for example:

- With the price of oil low, consumers (largely in the United States) are encouraged to further squander this limited resource in the interest of frivolous, often mindless entertainment, the price of which is to be borne by future generations: pleasure boats, RVs, ATVs, private airplanes, oversized motorcycles, outsized SUVs, 'personal watercrafts', snowmobiles, and similar non-essentials.
- People are inclined to move to remote suburbs, commuting long distances to jobs that may pay a few dollars more—again, enriching themselves monetarily at the expense of their children. At the same time, they abandon troubled neighborhoods, rather than expending the effort to improve living conditions there.

- This non-essential squandering of fossil fuels is damaging to health and to the environment, whether or not you agree that 'global warming' is part of that equation.
- The resultant depletion of fossil fuels is used as a convenient justification for expanding the use of hazardous nuclear reactors. (And who profits by building these reactors? Big corporations like Westinghouse, who buy their agendas from our corrupt *Republicrat* politicians.)

In a *true* free-market economy, a commodity like oil, which is at once limited in quantity, irreplaceable, essential to many industries, and in high demand, would level off at a price more representative of its true value. People would be far less inclined to squander it zipping around the waves in their little jet-skis, or barreling down the highway, going nowhere essential, in houses-on-wheels. These 'recreational activities', however, are wonderful diversions. So long as people are indulging themselves in mindless pastimes, they are less inclined concern themselves with what their politicians are up to.

Keep them occupied and happy, and we can go on doing whatever we like.

And *how* are oil prices maintained at these absurdly low prices? By subsidizing the oil industry with *your* tax dollars.

Hey! Wait a minute—what ever happened to our suspicion and disdain for all things *Socialist*? As we saw quite clearly during the 2008 financial meltdown, and the subsequent bailout of Wall Street criminals, the law of our land has become: Socialism for the rich, Capitalism for the poor; Socialism for the connected, Capitalism for the citizen; Socialism for the corporations, Capitalism for the workers.

Instead of subsidizing the oil companies, who are already making record profits, wouldn't it make more sense to allow oil prices to reflect the value of the commodity itself, and subsidize the essentials, such as heating oil? It would ***if*** poor, elderly people were able to generate billions of dollars in payola for 'their' representatives, the way the oil companies do. It would if the manufacturers of gas-driven recreational devices didn't lavishly spread their wealth around Washington. It would if the companies raking in unprecedented profits by moving goods across the globe, in order to deprive Americans of their jobs, weren't greasing the rapacious palms of *Republicrat* lawmakers,

This, of course, would represent Capitalism employed in a responsible manner, as opposed to the greed-driven abomination into which they have turned it. As Ron Paul has observed: "Capitalism should not be condemned, since we haven't had capitalism."

Unfortunately, as we've seen repeatedly, the average brain-dead American can't palate the bitter taste of truth; preferring instead the artificially-sweetened pablum of deceit spoon-fed to them by their lying politicians.

So, what we are doing is indulging in exorbitant convenience, luxury, and entertainment, at the expense of a debt that will not only be burdensome, but indeed, will likely threaten the very existence of our species. This is not conservatism. This is not liberalism. What it is, is a crime against humanity, a crime against nature, and a crime against all reason.

This brings up yet another aspect of this problem: the environmental impact of this out-of-control hedonism.

The question of human-driven climate change is beyond the scope of the current discussion, other than to reiterate the points presented earlier: The traditional meaning of the word 'conservative' is: "marked by moderation or caution…a cautious or discreet person" (*Merriam Webster's 11th. Collegiate Dictionary*). From this perspective, even *if* man-made greenhouse gas production proves to be harmless, we have lost nothing, other than, perhaps, some transitory and ultimately nebulous and meaningless wealth, and will have conserved a large amount of oil that will, by that time, be even *more* valuable, thereby resulting in even greater monetary remuneration Thus, the *true* conservative (as opposed to the greedy, irresponsible, self-serving wealth builder) would make a conscious choice to err on the side of safety. The fact that so vast a majority of those who *call* themselves political Conservatives take precisely the opposite position is an apodictic[1] argument that they are, in fact, merely greed-driven criminal scoundrels, rather than the responsible idealists they present themselves as being.

Whether or not this irresponsible exploitation of petroleum leads to catastrophic climate change, there are other undeniable downsides to this dithyrambic style of commerce made profitable by subsidized dissipation. Even something as seemingly trivial as the excess packing material needed for all this profit-driven commerce represents a huge deferred debt, both in terms of resources consumed as well as waste requiring disposal (and, of course, the additional energy needed to accomplish both). Considering that we've only been using fossil fuels for a bit over a century, and in that time have managed to deplete a huge portion of known reserves, one would *think* that the conservative position would be to treat short-term financial gain as a secondary consideration, both in terms of conservation and the development of alternative energy sources.

Nor is oil the only industry focused on raping the planet in pursuit of a quick buck, leaving future generations to survive on whatever rubble we happen to leave behind.

[1] Apodictic — From the field of formal logic, an assertion that is incontrovertibly or demonstrably true as a result of having been deduced systematically, in a stepwise manner, from incontestable foundational principles, in such a way that denying it leads to a contradiction.

The Rape of our Oceans

As a result of the proliferation of big, industrial-scale fishing operations, seventy percent of the oceans' commercially-targeted marine fish stocks have been exploited beyond ecologically safe limits. One-quarter of all the fish pulled from the sea never make it to market. Twenty-seven million tons of unwanted fish are thrown back each year on average. Most don't survive. Twenty-seven million tons of wasted fish represent more than half of all fish produced annually from marine capture fisheries for direct human consumption.

Populations of top predators, a key indicator of ecosystem health, are disappearing at a frightening rate, and 90 percent of the large fish that many of us love to eat—tuna, swordfish, marlin, cod, halibut, skate, and flounder—have been fished out since large-scale industrial fishing began in the 1950s. The depletion of these top predator species have caused a shift in entire oceans' ecosystems where commercially valuable fish are being replaced by smaller, plankton-feeding species. This century we're already seeing bumper crops of jellyfish replacing the fish consumable by humans.

These changes endanger the structure and functioning of marine ecosystems, and hence threaten the livelihoods of those dependent on the oceans, both now and in the future.

The over-exploitation and mismanagement of commercial fishing has already led to some spectacular fishery failures. The cod fishery off Newfoundland, Canada collapsed in 1992, leading to the loss of some 40,000 jobs in the industry. The cod stocks in the North– and Baltic Seas are now heading the same way and are close to complete collapse.

Instead of trying to find a long-term solution to these problems, the fishing industry's eyes are turning towards the Pacific—but this is not the answer. Politicians continue to ignore the advice of scientists about how these fisheries should be managed and the need to fish these threatened species in a responsible, sustainable manner. Why? Here again, we are compromising the survival of our species in a quest for immediate profits for a few psychotically greedy individuals, who grease the waiting palms of *Republicrat* politicians in order to maintain their exploitation.

More often than not, the fishing industry is given access to fish stocks before the impact of their fishing can be assessed; with the industry being regulated, predictably, by the same government industries that are on their lobbying payroll.

Is it merely coincidental that many of the same politicians who support the continued rape of our planet are simultaneously working hard to compromise the rights of *women* who are sexually assaulted, both by raising the bar for what constitutes a sex crime, and by preventing them from ending a pregnancy that results from a sexual assault? I suppose it's a small step from raping another human being to assaulting an entire planet: "Hey, she was *asking* for it...."

Technological Issues

Huge segments of *our* tax dollars are funneled into supporting supposedly innovative research and other scientific endeavors, but it's not difficult to see that the vast majority of this money goes to the familiar cronies of those controlling the purse strings: big oil, the nuclear industry, coal, and others who are already raking in obscene profits (with the usual backflow of cash to those who pass the enabling legislation.)

Alternative energy, principally solar and wind, is a prime example of how the profit-making interests of entrenched corporations trump logic and the good of both the people and the nation. As such, it could be argued that those who press their own agendas in so critical an issue are, indeed, traitors.

The first thing we have to understand about wind/solar technology is that it's proven, well understood science. This makes it fundamentally different from, say, developing fusion power. In the latter case, throwing money at the problem might or might not ever result in a breakthrough. In the former, we're dealing with something that we *know* can work.

Let's look at some numbers:

According to the 2000 census, there are 69,865,957 detached, private dwellings in the United States. For the sake of argument, suppose it currently costs approximately $20,000 to install a complete (on-grid) solar panel system on an existing dwelling. Multiplication gives us a total cost of $1,397,319,140,000.00, just under $1.4 trillion, to install this technology on *every* private dwelling in the U.S.

Forgetting for the moment the objection that someone might (heaven forbid) get something they didn't earn, [fn: Is it not astonishing how the very same people who bristle at the possibility that someone might get something they don't deserve, are the ones who think nothing of the likelihood that a death-penalty might be imposed on someone who isn't guilty?] suppose the government were to make this conversion available in the form of loans (which funds would be recovered later, as discussed below). Indeed, considering that, as a result of the recent financial meltdown, Americans lost somewhere around $15 Trillion out of their bank accounts, their investments, their retirement funds, etc., these wouldn't be a give-away at all, but a very small compensation for the damage done by this government's corrupt policies.

How much would such an infusion force the price to go down? ½? ¼? To give us an even number to deal with, let's say the total bill is $750 Billion—which is pretty conservative. (Consider what production volume did to the price of fiber optics since their advent in the mid 1970s.)

A large number, true, but no more than was pumped into resuscitating the corrupt institutions whose malfeasance resulted in the collapse of the world economy. How much *has* the US government pumped into 'conventional' energy subsidies, thereby bolstering an obsolete and destructive technology?

As I write this (April, 2011), oil companies are announcing record profits, up as much as 55% compared to last year, *while* gasoline prices are inching past $4/gallon at the pumps, and, they are *still* being subsidized with tax payer money to the tune of $45 billion/year, ***and*** have the unmitigated gall to say that the additional tax breaks they're requesting, which average about $4 billion a year according to various government reports, "are a bargain for taxpayers"!

Need I offer any further defense for my use of the word '*scumbags*'?

Just in *case* anyone is even *thinking* about questioning this debacle, scumbag Jack N. Gerard, president of the American Petroleum Institute, warns that "any cut in subsidies will cost jobs."

Sima J. Gandhi, a policy analyst at the Center for American Progress, argues that: "We're giving tax breaks to highly profitable companies to do what they would be doing anyway. That's not an incentive; that's a giveaway."

Now, if you're one of those people who are inclined to knee-jerk to the contrary position just because this observation comes from someone you're told is a Liberal, well…what more can I say? Have fun the next time you fill the tanks on your pickup truck.

Of course President Obama, in a virtual word-for-word repeat of a corresponding announcement by President George W. Bush, has promised that: "We are initiating an investigation into price gouging…." Which *color* of *scumbag* do you prefer? You see? The American People *do* have a choice after all!

Nor are the oil criminals the only old cronies receiving corporate welfare payments directly from *your* pockets. The U.S. coal industry enjoyed subsidies of around $17 billion between 2002 and 2008. Natural gas drillers (who, at the time of this writing, had just discharged thousands of gallons of toxic drilling fluid into the once pristine Pennsylvania environment), also benefit from massive subsidies, *and* preferential treatment, including the total exemption from Clean Water Act protections, courtesy of that champion of fair play, Dick Cheney.

One last point to consider: Who, precisely, *owns* the vast resources beneath the North American continent? Can it not be reasonably argued that these giant corporations, funded by tax dollars, are exploiting the wealth that legitimately belongs to the American People, and then selling these resources *back* to the legitimate owners at obscene mark-ups? And are they not getting *away* with this blatant thievery by virtue of using these ill-gotten gains to bribe those who are supposedly representing *our* interests with the very money they are stealing from *our* pockets?

Nice business model. Is it any wonder their profits are up 55%? Oh, sorry, I forgot: this is a "bargain for taxpayers."

SCUMBAGS!

Skeptics are fond of summarily dismissing clean energy technologies such as solar and wind power by arguing that these technologies "can't compete on price without public subsidies." However, the history of coal, oil, natural gas, and nuclear power demonstrates that *no* energy sector was developed without subsidies. Indeed, in the case of nuclear energy, the United States government underwrites the insurance of *all* nuclear power facilities. Why? Because, within a normal *market-driven* business environment, *no* insurance company will undertake such a risk! What is this if not corporate socialism? When (not *if*) the next accident occurs, who, precisely, is going to foot the bill if not the taxpayer? But don't forget: this, too, is a *bargain* for *you*. Good thing our politicians are there to watch out for *our* interests!

What would be the effect of replacing these blatant give-aways with *investments* in more forward-looking technologies?

How many jobs would be created?
What would be the effect on greenhouse emissions?
What would be the effect on our dependence upon fossil fuels?
What would be the financial benefit of the US becoming the leader in this technology, and making it available to others (as China is well on the way toward doing)?

And to pay for it? Simple: Install electric meters, and charge the beneficiaries the same rate they're currently paying to the big utilities, until the government's *investment* is recovered. Notice, I said 'investment', not 'subsidy', or 'hand-out', or 'give-away'.

Of course, to be equitable, we have to consider the negative financial impact to the existing energy businesses, including investors, retirement funds that have invested in them, and so forth, but this is another issue entirely. In a true free-market economy, some benefit, some lose, and in this case, those who might lose are the ones whose benefits have been artificially facilitated right from the beginning, as a result of blatant corporate socialism.

There are undoubtedly other positive aspects, such as the strategic advantage of decentralizing the power grid; environmental impact of not having to resort to hydraulic fracturing to recover natural gas, the installation of gas lines, the installation of more power lines, the electromagnetic impact of high-voltage lines; and others I'm sure we won't even know about until the tumors start showing up in our children's internal organs.

One needn't dig too deep to discover corporate interests at work in innumerable other technological areas.

Just look at agriculture, where genetically manipulated plants, deliberately created so as to render the seeds infertile, ensure that farmers have to keep coming back to the seed company year after year. But consider the *implications* of relentlessly replacing natural plants with ones incapable of reproduction. One attacker—insect, blight, bacteria, or whatever—could, as a result of this lack of diversity, lead to global famine, or even leave the planet incapable of supporting life. Is this a reasonable trade-off in return for short term profit? To those driven by selfish, pathological greed, perhaps, but not to anyone remotely deserving of the term 'human'.

Going even further, these plants are, whenever possible, bred so as to necessitate the use of specific chemical fertilizers, and specific chemical pesticides, and specific chemical herbicides, also, conveniently, held in a lock grip by the same corporations. Thus, the farmer is totally at the mercy of the company. (In fact, as I write this, farmers have identified a new, 'RoundUp-Resistent' strain of hogweed, which, due to the genetic uniformity and lack of diversity in their crops, threatens to decimate their farming operations.)

In India, a coordinated program of subsidies, manipulated seed sources, specialized fertilizers, pesticides, and herbicides have poisoned consumers, destroyed crops rendered more vulnerable by lack of diversity, and driven small farmers into such horrendous levels of debt that thousands have committed suicide. Is this a reasonable trade-off for generating obscene wealth for a few greedy enemies of humanity?

I suppose it is, *if* you're a greedy, degenerate enemy of humanity.

Huge corporate farms employ obnoxious practices such as fertilizing crops with human sewerage, which has on numerous occasions led to illness and even death. In a completely analogous fashion, our corporate meat factories deliver food to the consumer saturated with powerful antibiotics necessitated by the abysmal conditions in which these animals are forced to live. We have already seen the preliminary by-products in the form of antibiotic-resistant strains of deadly contagions, and a growing array of new threats to human health. Is it in any way 'conservative' to risk the health of millions of human beings, if not the outright obliteration of the species, so that a few cronies can get even richer than they already are?

As previously shown, high-tech fishing vessels can virtually depopulate entire regions of our oceans, catching, processing, and packaging their spoils right on board, so as to eliminate the necessity of interrupting the devastation with frequent port calls. Many scientists agree that even with the damage already done, huge regions of the sea have had their ecosystems so drastically impaired so as to render them incapable of supporting life. Is this in any way representative of the conservative, capitalist philosophy? Destroying resources for generations to come, so that a few privileged members of *this* generation can accumulate more than any human being could ever live long enough to enjoy?

In the pharmaceutical industry, government tax incentives and give-aways are used to support the manufacture of new diseases to go along with whatever new drug they happened to develop. A typical example is the medication for toe nail fungus, among whose side effects are heart disease, stroke, and death. Rather than expend valuable resources toward addressing *real* diseases, the profit-driven mentality guides the direction of research into whatever will make the most money.

Research grant dollars given to universities and private organizations finance the development of cataclysmic weapons of ever increasing virulence and destructive capability. Can one *possibly* envision a scenario in which our existing arsenal of tens of thousands of nuclear weapons, nerve gas, and biological agents wouldn't provide adequate deterrent to any aggression? (Not to mention the obvious fact that the entire 'deterrent' strategy hinges on a tacit acknowledgment that retaliation against an enemy's civilian population could ever be a morally justifiable tactic.)

The Medical Field

Any in-depth discussion of the medical industry, the drug industry, or the health-insurance industry is such an immense topic as to defy detailed analysis in a single treatise, even if that were the central topic of this book. On the other hand, it's clear that healthcare is an integral part of the economic collapse in a number of ways, and these *do* merit some discussion here.

Although there are obviously many committed, dedicated professionals in the medical field, as there are in all others, for many, the field has become commercialized to the point where they are identical to any other cut-throat enterprise, with little or no thought given to the reality that people's lives and health are the primary outcome, and not merely a peripheral by-product of doing *business*. Indeed, the underlying attitude of customers as marks, of unprincipled exploitation, is in every way identical to that in other industries.

The distinction between true capitalism and *AmeriCapitalism* is exemplified by a paradigm in which, rather than identifying a need and attempting to meet it, the 'entrepreneur' simply develops what is most expedient, and then engages a massive marketing engine to convince the public that they can't live without it. The aforementioned example involving the prescription oral medication *Lamisil* (Terbinafin), approved by the FDA for treatment of toe nail fungus, is a perfect example. Known side effects? It is acknowledged to cause liver damage—some sufficiently severe as to have necessitated a liver transplant, or even caused death. (But your toe nails sure will look pretty.) How could our government approve such a dangerous treatment for a relatively benign complaint?

As in most such cases, the numbers tell the entire story:

Novartis, the patent holder for *Lamisil*, along with the other major pharmaceutical companies, employ 625 lobbyists to promote their agendas in Washington—that's more than one lobbyist for every member of congress. The bill for this team of lobbyists in 2000 alone: $92.3 million. Of these 625 lobbyists, more than half were either former members of Congress or others who previously worked in Congress or in other federal government positions. Nor are we talking about low-level public-service employees. Drug industry lobbyists include 33 who had served as Chief of Staff to members of Congress; 11 who worked for the powerful House Ways and Means Committee, which has jurisdiction over the Medicare drug bill; and 8 others who had worked for the key Senate Judiciary Committee, where drug patent law is crafted. In addition, six worked for the Bush I administration; five worked for former House Speaker Newt Gingrich (R-Ga.); four worked for former Senate Judiciary Chairman Orrin Hatch (R-Utah); five worked for (then) current Senate Health, Education, Labor and Pensions Committee Chairman Edward Kennedy (D-Mass.); four worked for former Senate Majority Leader Trent Lott (R-Miss.); and three worked for current Senate Finance Committee Chairman Max Baucus (D-Mont.).

The drug industry spent $262 Million on political influence in the 1999-2000 election cycle: $177 Million on lobbying, $65 Million on issue ads and $20 Million on campaign contributions. In fact, the drug industry spends more on political persuasion (i.e., bribes) than any other industry.

Might these factors have any bearing on a company being permitted to market a cure for toe nail fungus that can *kill* the user?

You *think*?

In return for their bribes, the federal government has conferred on the industry monopoly patents and patent extensions, tax credits worth billions of dollars a year, and research *subsidies* for both the most medically important drugs and also the top-*selling* ones. Nevertheless, these criminals, whom *you* have elected, persist in claiming that trying to lower drug costs to the consumer is socialism, while taxing *you* in order to reward those who pay them off, is not.

How do they get away with this blatant chicanery? Once again, by misdirection. Any time the American people are on the verge of getting wise to these criminal activities, they switch gears and shout out: "Hey, look what those (Republicans/Democrats) are up to!" Look over there, (at your neighbors) not at what *we're* doing.

Ever hear that rather rude expression: "Money talks, bullshit walks"?

Any confusion as to which segment *you* represent as far as *they're* concerned? A quick glance at whose talking and whose walking should give a pretty clear indication of what our politicians think of the American People as a whole!

Pharmaceuticals, of course, represent only one segment of an overwhelmingly corrupt and dysfunctional commercialized medical establishment.

Laurie Johnston and Janice Laporte were both subjected to radical mastectomies, even though all evidence proves that their doctor *knew* they did not have cancer, and went ahead with the surgery anyway, three days *after* receiving the pathologist's report saying the patients/victims did *not* have cancer.

The doctor's explanation?
"I'm sorry. I made a mistake. I did not read the (pathology) report fully."
Well then, I guess all should be forgiven.

Note, parenthetically, how many politicians are fighting to place a cap on medical malpractice judgments, when, in cases like this, real justice might entail cutting off some piece of the *doctor's* anatomy.

Unfortunately, when we embrace a philosophy in which the bottom line is the sole consideration, this type of abuse is only natural.

A few personal anecdotes to conclude this chapter:

A few years ago, after losing two teeth that could have been saved if I'd been in a position to cover the insurance co-pay on root-canals and crowns rather than less expensive extractions, I decided to refinance my home in order to protect my remaining oral apparatus.

The dentist I'd been using for several years was a 'specialist'—meaning she only did high-profit routine dentistry, and outsourced root canals, extractions, and so forth. Hence, I went to her, explained the situation, and obtained a quote for 'her part' of whatever work would be necessary to address all existing issues. Then I went to the endodontist she recommended, and obtained a similar quote for what I would need to cover out of pocket. Then I hocked my home, and commenced treatment, secure that I would at least end up with a baseline that would prevent future avoidable losses.

The first procedure was completed without incident. The root canal was done, the crown installed, and we moved forward.

Then, things became complicated.

First, after one tooth (#18, I believe) was root canalled, my original dentist thought she saw some kind of anomaly beneath it, which she believed might be an abscess. She conferred with the endodontist who assured her that he knew what she was referring to, but had concluded that it was not an issue. He advised her to proceed with the crown installation. Nevertheless, she decided it would be best to wait for three months, just to be sure. When I returned after the appointed duration, she took another x-ray, and, still not satisfied, wanted to wait another three months. Once again, I complied, returned three months later, and once again, was told to wait for *another* three months. Three weeks later, the tooth fractured.

When I tried to make an appointment with her to determine what might be done, I was told that she could no longer see me because she had stopped accepting my dental insurance plan.

In the interim, we had completed work on several more teeth. Out of nowhere, after having paid the co-pay for each procedure as completed, I received a bill for several thousand dollars from the endodontist for fees not covered by the insurance company. When I questioned this divergence from his original quote, he referenced some fine print in the paperwork I had signed saying that if the quote was incorrect, I would be responsible nonetheless. Since I did not have any more money to pay this bill in full, he refused to see me to discuss salvaging the broken tooth that he had originally treated, saying only that he had told my dentist to go ahead and crown it, and so it was not his problem.

(As it later turned out, the *reason* for the discrepancy in the insurance coverage was because his office had failed to obtain the required pre-authorizations after the initial procedure, and hence, had been covered at a lower, 'out of network' rate. At that point, however, he had already impaired my credit report, and only after I engaged an attorney did he agree to retract the claim.)

With no place else to go, I went to a nation-wide dental franchise (whose name is the same as a famous ski resort in Colorado, and which, as it turns out, is the target of a massive class-action litigation.)

After the initial 'free consultation', I was directed to their financial department. The person there went over the list of essential work, which included $4,000 for critical periodontal treatments, the need for which no prior dentist had ever mentioned. They offered several payment plans, but of course, no work would be commenced until the financial issues had been satisfactorily arranged. I opted to forego the periodontal work for the time, and concentrate on that broken tooth, and a second massive cavity which nobody else had noticed, and which I was told was questionable—if the filling didn't work, my only options would be a root-canal or extraction; which was precisely the situation I had hoped to avoid. The broken tooth, I was assured, was beyond help, and had to be extracted.

I agreed, and the work was commenced; first the cavity, then the extraction.

After the Novocaine wore off, I *thought* I could still feel the jagged remnants of that broken tooth, and called to question whether they had indeed gotten it all. They scheduled another appointment. When I arrived, I was told that the dentist who had done the extraction was no longer there, but one of their other interchangeable professionals would be seeing me.

He studied the x-rays, examined my mouth, and assured me that everything was fine, and what I was feeling was part of an adjoining tooth.

Fast forward.

My daughter recommended a dentist she'd discovered, some fifty miles from my home, and he agreed to take me on as a new patient. My initial surprise came when I tried to discuss finances with him. His response? Let's worry about saving your teeth first, and we can figure out the rest later.

Surprise number two?

"We should be able to save that broken #18 with a post and cap…."

Huh? Excuse me? #18 was *already* extracted!

He looked at me quizzically, consulted the x-ray, looked back in my mouth, and assured me it was still there.

In fact, the factory dentist had extracted the tooth *next* to it. Moreover, when I contacted the insurance company to request their records, they informed me that the dental factory had never submitted a claim for *any* extraction! Clearly, the second factory dentist, discovering the error, had hurried to prevent any billing that could ultimately provide evidence of their error.

Meanwhile, my new dentist has *saved* that broken tooth (yes, the one that the factory dentist assured me was beyond salvage), repaired that botched filling that the dental factory told me would be questionable, crowned them both (oh yes, did I mention that *this* dentist does the full range of work himself, rather than outsourcing), took care of a few other items, assured me that I do *not* need $4000 worth of periodontal work, and is accepting reasonable monthly payments for the portion not covered by my insurance.

What's *wrong* with this guy? What is he, some kind of goddamned *communist*?

No, he's just a *real* healthcare professional.

Oh yes, *all* of the factory dentists were foreign imports. This is not to suggest that there is any racial element to this issue, but rather, that the franchise is clearly hiring the lowest-cost, foreign-trained workers, regardless of qualification, or lack thereof. Profit first, quality and ethics a distant second.

Anecdote Number Two:

Both my brother and his wife are self-employed, and found the cost of medical insurance prohibitive. After doing some careful analysis—taking into account that they both adhere to an exemplary lifestyle, exercise regularly, eat carefully planned meals, and so forth—they established a conservative self-insurance plan consisting of meticulously banking a substantial sum each month to cover healthcare contingencies. This worked fine for several decades, leaving them with a reasonable surplus...until my brother was diagnosed with a malignant brain tumor.

His condition was quite serious when he arrived at the world-renowned Mayo Clinic. My brother, always an impressive athlete, had to be brought in with a wheel chair.

The doctors advised immediate surgery, and even then, declared that one-year survival would be an "excellent outcome." However, before beginning...$80,000...cash, if you please. No tickee, no washee.

Fortunately, between their medical savings, and help from parents and in-laws, the money was quickly raised, and the operation proceeded.

More amazingly still, today, some four years later, my brother has been cancer-free for over a year, due in large part to an intensive regiment of holistic measures in addition to traditional treatments. Oh yes, the post-operative medications? $800 per capsule, taken once/week for several months.

My brother was *lucky*. He had the financial support structure that allowed him to receive the essential treatments. If not, he would have been wheeled out into the gutter and left to die.

So, here's *my* question: Is the Mayo Clinic 100% self-funded? Do they receive *no* government assistance, funding, tax-exemptions, grants? What about the techniques and technologies they employ? Were these *all* developed *completely* within a free-market driven model?

I don't *know* the answer to these questions, but I strongly *suspect* that the answer is 'no'. Hence, to argue on the basis of free-market capitalist philosophy that people are entitled *only* to the care they can afford to buy is patently disingenuous.

Put this another way: *Without* all that publicly-funded research, technology, and so forth, no matter *how much money* an individual has, none of these treatments would be available. Through cooperation...*socialism*...society pools their efforts and resources for the mutual benefit of all, not just those who can pay. The notion of invoking capitalist principles or socialist ones when each suits your personal needs is both unreasonable and dishonest. Indeed, is it not completely analogous to a scenario in which all people pool their resources for federal disaster insurance, and then, when a calamity occurs, the wealthy neighborhoods are rebuilt, and the poor are instead told to simply sell the remnants of their property to rich people, at a fraction of their previous value?

So, to expand on Noam Chomsky's analysis, in America's particular implementation of capitalism, everything is for sale to those who can afford it, including freedom, justice, and even life itself; and even those commodities developed and produced at the public expense.

If this doesn't sound like blatant corruption to you, perhaps some education in basic ethics is indicated.

The Pinnacle of Greed

Although anyone with $1 million in the bank is technically a millionaire, it apparently takes a *lot more* money than that for the *merely rich* to feel *truly wealthy*. According to a survey of the ultra-rich by Fidelity Investments, most of these millionaires did not feel rich unless they had $7.5 million.

Keep in mind that one out of three Americans do not have one penny to their name, not even stashed in the beat up mattress. In fact, the average per capita income in the United States is $25,000, so it says something about the proliferation of greed to hear millionaires saying that they don't feel wealthy *enough* until they reach the $7.5 million mark. As it is, the top 1 percent already have over 40 percent of all financial wealth in this country, but apparently even this is not enough. What the survey found, implicitly, is the wealthy want even more from an already shrinking pie, and they are more than willing to sacrifice the American middle class to achieve their benchmark of wealth. In other words, they want more, and believe themselves perfectly *entitled* to take it away from those who already have next to nothing.

We now have *45,000,000* Americans on food stamps, and even though we have recently added more Americans to the employment rolls, we are still over 7,000,000 jobs short from when the recession started. Moreover, the vast majority of these new jobs are low-level, low-paying positions at places like Wal-Mart, with minimal benefits, pedaling the cheap imports that that are helping those *other* Americans achieve their coveted $7.5 million status level. Of course, the official propaganda machine wants you to believe that *everyone* is doing badly, and that we all have to tighten our belts and sacrifice; or so scumbags like Scott Walker would have us believe. I suppose that includes those whose 'suffering' entails squeaking by with only $6 million. (Let's not forget that the stock market is *up by 100 percent* from the March 2009 low.)

It's critical that we don't lose sight of the fact that the largest portion of the ultra-wealthy come from the production-sucking financial sector. Think of all the hedge fund managers and investment bankers that *made* money during the housing bubble, and those that made *billions* by betting on the *failure* of American households. These are the people getting giant tax breaks, while those for whom you voted keep telling you that they're supporting those tax breaks for *your* benefit.

In fact, the true effective tax rate for multimillionaires is *already* far lower than what is indicated by official government statistics. That's because those figures fail to include the additional income that's generated by many sophisticated tax-avoidance strategies.

Typical schemes involve complex loans that are designed to never get repaid, netting the beneficiaries hundreds of millions in tax-free cash. From 2003 to 2008, for example, real estate developer Frank H. McCourt Jr., owner of the Los Angeles Dodgers, paid *no* federal or state income taxes. What kinds of laws do you *expect* will be favored by the *next* multi-millionaire who manages to buy his way into the presidency?

Moreover, since a large portion of the top 1 percent of wealth holders in this country directly benefit from the financial sector, it should come as no surprise that these individuals received a substantial portion of the banking bailouts, while working and middle class Americans foot the bill.

Nevertheless, many Americans continue to support politicians whose policies are actually detrimental to their own well being. How many of the new 'budget saving' measures include massive cuts that actually impact the working and middle class, like access to schools, infrastructure repair, Medicare, and other programs, while simultaneously lowering tax rates to the wealthy? Not only are these politicians cutting *every single program* that actually makes an impact on the lives of the working and middle class Americans, while lowering the tax burden on the rich, they've convinced you that it's in *your* best interests!

Three cheers for Scott Walker and the Koch Brothers! Go team!

As the vast majority of normal human beings can comprehend, one can only buy so many toys, only see so many sights, only conquer so many women. Why, then, the quest to acquire such mammoth fortunes?

While there are some exceptions, the bulk of such people want to establish a *dynasty*. They want to confer their great wealth to their progeny, so that *they* will have a maximal advantage over the progeny of everyone else. They want *their* children to be able to attend the finest schools, regardless of whether or not they're qualified, so they can get the best jobs, regardless of whether or not they're competent, so that they will make the most money, and pass it on to *their* progeny.

Since only one out of four Americans has a bachelor's degree, an education is critical to moving up in life; yet these 'austerity measures' will force many more to opt for the student loan debt landmines being set out in our country, particularly by for-profit schools.

While it is an intrinsic part of nature for each entity to do its best to maintain its own line of DNA, survival of the fittest, under normal circumstances, works to improve the *species*. But is that what is happening? Are the spoiled, self-absorbed offspring of rich, amoral cut throats the genetic line most salubrious to the wellbeing of humanity? Or is exactly the opposite true? Is Paris Hilton to be the next stage of human evolution?

What these corrupt few have done, over the course of centuries, is twist the environment such that natural selection favors the most evil, most corrupt, most antisocial elements, and then tried to convince the rest of the tribe that *this* is what *they* should strive for as well. Perhaps the principle at work here might better be termed: Survival of the *feces*!

Consider one relevant parallel: Those in control of Monsanto have spent generations breeding plants that are incapable of natural reproduction, so that farmers will be forced to buy seeds from them. At the same time, they have actively worked to promote the extinction of all competing plants. The danger? By eliminating diversity, they ensure that a single blight could wipe out entire sources of food, and consequently, endanger all life in the planet.

Adolph Hitler killed six million people, driven by insanity, and a twisted theory of eugenics. These people would wipe out ***billions*** of people, motivated by simple greed. Now you tell me, which one is the bigger criminal? Which is truly the enemy of humanity? Which is the more despicable?

And who supports these companies? Legions of greedy investors, looking to make an easy buck while producing nothing on their own.

So, riddle me this: when 90% of the food is gone, and 90% of the water is poisoned, and 90% of the animal life is dead, whose children do you think will be getting the 10% that remains? Yours? Or the children of the rich?

Hence, when you stop and ask yourself: What kind of person would promote such policies? The answer becomes clear: Those who want to *kill your children,* in order to make more room for their own. So, yes, 'class warfare' *is* coming, and if the rest of us don't wage it with conviction, extinction shall be our destiny.

The whole intent of capitalism is that every individual has equal opportunity, and the freedom to go as far as their abilities and the value of their contributions can take them. It is not to perpetuate the power of a few inbred 'elites'.

Why aren't people on the streets revolting against this inequality that resembles that of the Great Depression or the period that led to the French Revolution? Why aren't these greedy enemies of humanity being dragged from their McMansions and marched up to the guillotines, to the cheers of the masses? Why this deafening silence from the victimized?

The reason is clear: the government's propaganda machine assures us that, if we keep sacrificing and working hard for our corporate massahs, one day *we* will wake up and have $7.5 million in the bank. And 'when' that happens, we don't want the government touching any part of *our* 'hard-earned' money, do we? Never mind that when you buy into that lie you're supporting the same Wall Street investment banks that robbed your home, crushed American jobs, and are stripping away the rights that working and middle class Americans have fought for over the last century. Never mind that, once again, one in three of us don't even have a dollar to our name, and our average per capita income is $25,000. Forget that the odds against you prevailing in this ongoing Ponzi scheme is as infinitesimal as hitting the lottery, or having Publisher's Clearing House show up at your door with one of those four-foot wide checks. Keeping on believing that there's such a thing as a free ride, and you're going to be one of the lucky ones to hop on board…***sucker!***

For a glimpse at the true pinnacle of greed, one need only consider the New York City-based Pinnacle Realty Company.

Unscrupulous landlords have always thrived in New York. But Pinnacle is unique in its scale and financing through the Praedium Group, a real estate investment trust (REIT) on steroids. REITs have been around for decades, but only in the late 1990s did big banks get in the action—just as New York State began allowing apartments with rents exceeding $2,000 to exit stabilization programs.

A handful of banks suddenly saw Harlem and the Bronx in a whole new light. "It's viewed as a decent investment," said Jerry Salama, a NYU professor and real estate expert. "The large investment banks are…going to Harlem and buying rundown multifamily homes and fixing them up."

Credit Suisse First Boston, one of the country's biggest investment banks, established Praedium in the nineteen-nineties. One Praedium REIT, Praedium Fund V, pooled $465 million from pensions, endowments and foundations to leverage $1.7 billion in acquisitions according to financial industry reports. The bulk of that went to buy New York apartment buildings. A Praedium spokesperson refused to comment on their individual holdings, but Kim Powell, a Pinnacle resident from Harlem, spoke candidly about Praedium, "They are not seeing that within their real estate work, there are habitants and human lives."

Now, to the staunch *AmeriCapitalist*, this is the way things are *supposed* to work, but when you stop and think about it, isn't this reminiscent of what was done to the Native Americans? First, we drove them off of all the desirable lands, forcing them, through treaties we had no intention of honoring, to live on the lands we thought were worthless. Then, when we found *gold* on those lands, or wanted to construct our railroads through them, or for any number of other reasons decided that they had some value after all, we simply evicted them and sent them to an even worse hell hole. Unless, of course, the bounty on Indian scalps is up, or tobacco pouch futures have driven up the value of Indian scrotums, making the business model more conducive to simply butchering them for their parts.

In the Pinnacle case, it's not as if these capitalists paid top dollar for these properties, only to have some meddling socialists force them to open the doors up to the poor. These are the same people who, year after year, refused to repair these properties, allowed them do disintegrate, refused to give heat to people in the winter, and now, when New York real estate has become so very precious, are ready to run these *people* out of their homes, and who cares where they live next?

AmeriCapitalists are fond of quoting Horatio Alger stories, and saying that anyone should be expected to pick themselves up by their bootstraps, while simultaneously ensuring that educations are available only to those with money, or those willing to indebt themselves for life.

An integral part of this mythos is the notion that these 'great philanthropists', by advancing the industrialization of the US, benefit all; but does this stand the light of scrutiny?

Were the mine owners *elevating* the miners when they hired Brinks men to murder those who dared to unionize? Or were they serving their own interests, and those of fellow greedy industrialists in the steel industry?

And what ABOUT those Brinks thugs? Are they not the same breed of unprincipled mercenary that we see today under the auspices of Blackwater, and even those donning the uniforms any big-city police department??

The philosophy of *AmeriCapitalism* is easy to perceive and to understand:

- Profit trumps human rights.
- Profit trumps democracy.
- Profit trumps the environment.
- Profit trumps animal abuse.
- Profit trumps property rights.
- Profit trumps the Constitution.
- Profit trumps safety.
- Profit trumps the future.
- Profit trumps life.
- Profit trumps *all else!*

If this pinnacle of greed, avarice, and irresponsibility is *your* philosophy as well, then by all means, continue to cast your votes for the Republicans and the Democrats who truly represent *your* professed interests. (But please don't complain when you find your head in a wicker basket!)

Taxation Without Representation

I consider it a great misfortune that the term 'Tea Party' has been preemptively hijacked by the same neo-conservative, corporate interests that already own the *Republicrats*, because it would otherwise represent a perfect rallying cry for intelligent, thoughtful people from all across the political spectrum.

Originally proposed as an acronym for "Taxed Enough Already," it's easy to see how this movement has been turned from something that *might* have united people against the ruling Junta, into yet another tool for dividing and distracting would-be opponents of the most corrupt regime in the history of civilization.

As I write this (4/2011), the federal government narrowly averted a shutdown, due to a budget impasse, with the Tea Party supposedly providing fuel to the conflagration. A close examination, however, reveals that this contrived drama is about far more than finance.

The Republicans, while *claiming* their motivation is to "cut spending," saddled their proposals with demands called *Policy Riders*, for such things as defunding planned parenthood and National Public Radio (NPR), *and*, tellingly, removing the enforcement power of the Environmental Protection Agency, and removing financial industry regulation. It is not my intent to debate the merits of these issues, other than to observe that they have absolutely nothing to do with the matter at hand, and in fact, seem to have been *purposely* injected in order to force a confrontation. Moreover, in the event of a government shutdown, guess who will continue to get paid. Our soldiers on the front lines? No. The FBI? Nope. Low-level clerks serving essential public needs? Not a chance. Congressmen? You better believe it!

We *all* have various hot-button issues that absolutely make our blood boil, and I agree that many of them are quite important. Nevertheless, if we're *really* setting out to solve this bourgeoning debt problem, does it not make sense to focus on that issue, and *only* that issue, since even in the absence of additional baggage, it promises to be a difficult problem to resolve?

Unless, of course, your really don't *give a damn* about reducing debt, but rather, simply want to give your constituents the appearance that you are a big, tough, macho guy who is fighting *their* battles against an evil opponent.

Of course, neither *Republicrat* faction questions the $2 billion ***per week*** hemorrhaging from our economy to support our adventure in Afghanistan (and that does not include the estimated $1 trillion liability being accumulated for the long-term care of the American soldiers being maimed there.) Might we attain greater security will a lesser expenditure? I don't purport to have an answer to that question, however, it *is* quite telling that nobody in power thinks the question is even worth *asking*, much less analyzing and debating. Of course, people like Ron Paul, are immediately marginalized, lest anyone take a moment to listen to what they have to say: "The moral and constitutional obligations of our representatives in Washington are to protect our liberty, not coddle the world, precipitating no-win wars, while bringing bankruptcy and economic turmoil to our people."

To understand who supports the war, just look at who *profits* by it:

- **Halliburton**: A March 2003 Pentagon e-mail reveals that action on a no-bid Halliburton contract to rebuild Iraq's oil industry was 'coordinated' with Dick Cheney's office. Halliburton's KBR, Inc. division bilked government agencies to the tune of $17.2 billion in Iraq war-related revenue from 2003-2006 alone. This is estimated to comprise a whopping one-fifth of KBR's total revenue for the 2006 fiscal year.
- Contract interrogators **CACI and Titan Corporation**, hired through no-bid contracts, and linked to the torture of detainees at Abu Ghraib and elsewhere. More than 92 percent of CACI's $843 million in revenues last year came from the federal government. 96% of Titan's $1.8 Billion 2003 revenues came from government contracts.
- Construction and engineering giant **Bechtel**, awarded a $2.4 Billion, no-bid contract, and renowned for reconstruction failures that range from shoddy school repairs to failing to finish a large hospital in Basra on time and within budget.
- **Aegis Defense Services:** A UK-based military contractor (mercenary force) engaged for $430 million despite lower bids from American companies in an effort to shield both sides of the transaction from accountability for any war crimes, since their actions fall outside the military codes of conduct.
- **General Dynamics**, which supplies the Army with everything from bullets to tank shells to Stryker vehicles, and whose profits have tripled since 9/11.

- **Nour USA Ltd.:** Incorporated shortly after the war began, Nour has received $400 million in Iraq contracts, including an $80 million contract to provide oil pipeline security that critics say came through the assistance of Ahmed Chalabi, whose misleading WMD information was instrumental in justifying the invasion of Iraq.
- **Blackwater:** who supplies the unanswerable mercenaries responsible for many of the worst war atrocities.
- **Raytheon, Boeing, Lockheed Martin, Northrop Grumman**...the list goes on...

This picture only comes into clear focus when we examine how much these companies 'give back', specifically, how much of these obscene profits they funnel back into the coffers of those responsible for *starting* wars and keeping them going. For example:

2000-2010 Political Influence Expenditures:

Halliburton *cut* their lobbying expenditures in half, from $1.2 million to $600,000, when former Halliburton CEO Dick ("deficits don't matter") Cheney took office; reasonable enough, since they then had their made man on the inside. Nevertheless, between 2000 and 2010, they have poured $1,130,813 into political contributions, and 5,827,000 on lobbying.

As shown in the sampling below, war profiteers think nothing of sinking half a billion dollars into buying their agendas. Think *you* can compete with *that*?

2000 to 2010 Lobbying Expenditures	
CACI:	$2,008,000
Halliburton:	$5,827,000
Titan:	$2,640,000
Bechtel:	$5,730,000
Aegis:	$250,000
General Dynamics:	$76,643,496
Nour:	$150,000
Blackwater:	$962,000
Raytheon:	$54,962,188
Boeing:	$122,694,310
Lockheed Martin:	$116,168,853
Northrop Grumman:	$147,921,147
	$535,956,994

Reality—What A Concept!

Okay, nobody like to be wrong. Nobody like to discover that someone in whom they believed, perhaps loved, isn't what they thought. We see it all the time —those tearful mothers who, despite overwhelming physical evidence, perhaps even a voluntary, signed confession, persist in proclaiming that their beloved son could not *possibly* be a rapist, serial murderer, cannibal…whatever. Loyalty is admirable. Giving anyone the benefit of the doubt is expected. Innocent until proven guilty; that's the *law*. But denial of reality is simply, well, pitiful. Indeed, when someone in whom you believed—someone you supported—turns around and betrays you, righteous indignation is the most appropriate reaction.

Such is usually the case, except in politics; which seems kind of absurd, does it not? After all, Barack Obama isn't your son. George W. Bush is probably not your father. Lyndon Johnson wasn't a close relative to most of us. Nevertheless, those whose relationship to these individuals went no further than casting a vote, putting a sign on their lawn, or maybe making some campaign phone calls, cling so tenaciously to a thoroughly debunked, expertly contrived, and slickly marketed *image*, that one would think detractors were impugning the purity of the Mother of God.

This may come as a flash, but Obama ain't Jesus, and neither is George W. Bush, Lyndon Johnson, or even our beloved Ronald Reagan. All did some good things—nobody is denying that—but all did some wrong as well, and failure to acknowledge that fact puts us in the same category as the followers of Jim Jones, dutifully swilling cyanide-laced Cool Aid at his mere command.

For those readers who would characterize themselves as 'people of faith', recall the *First* Commandment: *No gods before Me*. I would venture to say that this includes the deification of politicians as well!

It is now a widely known, completely documented, and irrefutable fact that the event Lyndon Johnson used to justify the invasion of Viet Nam…*never happened.* Maybe there were good reasons why we *should* have engaged in that war, maybe not. The plain fact, however, is that whatever the real reasons were, Johnson felt they were inadequate to convince the American People, and so, he made up a story to *deceive* the people into supporting his agenda.

Pretty tough to spin bald-faced lying into a positive character trait.

Would failure to have engaged in that conflict have seriously changed the current face of the world? No way of knowing, but consider this: China, whom we considered the greatest threat in that part of the world, recently walked into Hong Kong, a place then and now far more valuable and critical than Viet Nam, and we raised not a syllable in objection. China now *owns* American assets many times more valuable than Viet Nam.

Who is the real enemy? The Chinese, or those who sold America to them (for a metaphorical thirty pieces of silver)?

A more recent replay, of course, are our adventures in Iraq and Afghanistan, which bleed our already hemorrhaging economy to the tune of $2 billion/week. I have neither interest nor intention of getting into the whole 'WMD' issue; whether they ever existed, who might have known the truth, or when they might have known it. Although the very idea that someone would deliberately lie to promote some nefarious agenda, at the cost of trillions of dollars and thousands of lives, suggests a level of depravity on par with the worst villains in all history and literature, this is a matter that will probably never be resolved, so why go there?

What *can* be said with certainty is that there never existed, nor does there exist today, a single shred of evidence suggesting that any segment of the Iraqi government was in any way connected with the 9/11 attacks, or with any of the individuals or groups responsible. Attacking Iraq in retaliation for 9/11 was like bombing Sweden in response to Pearl Harbor. Indeed, the only connections that *can* be demonstrated with certainty are that:

1. Numerous members of the Bush II administration, including George W. himself, had pre-existing gripes with the Iraqi regime, possibly even including some element of Bush family honor, a notion of unfinished business, or a fully consistent need to show up 'Daddy' by succeeding where many had seen Bush Senior as having failed.
2. In the aftermath of 9/11, Americans were sufficiently riled that popular support would never be more propitious for whatever military engagement was suggested to them, even with the most far-fetched of connections, which is precisely what was presented to tie the invasion to the 9/11 attacks.

Somewhere in the aftermath of the 9/11 attacks, amidst the stammering attempt to connect Iraq to the terrorists, the discussion subtly shifted from that non-existent connection, to Saddam's acquisition of 'yellow cake' (raw material for making weapons-grade nuclear materials), and thence, to WMDs in general. Next stop: 'Shock and awe'. To punctuate the essential nature of the foregone invasion, George W. Bush uttered the (in)famous verbiage: "the smoking gun could come in the form of a mushroom cloud...."

Woe! Hey! Wait just one second. Let's stop and *think* about what's being implied here, shall we?

Even *if* this crazed madman was somehow able to get his hands on a nuclear (no, *not* 'nuqueler') weapon, or any weapon of mass destruction, how do you suppose he was going to use it against us? A slingshot? Fed Ex? The back of a camel?

The design and construction of a nuclear weapon is a formidable undertaking, but the engineering of an accurate ICBM, capable of delivering a payload halfway across the world, makes building the weapon itself seem like an automotive tune-up by comparison. Moreover, whereas a nuclear program can get quite far along in a secret lab somewhere, testing sub-orbital missiles is not something you can take beyond the paper stage without attracting attention.

If *that* was our concern, all we had to do was wait for their first test, take out their facility with one cruise missile, and let them expend as much money as they want starting again from scratch. Now *that* seems like a strategy *we* could keep up a whole lot longer than *they* could.

In fact, Saddam's crude Korean-built Scuds could barely hit Israel (and *that*, of course, might have provided some impetus for our rush toward confrontation.) The long and short of the matter is that all of our high-tech, super-secret intelligence prowess was hardly needed to prove that Iraq was not a threat, nor was it likely to become one in the foreseeable future.

The only way our enemies could possibly deliver such a weapon would be through some alternative means: in a shipping container, or smuggled across our borders. How are troops deployed all across Europe, Asia, and the Middle East serving to prevent *that* eventuality? Would it not be more effective to put them to work protecting our home soil, where the threat actually exists? For the cost of maintaining these strutting, ineffective, and expensive displays of machismo, could we not patrol our borders, inspect incoming freight containers, and, in the process, reduce the hatred, resentment, and animosity that are most likely to *motivate* such an attack in the first place?

Then, of course, there was Afghanistan.

This time, at least, there was some almost-plausible connection: Evidence *was* fairly conclusive that those responsible for the attacks had actually trained and hidden in the rugged mountainous wilds of Afghanistan; probably with the acquiescence, if not the outright support of ruling junta, known as the Taliban.

Now, if we're talking about good old, Old Testament, 'eye for an eye' vengeance, then fine: a barrage of cruise missiles killing an equal number, or ten times the number of innocent civilians, who had absolutely nothing to do with the 9/11 attacks, should have been adequate to satiate the blood lust of the American People and our leaders. This, however, is not what we're purporting to do. We've spent ten years occupying this inaccessible hellhole in order to…what? Prevent another similar attack? Okay, then what you're saying is that if we had invaded and occupied Afghanistan ten years earlier, then *that* would somehow have *prevented* angry Islamic men from boarding a commercial airliner and turning it into a weapon? (And no, citing the absence of subsequent attacks may be comforting, but it reveals absolutely no connection with what our troops are doing there. Indeed, our stopping of the so-called 'shoe bomber', and 'underwear bomber' suggest that far more effort needs to be devoted to intelligence gathering, analysis, and coordination, rather than fighting enraged tribesmen on their own home turf.)

Even *if* this were all being done with the most noble of intent (which it is not), it would reveal *such* monumental ineptitude as to demand the immediate ouster of all involved. Moreover, even if we *did* start this with honest motivations (which we did not), there can be absolutely no question that we remain there solely to save face. *We* will not allow the world to see us fail as did the Soviet Union, and Alexander the Great before us. $2 billion/week is a pretty steep price for maintaining prestige.

Of course, there does remain that one last justification: "We're fighting them *there* so we won't have to fight them *here*."

Fair enough. Let's question that premise. (We *are* still permitted to do that, aren't we?)

What I find most difficult to understand is that those who most often cite this justification are the same ones who are *least* in need of having anyone else do their fighting for them. Take my neighbor, Charlie. Around 60 years old, five-foot-eight and maybe a hundred and fifty pounds, I'd pity the 20-year-old who made the mistake of provoking a physical confrontation. Come hunting season, Charlie's always the first one with the biggest buck in his pickup truck, having bagged it further into the forest, and higher up the mountain than most of us have ever ventured; taken it with a single shot from a distance at which I couldn't even *identify* a tractor trailer; and dragged it out without breaking a sweat.

Let's be conservative and estimate that about half of Americans would describe themselves as more akin to our pioneering forbearers than, say, a young, upwardly-mobile, city-dwelling office worker who shudders at the thought of a firearm.

When George W. Bush boasted: "Bring 'em on…," it was with the bravado of someone who had, for whatever reason, managed to avoid combat; is probably the most protected individual in the world; and who has many thousands of armed proxies who will flex the muscle and bleed the blood to back up his tough-guy rhetoric.

The Americans *I'm* describing are a completely different breed.

I'm not talking about some backwoods bully itching for a fight, mind you; these are, in large part, the most non-confrontational people I've ever encountered. If they have something to prove, it's proven by the way they live their lives: Working hard, living independently, letting deeds reflect their beliefs, rather than loudly recited creeds. If they resent entitlements, it's because they themselves would never expect or accept a handout, and don't believe others should either.[1] One reason they *do* feel this way is because they are always the first ones to help another person whom they believe to be in need.

They are also people I would *most* want by my side if we were defending ourselves from any foreign invaders. Don't need any Predator Drones, don't need night-vision or Kevlar body armor, or high-tech weapons. I'd put my money on a hundred of these guys, with Model 1894 Winchesters, against any fighting force double that size from anywhere in the world, regardless of their high-tech toys.

If your only tool is an ICBM, every threat looks like The Soviet Union; but we're not talking about high-tech Soviet adversaries here. Ronald Reagan—in combination with expensive, unwinnable military adventures in places like... Afghanistan—in large part, took care of *that* particular threat. We're talking about cave- and tent-dwellers in sandals and robes, who can barely make it from one goat pasture to another, much less cross oceans in force. Moreover, if they have issues, they're not with the guys who are minding their business, raising cows, fixing lawnmowers, or plowing fields in rural America; it's with whoever is supplying *their* enemies with weapons of mass destruction that are obliterating their families; or propping up brutal dictators who have taken power from democratically-elected leaders who had the temerity not to bow to multinational corporate coercion.

I daresay most of people I know would agree with the logic of taking that ***Two Billion dollars each week*** that we're spending in Afghanistan, and applying it to tax relief. *We'll* take care of defending our turf, if and when those dread terrorists decide to move on our neighborhoods, thank you very much.

So, yeah, ***we*** can say "bring it on;" and if/when they do, we'll kick their camel-riding asses, and you can take *that* to the bank, Mister Bush, Mister Obama, and all you other big, tough-talking macho men in 3-piece suits and BMWs!

Naturally, that approach wouldn't sit well with people like *Blackwater*, or *General Dynamics*, or *Dow Chemical*, or *Raytheon*, or *Halliburton*, who profiteer from our high-tech, WMD-driven overseas adventures. How much of that money do *you* see? How many of *you* work in the defense industry, or get a substantial part of *your* income from defense-industry investments? Enough to have your interests prevail in a *real* democracy? If not, then *something* here is *seriously* amiss.

Of course, 'both' *Republicrat* factions would like you to believe that there are more sophisticated foreign threats, against which our provincial armed citizens would have little chance to prevail. But who, precisely, might *they* be?

[1] While this attitude may reflect a somewhat limited perspective with respect to the obstacles that are often stacked against certain groups—obstacles that these folks simply can't imagine—it differs markedly from the uncaring, mean-spirited, self-serving indifference that those who *do* embody those characteristics (e.g., *Republicrat* Neoliberals) try to attribute to the American rural Right.

Iran?

Ahmadinejad certainly has the intent, and is undoubtedly crazy enough to try…if he had the means. But in terms of conventional warfare, delivering a payload halfway around the world is not some elementary feat that one can accomplish merely by throwing money at the problem, and developing that kind of technology is not something you can do in secret, like building the payload itself. Even someone as insane as Ahmadinejad is portrayed as being couldn't believe that a program to develop ICBMs could ever succeed.

China?

We've already *sold* so much of this country to Beijing, that a confrontation with the United States would destroy their economy from two fronts at once. Their investments would be forfeit, plus they would incur the expense of a war. China has nothing to gain and everything to lose. Indeed, the only nation that could *possibly* present a threat to the US, either in terms of technology, the possibility of benefiting thereby, and having demonstrated the prerequisite treachery, not only to their enemies, but to a supposed ally, the US itself, is…***Israel***.

Lest we forget, Israel has spied on us while simultaneously accepting aid conservatively estimated at $114 billion dollars. They stole their nuclear weapons technology from America, and continue to blatantly lie about even having it. They repeatedly ignore our requests that they abide by international conventions, compromise our international positions and image in order to further their own selfish interests, and have even humiliated our government officials in plain sight of the rest of the world.

As Pat Buchanan observes in *A Republic, Not an Empire* (and undoubtedly the kind of statement for which he is undeservedly labeled an anti-Semite): "And though it has received $100 billion in U.S. arms and aid over the past thirty years.... Israel suborned the traitor Jonathan Pollard to loot our vital secrets, lied about it, and then sold the technology for our Patriot and Python missiles, and the AWACS and F-16, to Communist China.... Israel looks out for Israel first, and Americans must start looking out for America first. Because our interests as a world power are broader and greater, and may conflict with the annexationist agenda of Sharon, America must make known to the Arab and Islamic world that Israel does not have a blank check from the United States. We can no longer give preemptive absolution to an Israeli regime that could drag America into a war of civilizations with the Arab and Islamic world—and there is reason to believe this is exactly what Ariel Sharon has in mind."

I'm very sorry, but if *that* qualifies someone as an anti-Semite, then I suppose I'm one too. We tolerate from Israel what would result in a 'Shock and Awe' decimation of *any* other nation, because entrenched *Republicrats* are afraid of offending a large, powerful, influential, militant pro-Israel contingency. This is *not* a swipe at Jews. Judaism is a *religion*, just like Christianity, or Islam, or Buddhism, or Hindi. Israel is a *foreign nation*, which happens to be primarily Jewish, in much the same way as Italy is primarily Catholic.

This isn't even a criticism of Israel—every nation is expected to act in what it perceives as its own best interests, and when nations negotiate in good faith, they attempt to reach solutions that are equitable to all concerned.

The core issue here has to do with citizens of one nation whose primary allegiance is to a foreign nation, even in situations where the interests of that foreign nation conflict with those of the nation of which they are purportedly citizens. There is a word for such people, and that word is:

Traitor: *"One who is false to his allegiance to his sovereign or to the government of his country."*

I don't give a damn if you wear a turban or a yamaka or a propeller beanie; if you call yourself my neighbor, and then turn around and support those trying to harm me, you are a *traitor*, and deserve to be dealt with using *rope*.

This situation is tolerated for only one reason: The goals of the traitors who run our government, and those of the traitors who support the foreign government are tightly intertwined and interdependent. One unctuous, treasonous hand greases the other.

When my grandfather, himself an immigrant from Sicily, used to see those Italian-American Unity Flags that were prevalent in the early 1970s, he would mutter: "If you like the old country so much, why don't you go back there?"

Why indeed?

In the words of Teddy Roosevelt: "There can be no divided allegiance here. Any man who says he is an American, but something else also, isn't an American at all. We have room for but one flag, the American flag...and we have room for but one sole loyalty and that is a loyalty to the American people."

The connecting thread here is that the *Republicrat Junta* repeatedly, consistently, and constantly carries out the will of the rich, the powerful, and the influential, when those policies can be objectively shown to conflict with the principles, priorities, intentions, and wellbeing of the majority of the People. What we have just described is an illegal junta that his usurped the Constitutional government of the United States in a covert *coup d'etat,* and established in its place an kakistocracy of the rich, the influential, and the powerful.

As referenced by the title of this chapter, the cornerstone of the Tea Party movement, before it was co-opted by the *Republicrat's* faux-right faction was… taxation, and more specifically, *taxation without representation*. This, of course, was a situation to strike fear into every corrupt parasite in Washington, of both factions. What could possibly be *worse* than a clearly-defined issue on which Americans of differing principles can agree?

Their strategy should be obvious to perceptive people of every political conviction. Just like the supposed efforts to control the budget, the basic tactic is to muddy the clear waters by tossing in every polarizing, contentious, hot-button issue in order to destroy any consensus that might question their hegemony.

Just think about it. As suspicious as you might be of that guy up the road with the peace sign on his car; much as that dude with the 'Redneck' plate on his pickup truck might make you nervous; irritating as you might find that loudmouth feminist on the school board; if a hoard of goose-stepping invaders were to threaten your town, you'd be more than happy to put aside your differences for a while, and accept help from *all* of your neighbors. Given half a chance, you'd be amazed at how much you have in common, but *those in power* are highly motivated to prevent this realization.

But ***Taxation without Representation?*** *Isn't that a bit of a stretch? I still* ***vote*** *every year.*

Every time the populace votes on an issue, and the heavy-handed, overbearing federal government walks in and overrules the will of the citizens, even though the issue in question violates no tenet of the Constitution, that is exactly what's happening, and those affected should refuse to pay their federal taxes until the abrogation of their will is reversed.

Liberals might, rightly, hold up the various medical marijuana initiatives as examples, but those on the left must simultaneously accept the prospect that if the majority of citizens in, say, Alabama, want Creationism taught as a science, sorry, guys, that's the way it goes—move to California if you don't like it, or send your kids to private schools. You see, *everyone* seems to think they're *entitled* (there's that word again) to have things *exactly* the way they want, *wherever* they happen to be; and it just doesn't work that way. You have the right to vote. You have the right to abide by the results. You have the right to move somewhere more to your liking. Nowhere is it written that you have the right to make everyone else bend to *your* particular vision of utopia.

Of course, if it turns out that all the kids from Alabama can't compete in a technological workplace because they were taught ineffective scientific concepts, well, that's the way it goes. We'll always need people to spread asphalt, flip burgers, drive taxi cabs. Similarly, if everyone in California turns out to be too stoned to get anything done, the same argument applies. Eventually, people will discover that their state can't attract the kinds of skill sets they desire, and the law may be modified. Localized inefficiencies are self-correcting phenomena. But these are *not* Constitutional issues, except insofar as an illegal *Republicrat Junta* chooses to treat them as such.

The notion of *an* American mindset, or *an* American perspective is a nonexistent abstraction, of use *only* to those who wish to homogenize what has always been a culture defined by its diversity, in order to further their own ends.

Consider the diversity of American society even before we became an independent nation:

In New England, a culture evolved based on orthodox religious intolerance, the most visible manifestation of which occurred in 1692 when nineteen members of the community were executed as witches. In the South, a feudal society relied on involuntary servitude for the basis of its entire economy. Meanwhile, those who valued their personal freedom above all else tended to eschew these centers, pushing westward. Unlike the greedy empire-builders who followed later, these first pioneers embraced the 'live-and-let-live' philosophy that many profess but few practice. People like Daniel Boone, Davy Crockett, Lewis and Clarke, and others like them sought to establish friendly relations with the native inhabitants, and embodied the persona of self-reliance, fair-play, and decency that is cited to this day as the *American* self-image, too often with scant accuracy or justification.

As the nation coalesced, the cultures that developed in San Francisco, New York, Boston, Saint Lewis, Houston, Chicago, and New Orleans, were distinct and colorful, but those differences in no way diminished the national unity; quite the contrary. This could clearly be seen in WW-I and WW-II, as soldiers from every state stood shoulder-to-shoulder, *Americans* one and all.

Tea for *Who*?

The Tea Party movement is an interesting phenomenon from a variety of perspectives. Although an acronym for ***T****axed* ***E****nough* ***A****lready*, it arose more as an expression of general dissatisfaction with *how* our tax dollars were being squandered than a tax revolt *per se*. As such, it seemed like a perfect rallying point around which real, honest, intelligent Conservatives and Liberals could find common ground. We *all* agree that those in Washington aren't serving the will of *either* side. Let's set aside our differences for the moment, agree that those in power are scoundrels, if not outright traitors, throw the bastards out, and then, once we have a clean, honest slate, start squabbling about the small stuff again.

It would be astonishing if the *Republicrats* didn't reach the same conclusion, and indeed, it's easy to see how 'both' sides have scrambled to address this threat in their usual manner: by turning Americans against one another.

The Democrats blatant manipulation of their constituency takes the predictable form of painting all Tea Party supporters with the same broad brush of racism, orthodox theocracy, obstructionist, mean-spiritedness, and tyranny.

The Republicans, for their part, have opted to infiltrate and co-opt the movement: injecting into what would otherwise have been a movement with wide-based appeal, their own most reactionary agendas, secure in the knowledge that doing so would polarize public opinion, and weaken the movement to the point where it poses no threat to 'either' entrenched party.

Make no mistake: whichever side you might embrace on any particular issue, the motivations of the *Republicrats* are *not* based on *your* beliefs, aspirations, or principles; but only on their own, and those of their corporate cohorts.

The Homogenization of America

When I first left Brooklyn (NYC), in 1970, I moved around a lot, from one part of the country to another—South, West Coast, Rocky Mountains, New England. For the most part, all were positive experiences, and the thing that struck me was that all these different regions had their own unique culture, flavor, experience. Foods were different, stores were different, TV was different.

When I *last* traveled on business, in the late 1990s-2004 or so, all that was gone. The same malls contain the same chain stores carrying the same merchandise. The TV anchors all have the same bland accent. This, of course suits the mega corporations perfectly. They couldn't grow to such outlandish proportions *except* through the economies of scale. Rather than trying to serve the tastes of the customer, they have contrived to convince everyone that they all want and like the exact same things.

Welcome to bland, corporate America.

Moreover, our culture had essentially subordinated personal relationships to…to what? Our *careers*? And what, precisely, are *they*? Our contributions to corporate progress? We spend the decades of our lives—while our parents grow old and die, while our dearest friends marry, have children that we never meet, while our own children grow up and move away—scooting from one meaningless corporate cubical to another, encountering, perhaps, a handful of people we can tolerate, a friend or two, if we're lucky, and masses of those we consider obnoxious; and *this* is what we have traded for deep, lasting friendships and solid, dedicated communities?

Instead, we stay in touch by email and telephone, see one another on holidays, when it can be managed, and then one day, look around and ask where the time has gone?

This homogenization carries within it the seeds of its own destruction. By trying to devise a single central repository of principles, values, and priorities, the only thing we have ensured is that camps of obstinacy are formed, and agreement has become nonexistent.

Now, I'm not arguing for slavery, or Jim Crow laws, or lynchings; but if these are *all* you know about the South, then you've never taken the time to know *real* Southerners.

If people want to live with others of their own sensibilities, and according to their own principles, so long as they're not blatantly criminal, then they should have to right to do so. The problem is, everyone wants that for themselves, but not for 'the other guy'. Seems to me that if California wants to legalize drugs, provide health care, or whatever, then they should be free to do so. However, the flip side of that coin means that if the people in Texas want to teach their children creationism, well, that's their right, or their problem, isn't it? Perhaps we'd like to convince them otherwise, but we sure aren't going to force it down their throats.

I actually believe that such a system would regulate itself after a few generations—far better than any central government can through coercion. Hey, if you bring up your children to be ignorant, fewer of them will be getting into colleges. Sorry, sad for them, but we can't solve the ills of the world through force. Educated people, wanting the best schools for their children, the best culture for themselves, won't move to a place they perceive as lacking on those areas. Conversely, homophobic fundamentalists probably won't opt to live in California—just don't go there and expect everyone to change to suit *your* sensibilities.

Consider the attitudes many Americans hold toward the French. We may joke about their capitulation to the Nazis, or the unshaven underarms of their women, but for most, it's just a good-natured ribbing, devoid of the bitter rancor evoked by discussions of alternative *American* subcultures. Why? Because nobody is trying to *make* them live like the French. Unless manipulated otherwise, I believe that the majority of Americans prefer the 'live-and-let-live' approach to life.

It should not be too surprising that when prevaricating politicians utter the word 'diversity', what they have in mind is precisely the opposite; and the motivation, as always, is financial profit for themselves and their corporate owners.

Because 'equal but separate' is wrong when it comes to mandatory segregation, it doesn't follow that mandatory integration is the answer to every situation. Sometimes certain people simply want to spend time with others of similar beliefs, priorities, interests, or backgrounds. You may not approve of the criteria employed to define those boundaries, but the choice is ultimately theirs, as are the resultant rewards or losses. Personally, I can think of nothing more unpleasant than spending time in the company of people who don't want me there.

Back in the late 1990s, I spent a long weekend in Edgefield, South Carolina, the birthplace of the late Senator Strom Thurmond. It was a wonderful, picturesque, peaceful Southern town. On Saturday morning, I noticed a small group of elderly men, all black, sitting on chairs outside a store in the center of town. A little way up the street was a similar group of elderly *white* men, also just sitting, chatting, laughing, and enjoying each other's company. While there was no interaction between the two groups, neither was their any sense of distrust, anger, hatred, or violence. The were just *people*, enjoying the company of those with whom they chose to associate. Regardless of how any outsider might feel about the racial dividing line, regardless of the spin a cultural anthropologist might be able to put on the history that led to this particular grouping, the plain truth of the matter is that they were all precisely where they wanted to be. Perhaps in a generation, or two, or ten, that grouping might be more diverse, but can any rational person imagine that forcing some arbitrary re-distribution of these groups could ever result in anything *except* resentment?

When people share common concerns, goals, threats, and so forth, they naturally develop a bond that shifts the boundaries of who represents 'the tribe' and who is 'from outside'. However, the homogenization of America has had precisely the opposite effect. By dissolving regional identity, and emphasizing this huge national conglomerate, artificial groupings are created. The people living down the street from you, regardless of race, are frequently strangers, or at best, casual acquaintances. Your 'tribe', instead, is defined by nebulous connections—the television programs you watch, the music to which you listen, the political party you support, the kind of car you drive, the teams you cheer, even the form of alcohol you prefer.

Suddenly, the person up the road whose uninsured house just burnt to the ground is of little concern to you. *Your* tribe is more closely defined by the fact that all of your friends are sending money to earthquake victims in Haiti than by the calamity that befell someone less than a mile from your home.

To compensate for the resultant lack of support structures, the government takes it upon itself to create huge centralized programs—welfare, social security, and so forth. Often, these are viewed with resentment by those who see their resources being forcibly reallocated to people with whom they see little tribal affiliation, and no personal responsibility or sympathy. In other words, the government, for its own reasons (power and wealth), works to break down citizens' natural bonding tendencies, and then tries to compensate by imposing its own, less efficient, substitute in the form of mandatory social programs.

This is not to say that a completely *liaise faire* approach is the answer. The appropriate stance of the federal government is to play watchdog and ensure that the tribes adhere to our common social cornerstones—that everyone's rights are being respected by their tribes, that nobody is being deprived, and that the Constitution is being upheld.

Even if the intentions of our leaders were selfless and honorable (and the overwhelming preponderance of evidence suggests otherwise), the plain truth is that simply exercising those powers granted by the Constitution has thus far eluded them, much less trying to solve all social problems and implement a Utopian society. Show me you can handle the responsibilities you already have, and *then* talk to me about trusting you with more.

Of course, as we've seen already, the goal of these con artists is not unity, but rather, discord.

Even in this day of worldwide internet connectivity, the vast majority of people spend most of their lives in tightly circumscribed geographical, social, and cultural circles. This makes it easy for propagandists to portray *other* groups as grotesque caricatures that cannot be contradicted by personal experience.

So, to the Liberal, *all* Conservatives become rabid racists, dragging innocent human beings behind their pickup trucks because they disagree with their complexions, beating college students to death for being gay, arming themselves to murder physicians in church, and seeking an end to women's suffrage, a return to slavery, and the establishment of a Taliban-style theocracy.

To the Conservatives, all Liberals are portrayed as rabble-rousing Marxists, slavering to confiscate all weapons in order to facilitate an agenda of a totalitarian state, teaching homosexuality as a preferred lifestyle, and promoting the elimination of all private property and redistribution of wealth.

No *wonder* people hate and fear each other!

As someone who has travelled through, stopped at, and lived in diverse areas of these United States, starting in 1970 and extending through the millennium, I can attest that I have *never* met any of these grotesque, hateful, exaggerations. Nor have I simply limited my circle of acquaintances to a tightly constrained group of like-minded expatriates.

At the risk of interrupting the narrative flow, I think it would be useful to relate a few relevant anecdotes.

Americans I've Encountered

When I first moved to a small town in rural Pennsylvania, I bought a 'fixer-upper' for $55,000.00. It needed siding, a roof, and a new heating system, but was basically solid. Getting into it required every cent I could muster, and when I moved in, it basically represented all my worldly net worth.

I first tackled the roof, waiting for a time when the weather forecast predicted a two-week span of clear skies. Predictably, as soon as I had the old roof removed, the sky darkened and clouds began to roll in. Working alone, there was no way I would be able to protect my new home from total destruction. As I sat there on the roof, in utter despair, a pickup truck, occupied by several rustic-looking types, rolled by—staring, laughing, pointing at me. Enraged, I shouted out a typical New York obscenity and flipped them the bird. Fortunately, they were already gone before they could see or hear my rudeness.

Twenty minutes later the same vehicle returned, this time with several additional occupants in the bed, along with some ladders. They pulled into my driveway, disembarked, donned their leather tool belts, and after some brief introductions, set about installing my roof. A few minutes later, we were joined by a man driving a front loader, of precisely the right size for lofting those heavy bundles of shingles up to roof level.

The roof was completed just as the first swollen drops of rain began to fall.

As I sat on my porch, enjoying a beer with the last straggler, he mentioned that the local volunteer fire company was in need of help, and would I be interested in joining.

How could I refuse?

This was a tightly-knit town, where most of the families had lived for generations, and where one neighbor who had moved there forty years earlier was still known as "Jersey Jake." Nonetheless, within a year, I had been elected Captain of their newly-formed Fire Police division, in favor of several contenders from among the 'good old boys'.

Now, these were, by any description, the very image of rural, right-wing America. They cherished their guns, gathered at *Jimbo's Garage* on Friday nights for beer and poker, and were in no way shy about employing a discourse rich in words like 'nigger', or 'faggots', or 'gooks', and so forth. I struggled to find some sense of balance between these people whose actions proved time and time again that they would do *anything* for those in need, including risking their very lives, but whose sentiments so embodied attitudes I had come to reject.

Clarification came when I had lived there a little over a year.

Gossip at the local country store revealed that the anticipated new minister at the Methodist church was…a *black* man…and one from *Zimbabwe* at that!

I steeled myself for the prospect of burning crosses and *Strange Fruit*.[1]

Shortly thereafter, a town meeting was called to "discuss the new minister…."

I attended with some trepidation, wondering if I would have the courage to voice my beliefs against what would certainly be overwhelming opposition. As it turned out, my concerns were wildly misplaced.

"These people come from *Africa*," one old farmer observed. "They have no idea what the winters are like up here…."

"And that old minister's residence is a sonofoabitch to heat," another chimed in. "Got no insulation at all."

"Furnace is a piece of shit," our local handyman added. "I been servicing it for years, and it's a miracle it works at all."

"They're gonna need warm clothes," one of the town's matriarchs suggested.

By the time the meeting was adjourned, committees had been formed to stockpile firewood, gather warm clothing, spruce up the old house, which the several former ministers had not occupied, and a variety of other essential tasks.

The following summer, some of the local ladies taught the minister's wife to drive, and she taught them about growing yams and some other African staples. Their daughter and mine became the best of friends, and remained in touch for many years after the Minister was rotated out to another parish.

It took me a long time to understand this seeming dichotomy between the way people talk, the things they say, and they way they *act* when abstract theory is replaced by concrete reality.

[1] A reference to the song *Strange Fruit,* by Billie Holiday, which describes the bodies of lynched black people hanging from trees like strange fruit.

It's critical to realize that these are people who have spent their entire lives never straying beyond 50 miles from where they were born. All of their neighbors are *people*, with names, and faces; members of the same tribe, the same clan. Everyone else is an outsider, to be regarded with suspicion until they have proven themselves to be trustworthy. This is completely natural and understandable.

When Brenda, the Minister's daughter, started school, she was the *only* black student in the district. Nevertheless, she was not harassed, ostracized, or subjected to any ill treatment.

For people who have never personally encountered a particular phenomenon—bet it a person of color, or spacecraft from another galaxy—caution is not only prudent, it is often essential to survival. Faced with unfamiliar situations, people rely on advice from sources they trust and respect: the government, and the media. Therefore, it makes sense to examine what these 'trusted' sources *show* them, versus what they might *tell* them.

First of all, it's crucial that we begin to at least *consider* the proposition that commercial, corporate media is little more than an organ of the ruling 'two'-party junta. This is why Conservatives see the media as a mouthpiece for the left, while Liberals similarly decry it as an instrument of the right. The answer is that both are correct, and both are wrong. What it *is*, is a servant of the Republicans and the Democrats, *neither* of which remotely represent the will of the true Conservative or the true Liberal; in other words, it is the official, sanctioned channel of the illegal *Republicrat Junta*.

Overtly, these complicit scoundrels preach universal tolerance, civil justice, and brotherhood. Simultaneously, they bombard the public with subliminal imagery calculated to evoke precisely the opposite response. The words simply don't match the pictures, and they know with a high level of certainty which will ultimately prevail. Hence, when the honest, hard-working middle-American sees black people on the news, he or she is shown lawless, hooting hooligans, looting wide-screen televisions from shattered store fronts. Hispanics are associated with violent gang bangers, or invading hoards sneaking across our borders, bringing drugs and violence. Conversely, the mild-mannered, urban intellectual sees a violent, armed, racist militia bent on murdering physicians, denying science, bombing clinics, and murdering innocent minorities.

An interesting corollary of this phenomena is that virtually *everyone* I know, from every point on the political spectrum, knows and respects one of 'them'...however, they assure me, *they* are one of the *good* ones. In fact, very few I've met can ever identify one of 'them' whom they know personally who is one of the *bad* ones. How strange is *that*? Indeed, the only ones *everyone* seems to agree are real scumbags are the ones in government—on *both* sides of the aisle. Once again, I pose the rhetorical question: Who *benefits* when Americans who would normally be inclined to find common ground are manipulated toward divisiveness?

Stereotypes

Stereotype n: *something conforming to a fixed or general pattern; especially: a standardized mental picture that is held in common by members of a group and that represents an oversimplified opinion, prejudiced attitude, or uncritical judgment. A preconceived and oversimplified idea of the characteristics which typify a person, situation, etc.; an attitude based on such a preconception. Also, a person who appears to conform closely to the idea of a type.*

We are taught/indoctrinated to accept as a tautology that stereotypes are universally inapplicable and inappropriate, but neither conclusion is accurate. Stereotypes become problematical only insofar as we misconstrue their boundaries. For example, the stereotype of violent, dangerous bikers—long hair, beard, unwashed, leather jacket, gang 'colors', spreading mayhem in their wake—might strike terror into the heart of an elderly grandmother each time she sees a college geek on a Vespa, inappropriately. However, if you encounter a hundred or so guys, all with jackets that say "Hell's Angels," or "Alien Nomads," you would be well advised to embrace that stereotype, and avoid any words, actions, or gestures that could be interpreted as adversarial.

For some people, the stereotype of the Italian-American is something out of *The Godfather*, or *Goodfellas*. If you mark your place and glance up at the right-page header, you'll notice that *my* surname ends in a vowel, and in fact, is of Sicilian origin. I *did* grow up on the largely Italian Bensonhurst neighborhood of Brooklyn, NY. Nevertheless, I don't think I would be accurately characterized by this particular stereotype. That said, I can say with the authority of experience that such people *do* exist, and indeed, are quite fairly represented by the stereotype.

In these examples, the stereotypes of outlaw biker and Mafioso wise-guy are inappropriate when applied to motorcyclists or Italian-Americans generally, but are completely valid when applied to violent motorcycle gangs or Italian-style organized criminals.

Difficulties arise, however, when certain stereotypes become social fashions.

In the movie *Wild Hogs*, four middle-aged suburban biker wannabes set out in search of adventure on their shiny new Harley Davidson motorcycles, but get more adventure than they bargained for when they encounter a *real* outlaw gang in New Mexico. Similarly, when I was a teen, all of us middle-class, white city-boy guitar players went through a phase when we tried to affect clumsy backwoods southern accents, and dubbed ourselves 'blues-man' monikers like Catfish, or Kentucky Lou, or Gator Joe…."

The point here is that things get a bit slippery when those stereotypes are embraced by a group to reflect their admiration for some of the more colorful, and admirable, features of the originals, without necessarily even *considering* the more negative connotations. That young, African-American guy in the fluorescent sneakers and baggy trousers could well be a straight-A student at a prestigious prep school. More pointedly, those beer-swilling, NASCAR-watching guys, with the Winchesters in their pickup trucks and their "'N-word' this," and "'N-word' that" jargon, while perhaps not people you'd want to accompany you to a Fleetwood Mac concert or the opera, are not necessarily the cross-burning, bomb-throwing, monsters the nearest stereotype might suggest.

Here's a perfect example.

My wife 'met' Lamar on an online equestrian chat room. We were living in South Carolina. We had recently bought my daughter a trained Arabian hunter-jumper mare, and we were trying to get up to speed on horse keeping. Over the next six months or so, we acquired a second horse, and decided to move to a small farm in North Carolina where we wouldn't have to pay exorbitant boarding fees. Although we had learned quite a bit, we were still novices. Of course, she kept all her online friends up on our progress.

In the weeks and months that followed, we became (and still remain) close friends with Lamar. A Vietnam-era ex-marine from West Texas, Lamar had actually been a working cowboy, but now earned his living as a long-haul trucker. He taught me to ride, how to do my own farrier work, how to arc-weld, basic gunsmithing, and a number of other valuable skills.

Lamar was also the *most* racist individual I have ever met—a label he would acknowledge with pride. I knew for a fact that he was a card-carrying member of the John Birch Society, and if he wasn't actually a Klansman, he made no secret that his sympathies leaned in that direction. It was a difficult set of realities for my basically tolerant nature to juggle, and for the most part, I simply filed the dichotomy away, like the knowledge that Quantum Mechanics and General Relativity are mutually incompatible, but both appear to be completely true.

One day, Lamar phoned to say that his primarily duct-tape and bailing wire pickup truck had broken down at a truck stop in Tennessee, about midpoint in the 100 mile distance that separated our respective domiciles. The situation was complicated by the fact that he was pulling his horse trailer, with horse. After all the help he'd given us, I was delighted to be able to reciprocate, and set out with my own truck to tow him and his livestock back to his home, and then see what we could do about the vehicle.

I spotted Lamar's truck, trailer, and horse immediately, but the cowboy himself was nowhere to be seen. After circling most of the massive truck stop I spotted him.

A trucker with a load of logs had parked for the night, and was having problems getting his landing gear up in preparation for departure. Lamar was under the truck, black, shiny grease up to his elbows, drenched in sweat and swinging a sledge hammer at the recalcitrant hardware. I watched for about twenty minutes until he finally managed to crank up the steel legs for the grateful driver. Then he wiped off enough of the grease to accept the driver's handshake.

"Thanks, brother," said the ***African-American*** driver.

"Any time," replied Lamar, patting him on the back like a long lost friend.

Then he joined me and headed back toward his trailer, muttering: "Fucking niggers, dumb as a box of rocks."

Suddenly, all the pieces seemed to fall into place. Lamar would no more harm another person without provocation as refuse aid to a fellow trucker, regardless of his race. This was simply a persona that, for whatever reason, Lamar felt best represented the image he chose to display to the world at large. Is it one *I* would care to wear? Certainly not, but then…I abruptly remembered a rather shameful episode from my childhood.

I was in seventh grade, at Saint Patrick's Military Academy in Harriman, New York. My class had been paired off into two-person teams to work on some project or other, and my partner was a classmate named Pedro Estella.

Although Saint Patrick's wasn't a *reform* school, its strict discipline made it a final stop for kids who's next step *would be* such an institution, and whose parents could afford this alternative. As a result, a goodly portion of the 'cadets' were big-city toughs, who had been busted for various crimes, including car theft, assault, and what have you. Unlike these others, Pedro was a well-mannered, soft-spoken, thoroughly likable fellow, and I was delighted to have drawn him as a partner rather than one of those loud, blustering tough guys.

Now, part of my early training in proper discrimination included the heuristic that Italian names typically ended with a vowel. Naturally, I assumed that 'Estella' indicated a goombah (never mind that I myself was only *half* Italian). So, my attempt at friendly, lightweight banter naturally included the confidence that "I hate all niggers and spicks." Pedro calmly informed me that he was, in fact, Hispanic. Flustered, I tried to regain my moral high ground by explaining that I didn't mean *Spanish* people, of course; I was referring to them damned 'PRs'. Again, he softly enlightened me about his pure, 100% Puerto Rican heritage.

Humiliation doesn't quite capture what I experienced at that moment. More than anything else, I was mortified at the certainty that I had hurt the feelings of someone I was certain was a fine and sensitive human being.

I suppose that might have been a turning point in my life; an awakening to the reality that my father wasn't the word of God, didn't know *everything*, and wasn't always completely right about all topics, which is a worshipful posture that he actively encouraged in all around him. Within another two years I was fully invested in the Hippie culture, and tolerance had largely supplanted prejudice as the image I chose to convey; but the point is that I, of all people, should have understood the danger of judging anyone by the stupid things they might say in an effort to impress their peers.

Unless you're someone who has *never* said a dumb thing—something that didn't even reflect your true feelings—and then felt yourself irreversibly categorized by someone whose assessment really mattered to you, then it certainly behooves you to give the other guy the benefit of the doubt.

For our current purposes, the critical point to recognize is that those in power, in their blatant efforts to deflect attention from their own nefarious actions, are actively encouraging people to react viscerally to these relatively meaningless charades. Hence, Liberals are provoked to equate *any* Conservative with drunken, mean-spirited, thugs, hooting, hollering, and swilling beer as they drag an innocent African-American to death behind their smoke-belching pickup truck. Simultaneously, they incite the righteous indignation of the Conservatives as they project a two-dimensional silhouette of all progressives as effete snobs, fixated on releasing criminals, murdering innocent unborn infants, confiscating firearms, outlawing religion, and taking the income of hard-working people for redistribution to lazy inner-city ne'er-do-wells.

Do these groups have philosophical differences, some of them quite profound? Indubitably. Are there absolutely *no* areas of agreement? Well, there's *one* that comes to mind, and it's precisely the one that our politicians don't want us to get friendly enough to explore: That virtually *all* of our politicians are scheming, dishonest scumbags, who are representing *their* sponsors, contributors, and ultimately, their own selfish interests, rather than the wellbeing of their constituencies.

Seems to me that's a pretty damned persuasive tract of common ground, isn't it? It's like: "Yeah, we disagree on everything except the fact that our country has been invaded by a foreign army and we're all in the process of being disenfranchised and turned into their serfs." Maybe; just ***maybe*** it's time to set all those other differences on a back burner, and turn our attention to ***kicking those bastards out.*** All that other stuff will still be there when we get back to it; this much I *can* promise.

- *"If we try to keep a sense of balance, the exposures of the past several months are analogous to the discovery that the directors of Murder, Inc. were also cheating on their income tax. Reprehensible, to be sure, but hardly the main point."*—Noam Chomsky.

Entitlements

A favorite gripe of the *Republicrats'* pseudo-conservative contingent are *entitlements*. In their typical parlance, this is a codeword for hand-outs to lazy ne'er-do-wells who would prefer to remain on the government dole than get off their lazy asses and go to work. But are these indeed the *only* people in our society who believe they are entitled to some kind of special treatment based on their social position?

In Andrew Bergman's 1990 movie *The Freshman,* a hapless student becomes embroiled in a Mafioso operation which runs a "gourmet club" specializing in endangered species. Unsubstantiated rumors abound of similar but even more egregious clubs where wealthy diners can actually feast on human flesh. All of which raises the question: does great wealth *entitle* the possessor to *anything* their money can facilitate?

Is the wealthy cattle baron *entitled* to dam up a river on his land in order to deprive those downstream of *their* livelihood?

Some years ago, one enterprising entrepreneur charged massive prices for the disposal of dangerous toxic wastes, which he then stored at his residential property in Staten Island, New York. Did the principle of property ownership entitle *him* to endanger the lives and destroy the property values of his neighbors?

In the 1960 cinema classic *The Magnificent Seven*, vicious Mexican bandit Calvera, played by Eli Wallach, justifies his exploitation of poor villagers with the dismissive words: "If God had not meant them to be shorn, He would not have made them sheep."

These are the hidden entitlements that we accept without question: ***I am entitled*** to do anything that ***money*** can facilitate.

I am entitled to drive a Hummer and squander the earth's resources, just because I can.

I am entitled to destroy nature because another entitled hypocrite gave me a deed saying this land is mine.

I am entitled to have multiple cars, motorcycles, pleasure boats, travel trailers, SUVs, even though doing so means the entire planet may one day have to go without heat as a result.

I am entitled to cheap clothing, cheap food, cheap appliances, even though they are kept cheap through the exploitation of others, because I happened to be born in 'the shining city on the hill'…; because I am…*exceptional.*

I am entitled to low-priced meat, even thought it means the animals from which it comes live lives of agony and deprivation, never seeing the light of day, in high-profit factory farms.

I am entitled to send overwhelming forces into other nations, kill civilians, usurp the will of the citizens, because my technology enables me to do so.

I am entitled to scheme, cheat, steal, swindle, betray, so long as I can get away with it.

I am entitled to abuse my slaves because they are my property, and we all know that the Holy Capitalism is all about possession and property.

Masters and Slaves

The *Republicrat Junta* would have us believe that a free market system is the be-all and end-all, and *obviously* the *only* necessity for a self-regulating society; but is it really? Or is what they're advocating more akin to a nicely sanitized implementation of plain old slavery?

The most obvious example, of course, is in the workplace. While other advanced nations have encouraged an increase in leisure time for workers, America has gone in precisely the opposite direction. American workers now put in more uncompensated hours, for less purchasing power, while their corporate masters rake in ever growing profits for themselves and their investor cronies. They protect this status quo by ensuring that every worker *so* fears the loss of his or her job that, increasingly, workers are even afraid to take the paltry vacation time to which they are entitled, lest they return to find their jobs eliminated.

Wage slavery refers to a situation where a person is dependent for livelihood on the wages earned, especially if the dependency entails an unequal bargaining situation between labor and capital, or where workers are paid unreasonably low wages (e.g. sweatshops). Some observers point to similarities between owning and employing a person, and extend the term to cover a wide range of employment relationships in a hierarchical social environment with limited job-related choices (e.g. working for a wage under threat of starvation, poverty or social stigma).

Although the concept began as hyperbole, it's not difficult to see how it has become increasingly literal. Saddled by credit, stuck in negative-equity situations with homes they cannot sell, workers who could once simply seek alternative employment no longer have these alternatives. As their options dwindle, employers feel empowered to demand concessions in wages, benefits, working conditions, and productivity, to the point where employees, increasingly, are virtually indistinguishable from slaves.

As in the case of the nefarious Koch Brothers, employees are even being told how to vote. Indeed, the rise of labor unions was a direct result of the slave-like working conditions prevalent in the 1800s, so it is hardly surprising that greedy, inhuman corporations have recently fixed their sights on eliminating this final challenge to their complete control over their slaves. As we've seen in Wisconsin, when those doing the jobs we can't outsource become too 'uppity', the answer is to simply pass laws curtailing their right to complain, organize, or bargain. What is this but slavery, or indentured servitude at the very least? Does this differ substantially from the treatment of black slaves in the antebellum South? Not by much. The main thing that's changed is that the 'massahs' have refined the model, and morphed it into something that is even *more* profitable, and easier to sustain. The only twist is the dangling carrot of 'capitalism', promising the slaves that if they work hard enough, they, too, might become massahs of their own plantations.

When our domestic slaves become too costly to maintain, the answer is inevitable: get our slaves from abroad, just as we did in the formative days of our nation. The only difference is that now, with more efficient commerce and communication, we can avoid the expense of actually relocating these poor souls, and can leave their management to their local overseers.

With deplorably few exceptions, exploitation is the only objective of those who encourage 'outsourcing' and overseas manufacturing. Rarely is the goal, even parenthetically, to raise the standard of living of those in developing countries. On the contrary, we use our massive buying power to ensure that the downtrodden remain that way. When, on occasion, these people manage to elect a democratic government that might favor the wellbeing of their citizens, at the expense of the profits of their foreign masters, our government (ruled by the big corporations) steps in to overthrow these upstarts and install a more compliant ruler—invariably a brutal right-wing dictator capable of keeping the peons in line.

This, of course, is nothing new. Under the guise of democracy, the *Republicrat Junta* has, in practice, *opposed* democracy in favor of a corporate-dominated kakistocracy since they seized power.

While we rattle our swords and make a big noise about 'illegal aliens', the plain fact of the matter is that the average American *wants* their grapes and lettuce to cost 89¢/pound, and not $2.00/pound. Who *cares* who has to pick them, or what kind of conditions they and their children must endure…just so long as *we* don't have to pay for their health care! Similarly, we whine and moan every time the minimum wage goes up by fifteen cents an hour, arguing that the result will be to 'hurt small businesses', but the truth of the matter is that we just want to ensure that our beloved McDonald's dollar-menu' artery-cloggers don't end up costing us a buck and a quarter. So *what* if those who flip those greasy little treats for us can't manage to support themselves on what they are paid? Fuck them! They are, after all, our inferiors…our *slaves*. How many jokes can you recall that end with:

"You want fries with that, mister?"

Recently, presidential hopeful Michele Bachmann had what was either the utter callousness, abject ignorance, or complete stupidity to suggest that our current unemployment problem would benefit from the removal of the minimum wage! The federal minimum wage, as I write this, is$7.25/hour. That means if you're working a full time job, you're grossing the princely sum of $14,500/year. Guess that qualifies as living high on the hog, in Michele Bachmann's book.

As of 2011, poverty level in the United States for a family of 4 is $22,350. How low must one's compensation go before they can qualify as slaves? At least in the Antebellum South, slaves received a roof over their heads, and enough food to keep them alive. I seriously doubt that one could accomplish that even on an exorbitant $14,500 annual salary.

Of course, we have to ensure that the rich can continue to increase their standards of living, and investors can continue to receive ever higher returns. I defy anyone to show me how this in any way differs from "Let them eat cake," or explain to me why the outcome should in any way differ from that of the French Revolution!class holocaust, and those who perpetrate it should be tried and executed for crimes against humanity.

PART III

THE JUNTA

The Republicrat Junta

Remember that 1984 movie *Red Dawn* (and the 2011 remake)? In it, Americans awaken one day to find foreign invaders—Russian in 1984, North Korean in 2011—overrunning the country. What do they do? Fight back, naturally. Fight back using every resource at their disposal, and ultimately, eject the usurpers and restore freedom, democracy, and the American way. Go team![1]

But suppose this coup had taken the form of an more insidious infiltration, rather than a full frontal invasion? What if our beloved government was gradually replaced by...*pod politicians*?

Of course, there are a few still running around that have not been assimilated—Dennis Kucinich, Pat Buchanan, Ralph Nader, Ron Paul—but nobody listens to *them*, because the *pod politicians* have told us that they are crazy.

Every judge, lawyer, lawmaker, and law enforcement officer in our country swears an oath to support our Constitution, to recognize it as the supreme law of our land, and to uphold ***only*** those laws that are in ***conformity*** with the Constitution. To violate this oath by subrogating the Constitution to conflicting legislation, or by ignoring its safeguards to further any other policy, is usurpation of the only legitimate form of government recognized by *the People*. Disregarding or ignoring the Constitution, or treating its mandates with indifference, is essentially a *coup d'etat*. Purposely violating one's oath of office to uphold the Constitution as the supreme law of the land is akin to levying war against the legitimate, Constitutional government. Violating one's oath of office adheres to and aids the enemies of Constitutional government. In other words, it is nothing short of *treason*.

In the United States, the punishment for treason is set forth in Title 18, USC § 2381:

[1] Of course, from the perspective of the *invaders*, these freedom fighters would be labeled as 'terrorists'.

Whoever, owing allegiance to the United States, levies war against them or adheres to their enemies, giving them aid and comfort within the United States or elsewhere, is guilty of treason and shall suffer death, or shall be imprisoned not less than five years and fined under this title but not less than $10,000; and shall be ***incapable of holding any office under the United States****.*

If we can demonstrate, unequivocally, that any serving member of government, or any police officer, is in fact guilty of treason, then we can say, at the very least, that they must be immediately removed from office, and at worst, should be executed.

I would venture to surmise that the vast majority of readers, at this very moment, could name *at least* one politician, living or dead, whom they suspect might fall into this category. Right, left, Conservative, Liberal, Republican, Democrat...if you've watched at all, then you've certainly seen something *so* obvious, so egregious, so unequivocal that is just *had* to rise to the standard of treason, as described.

One would *think* that at least *some* of these brazen cases would have *so* incensed the general populace that they would have put aside their petty differences long enough to bring their mutual enemy to justice. I mean, if the criminal is *their* guy, then hell, it's a no-brainer. If the betrayer is someone *you* supported, then by all logic, you should be even *more* offended; after all, he or she has made a fool out of you, and to continue supporting that person despite all reasonable evidence, makes you look like an idiot or a hypocrite, or both.[1] Why, then, do we not see at least *some* of these traitors hanging from trees, (figuratively speaking, of course)?

The answer is a classic instantiation of the infamous *Catch 22*.

First published in 1961, Joseph Heller's satirical novel *Catch 22* is frequently cited as one of the great literary works of the twentieth century. Its title has become common idiomatic usage meaning 'a no-win situation' or 'a double bind' of any type. Within the book, *Catch 22* is a military rule whose self-contradictory, circular logic is such that anyone who seeks to challenge it is automatically wrong.

Set during World War II, the novel focuses on Airmen of the fictional 256th. squadron, who struggle to deal with a situation in which the maximum number of combat missions needed to rotate out of combat keeps increasing, always remaining just beyond attainment. The protagonist, Capt. John Joseph Yossarian, attempts to get himself discharged on the basis of mental incompetence; he claims that his fear of combat has driven him crazy. *Catch 22*, however, states that anyone would have to be crazy *not* to be afraid of combat, therefore, if fear of combat has driven him crazy, he is obviously sane.

[1] As a prime example of how a man of integrity reacts to such a betrayal, just consider George Stephanopoulos, former White House Communications Director to President Clinton, who resigned after learning that Clinton, a friend to whom he had shown unwavering loyalty, had in fact lied to him.

Catch 22 appears in various guises throughout the novel, always to justify various bureaucratic abuses. Harassment by military police is justified by a *Catch 22* provision that states: "agents enforcing *Catch 22* need not prove that *Catch 22* actually contains whatever provision the accused violator is accused of violating." It is subsequently explained that: "*Catch 22* says they have a right to do anything we can't *stop* them from doing."

Yossarian comes to realize that *Catch 22* does not actually exist, but because the powers that be *claim* it does, and the world *believes* it does, it nevertheless has potent effects. Indeed, *because* it does not exist there is no way it can be repealed, undone, overthrown, or denounced. The combination of force with specious legalistic justification is one of the book's primary themes.

If *Catch 22* sounds too absurd for reality, recall the following:

According to (the specious *Republicrat* interpretation of) the legal precedent of *Marbury v. Madison,* the U.S. Supreme Court ruled that the U.S. Supreme Court has the authority to determine what the U.S. Constitution says, *regardless of its apparent or obvious meaning.* Words, in other words, will mean precisely what the U.S. Supreme Court *says* they mean, at least according to...the U.S. Supreme Court.

Remember Bill Clinton trying to exculpate himself from perjury charges after stating, under oath: "I did not have sexual relations with that woman, Ms. Lewinsky...," by disputing the meaning of the word "is"? (And yes, Bill Clinton *is* a lawyer.)

Hence, if you tied to prove that the Chief Justice of the Supreme Court is guilty of treason, he could simply rule that "treason" means "cream cheese". Case dismissed!

This deceptive process of interpreting away Constitutional protections—common knowledge among our legislators, most of whom are lawyers themselves—represents the execution of a *coup d'etat* just as surely as any bloody military uprising, and serves to underscore the treachery of these duplicitous usurpers of democracy.

The Supreme Court's decision in the *Citizens United* case is a prime example of doublespeak that was recognized and decried by over 90% of the citizens of this nation. Though shrouded in legalese, and obfuscated with pseudo rationalizations, the essence is within the intellectual grasp of most citizens: The rights of huge corporations to expand their use of graft will be protected, and the more money they spread around, the more their influence will prevail over the will and wellbeing of ordinary citizens. Corporate hegemony is hence granted precedence based on the power of their bribery.

Judge Stevens' dissenting opinion concluded:

"At bottom, the Court's opinion is thus a rejection of the common sense of the American people, who have recognized a need to prevent corporations from undermining self government since the founding, and who have fought against the distinctive corrupting potential of corporate electioneering since the days of Theodore Roosevelt. It is a strange time to repudiate that common sense. While American democracy is imperfect, few outside the majority of this Court would have thought its flaws included a dearth of corporate money in politics."

Unfortunately, the majority of the court had already been bought and paid for by corporate interests, and showed themselves to be the traitorous *scumbags* they are through this despicable and patently corrupt ruling.

Bad as this decision is on its own, its abject corruption and inconsistency becomes fully apparent only when considered in combination with other rulings regarding corporate shenanigans. So, on one hand, these double-dealing traitors in black robes assert that corporations are the same as people, but then, when they have engaged in criminal activities that have destroyed the economy of the entire world, *then* they are different—in *that* case, they are too big to fail, and hence, instead of being punished, they are bailed out at the citizens' expense.

Then, once again, there is the aforementioned case of General Electric, deemed immune from taxation, as are many others who fill the pockets of our illustrious politicians.

More recently (4/2011) in yet another ruling termed "a crushing blow to American consumers," and "a resounding victory for businesses" (what a surprise!), the Supreme Court overturned a 2005 California Supreme Court ruling allowing customers who signed arbitration agreements to form a class with other buyers who had similar grievances. Particularly grievous is the fact that this ruling allows *employers* to include such clauses in employment agreements: if you want to work in this economy, then you give up your rights to sue the employer as part of a class for such common injustices as gender, race, or age discrimination.

Working its way up toward the Supreme Court is a case which claims that some companies, particularly Wal-Mart, (a company with a long history of documented discrimination; and a long history of bribing government officials), is "too big to sue." (Gee, wonder how *that* one will turn out?...) Is this yet another example of "helping *small* businesses?" I can't help but wonder whether these same duplicitous scumbags would have ruled Nazi Germany too big to be guilty of war crimes. I suppose that would depend on how many Deutschmarks Himmler had deposited in Chief Justice John Roberts' Swiss bank account.

Think it's an exaggeration to suggest that the conspirators of this *Republicrat Junta* have deliberately violated virtually every tenet in our Constitution? Read the next chapter and decide for yourself.

The **Indictment**

Those who swear an oath to uphold the constitution, then fulfill that duty in an honest and forthright manner, are leaders and statesmen. Those who abrogate the Constitution, connive to circumvent its intent, or conspire to misapply the tenets set forth in the Constitution are, by definition, traitors, criminals, and enemies of both the American People and the legitimate government of the United States. Those who support honest leaders are upholding the law as public servants, and patriotic Americans. Those, on the other hand, who support traitors, are nothing more than criminal mercenaries, regardless of the uniform they might wear, badges they might display, or authority they purport to wield. Honest, patriotic law-enforcement officials deserve our respect and support. Paid mercenaries working in service to an illegal junta merit only our wrath.

> ***"This Constitution, and the Laws of the United States which shall be made in Pursuance thereof; and all Treaties made, or which shall be made, under the Authority of the United States, shall be the supreme Law of the Land; and the Judges in every State shall be bound thereby, any Thing in the Constitution or Laws of any State to the contrary notwithstanding."***
> **—SUPREMACY CLAUSE -U.S. Constitution. Art. VI, Paragraph 2.**
>
> ***When a judge acts intentionally and knowingly to deprive a person of his constitutional rights he exercises no discretion or individual judgment; he acts no longer as a judge, but as a " minister" of his own prejudices. [386 U.S. 547, 568].***

In the final analysis, it is up to each American citizen to honestly assess the evidence and decide for him– or herself, which groups or individuals are best characterized as one or another of these categories. Evidence consists of *facts*, not opinions, and certainly not the propaganda disseminated by those with vested interests or self-serving agendas. The following are some *facts* to consider in supporting or repudiating the thesis that the fundamental laws of our land have been deliberately violated or circumvented:

What the Constitution says: Article I, Section 10 of the Constitution makes it illegal to "make anything but gold and silver coin a tender in payment of debts;"

What Congress has said: TITLE 18 > PART I > CHAPTER 25 > § 486 : Uttering coins of gold, silver or other metal—Whoever, except as authorized by law, makes or utters or passes, or attempts to utter or pass, any coins of gold or silver or other metal, or alloys of metals, intended for use as current money, whether in the resemblance of coins of the United States or of foreign countries, or of original design, shall be fined under this title [1] or imprisoned not more than five years, or both.

Crimes Committed: Counterfeiting, Forgery, Treason.

Typical Penalties: Stipulated in U.S. Code Title 18, Part I, Chapter 115 - Treason, Sedition, and Subversive Activities.[1]

What the Constitution says: Article I, Section 9, Clause 2 of the Constitution states that "The privilege of the writ of habeas corpus shall not be suspended, unless when in cases of rebellion or invasion the public safety may require it."

What Congress has Done: The Department Of Justice, in contradiction to Article 1, Section 9, Clause 2, and, in contradiction to *Posse Commitatus*, has allowed the military to be used against citizens in the united States of America, resulting in the deaths of minor children and adults. H.R. 5122, the John Warner Defense Authorization Act for Fiscal Year 2007, signed by the president on October 17, 2006, gives the president the power to employ the armed forces to restore public order in any state of the United States.

Crimes Committed: Treason.

Typical Penalties: Stipulated in U.S. Code Title 18, Part I, Chapter 115 - Treason, Sedition, and Subversive Activities.

1 TITLE 18 - CRIMES AND CRIMINAL PROCEDURE, PART I - CRIMES, CHAPTER 115 - TREASON, SEDITION, AND SUBVERSIVE ACTIVITIES Sec. 2383. Rebellion or insurrection. STATUTE: Whoever incites, sets on foot, assists, or engages in any rebellion or insurrection against the authority of the United States or the laws thereof, or gives aid or comfort thereto, shall be fined under this title or imprisoned not more than ten years, or both; and shall be incapable of holding any office under the United States. SOURCE: (June 25, 1948, ch. 645, 62 Stat. 808; Pub. L. 103-322, title XXXIII, Sec. 330016(1)(L), Sept. 13, 1994, 108 Stat. 2147.)

What the Constitution says: Article I, Section 9, Clause 3 of the Constitution states that "No bill of attainder or *ex post facto* Law shall be passed."

What Congress has Done: The Department Of Justice, in contradiction to Article 1, Section 9, Clause 3, ***has*** allowed *ex post facto* laws to be passed (including retroactive taxation). Indeed, the Supreme Court first violated this tenet of the Constitution in *Calder v. Bull* (1798), when, without any basis in the Constitution, it ruled that this applied only to criminal, and not civil cases. This law has been routinely violated ever since, whenever convenient to the ruling junta.

Crimes Committed: Treason.

Typical Penalties: Stipulated in U.S. Code Title 18, Part I, Chapter 115 - Treason, Sedition, and Subversive Activities

What the Constitution says: Article I, Section 9, Clause 7 of the Constitution states that "No money shall be drawn from the treasury, but in consequence of appropriations made by law; and a regular statement and account of receipts and expenditures of all public money shall be published...."

What Congress has Done: So called 'black budgets' have been authorized, and, at least in some known cases, been utilized against the citizens of the United States—examples include the CIA MKULTRA project, in which dangerous psychotropic drugs were administered to citizens without their consent or knowledge, administration of dangerous radioactive substances to pregnant women, the mentally disabled, and prisoners, without their knowledge or consent.

Crimes Committed: Treason, Crimes against humanity.

Typical Penalties: Stipulated in U.S. Code Title 18, Part I, Chapter 115 - Treason, Sedition, and Subversive Activities. Death by hanging.

What the Constitution says: Article 3, Section 2 states that: " The judicial power [of the Supreme Court] shall extend to all cases, in law and equity, arising under this Constitution..."

What The Supreme Court has Done: This provision of the Constitution means that it is the sworn duty of the Supreme Court to declare laws passed by the US Congress to be null and void if such a law or laws was/is in violation of the Constitution.

Crimes Committed: The acquiescence of the Supreme Court in each of the violations described in this chapter represent, at best, dereliction of duty, and at worst, conspiracy to overthrow the government of the United States.

Typical Penalties: Article 3, Section 1 of the Constitution states: "the judges, both of the supreme and inferior courts, shall hold their offices during good behaviour..." Hence, the minimal penalty should be removal from their posts, and if guilty of more serious crimes, additional penalties as provided by law.

What the Constitution says: Article 4, Section 4 states that: "The United States shall guarantee to every state in this union a republican form of government, and shall protect each of them against invasion;"

What the Federal Government has Done: The Legislature has failed to pass comprehensive laws, and the Executive has failed to enforce such laws as already exist to control our borders; and, moreover, have abrogated the guaranteed republican form of government of states that have sought to control their borders on their own. The Supreme Court has, additionally, ruled against these States that have acted to control their borders in the failure of the Federal Government to carry out its responsibilities as required by the Constitution. This is not to endorse racial profiling, or argue for the justice of existing laws; but rather, to observe that politicians, more concerned with their own re-elections, refuse to carry out their duty for fear that doing so might offend one or another segment of the voting public. (They are also refusing to enforce Title 8, Section 1325 of the U.S. Code, "Improper Entry by Alien.")

Crimes Committed: Incompetence at the very least, dereliction of duty.

Typical Penalties: Removal from office.

What the Constitution says: Article 5 of the Constitution deals with the duty of Congress to call a convention to consider amending the Constitution when requests from the States reach a specific threshold. This threshold has been met, by all 50 States, on a variety of issues.

What Congress has Done: The Legislature has obstinately and steadfastly refused to convene an Article 5 Convention. The rational used by many revolves around a baseless claim that amendments must be "contemporaneous," that is, that they must have all occurred around the same time (whatever that means), and that the period for amending the Constitution is therefore expired! Any reasonable American can easily understand that the intent of the Founding Fathers was that the Constitution should evolve to meet unforeseen circumstances, and such changes are, *ipso facto,* the domain of the future. Hence, this is a clear violation of law. Some of the requested topics suggested for consideration as amendments include: Balanced Budget (50 States, since 1961), General Call for an Article V Convention (50 States), Limitation on Federal Indebtedness (50 States), Direct Election of Senators (50 States).

Crimes Committed: Minimally, dereliction of duty, obstruction of justice; however, looking at the issues involved (and the financial disasters that have ensued), far more serious crimes are certainly involved. Moreover, the *deliberate refusal* to address a universal call for reform of election laws—hose laws that serve to keep the lawmakers in power—further argue for the thesis of the current government being an illegal ruling junta.
Typical Penalties: Minimally, removal from office. Additionally, as stipulated in U.S. Code Title 18, Part I, Chapter 115 - Treason, Sedition, and Subversive Activities.

What the Constitution says: Article 6, Section 3 of the Constitution says: "The Senators and Representatives before mentioned, and the members of the several state legislatures, and all executive and judicial officers, both of the United States and of the several states, shall be bound by oath or affirmation, to support this Constitution;"
What the Federal Government has Done: As described in this chapter, and throughout this book, all three branches of the Federal Government have, repeatedly, deliberately, and with demonstrable forethought, flagrantly violated multiple provisions of the Constitution, and have done so to further their own individual and party interests, and those of others who have purchased their influence, including foreign powers inimical to the United States.
Crimes Committed: Treason.
Typical Penalties: Stipulated in U.S. Code Title 18, Part I, Chapter 115 - Treason, Sedition, and Subversive Activities.

What the Constitution says: The Fourth Amendment prohibits unreasonable search and seizure, and states that: "The right of the people to be secure in their persons, houses, papers, and effects, against unreasonable searches and seizures, shall not be violated, and no warrants shall issue, but upon probable cause, supported by oath or affirmation, and particularly describing the place to be searched, and the persons or things to be seized."
What the Federal Government has Done: While the most recent and visible violation of this law are the intrusive full-body-scans and intimate pat-downs instituted under the auspices of 'Homeland Security', the emotional issues involved are too fresh to permit a dispassionate analysis. Instead, we'll focus on the long-standing and patently egregious property-seizure laws. Across America, the Drug Enforcement Administration is seizing the luggage, cash and cars of hapless travelers. Under America's new civil forfeiture laws, mere possession of a large amount of cash or a drug dog barking at your luggage is sufficient probable cause for police to legally seize everything you are carrying. For example:

- In Albuquerque, N.M., in February 2000, DEA agents detained Sam Thach, who was traveling on Amtrak from Fullerton, Calif., to Boston, and seized $147,000 in cash he was carrying. Thach had no drugs. His crime? He had bought a one-way ticket with cash and didn't give Amtrak his phone number.
- The DEA seized $640,000 from Jennifer Leigh Ames while she was traveling on Amtrak on April 5, 2001. Agents say she looked nervous and had refused permission to search her luggage.
- Former Newark, N.J., policeman Carlos Hernandez discovered police searching his Amtrak sleeper cabin and demanding to search his luggage on July 22, 1999. Hernandez's crime? He's Hispanic and paid for his $694 ticket in cash.
- At Houston's Hobby Airport, police stopped 49-year-old Ethel Hylton and seized her luggage because a drug dog had scratched it. Agents searched her bags and strip-searched her but found no drugs. They did find $39,110 in cash from an insurance settlement and her life savings, accumulated through over 20 years of work as a hotel housekeeper and hospital janitor. Ms. Hylton completely documented where she had gotten the money and was never charged with a crime. But the police *kept her money anyway.* Destitute, she had no way to fight them.
- In Montgomery, Ala., police seized the home of 69-year-old Gussie Mae Gantt after videotaping police informants buying drugs in her yard. Ms. Gantt had previously called the police, complaining about drug dealing in her neighborhood, and had posted no-trespassing signs, but the drug dealers ignored them. Police waited until there was a drug deal in her yard and then seized her home.

These outrageous seizures are 'completely legal' and have been upheld by the highest courts in the land, including the US Supreme Court. The DEA's Web site claims, "Property is seized by the DEA only when it is determined to be a tool for, or the proceeds of, illegal activities such as drug trafficking, organized crime, or money laundering." But the above examples show the reality.

Under civil asset forfeiture, your property—not you—is charged with a crime. Hence the bizarre titles of civil forfeiture cases: "United States vs. one 1998 Mercedes Benz," "California vs. 1711 Main Street," and so forth. Once your property is charged with a crime, it can be seized and kept by police, even if you are never convicted of anything. An appeals court in Florida even ruled that police can personally receive bounties of 25 percent of the value of anything they seize from you, such as your car, bank accounts or home.

There are now more than 400 federal offenses and thousands of state and local offenses for which your cash, car, bank accounts and home can be seized—including playing a car stereo too loud (New York), and merely *discussing* violation of any law ("conspiracy"), such as underpaying your taxes. More than *$1 billion* in property is now seized without trial each year from innocent Americans, according to the National Forfeiture Defense Organization.

Once 'police' (thugs) seize your property, the burden of proof is on *you* to *prove your property's innocence.* Any suspected illegal actions of your relatives, guests, friends and employees on or even near your property are sufficient grounds to seize it. Once your home, car, or bank accounts are seized under civil asset forfeiture laws, you can pretty much forget about ever getting them back. It's you versus the police and courts, who divide up the proceeds from your property according to formulas such as "80 percent for police, 20 percent for the court."

If you want to fight seizure of your property, expect to spend at least $15,000 just to hire a competent asset defense attorney. Also expect the police to introduce hearsay evidence and to go through trial after trial, because the normal constitutional protections afforded criminal suspects don't apply to civil forfeiture of your property. *Their* attorneys are on payroll, while *yours* bill by the hour.

With all of this easy confiscated money, asset confiscation is now big business across America. In Volusia County, Fla., police seized more than $8 million worth of cars from motorists stopped for minor traffic violations along Interstate 95. In Alameda County, Calif., police auction off hundreds of seized cars and boats every month. The State of North Carolina was a pioneer in these fascist police methods when they instituted blanket roadblocks on interstate highways, purportedly to intercept drunk drivers, then used their powers to *search vehicles* and confiscate property without even a pretext of due process.

The latest wrinkle in civil asset forfeiture is police working with Amtrak, Greyhound, airlines and hotels to seize cash from travelers. The Albuquerque Journal reports that Amtrak gave the Drug Enforcement Administration access to its booking system in exchange for 10 percent of any monies seized (i.e., kickbacks) by police. The DEA has similar deals with airlines at major airports and many hotel and motel owners in Los Angeles, Las Vegas and other large cities. DEA agents are now permanently stationed at major airports and hotels.

On 5/16/2011, in yet another blatant exhibition of treason, the so-called 'Supreme Court' ruled in an 8-1 decision that police no longer need a warrant to kick in your door if, like the truffle-sniffing pigs in France, they smell evidence being destroyed. Justice Samuel A. Alito Jr., writing for the majority, said police officers do not violate the Fourth Amendment's ban on unreasonable searches by kicking down a door after the occupants of an apartment react to hearing that officers are there by seeming to destroy evidence. While this particular act of treason was specifically defecated with respect to the sniffing out of marijuana burning, it would also apply to just about anything else–the smell of gun oil, perhaps? The smell of paper currency? Indeed, the wording of the decision is such that any time 'law enforcement' claims they hear, smell, or in any way sense anything that leads them to believe that evidence is being destroyed, they are empowered to enter without a warrant.

Finally, consider that while violation of the Constitution *is* a crime, the purported justification—violation of drug laws—are *not* violations of the Constitution, and in fact, are in many cases protected under an individual's right to privacy.

Crimes Committed: Treason under multiple articles of the Constitution. Denial of due process. Theft. Robbery.

Typical Penalties: The appropriate penalties run the gamut, but at the very least, every American is empowered by the Constitution, and in particular, by the Second Amendment, to employ whatever force is necessary to protect their property against lawless invaders, which is precisely what the jack-booted thugs in black masks, or porcine pirates in blue uniforms are. These laws are also in flagrant violation of the Fifth Amendment. Penalties for treason, as stipulated in U.S. Code Title 18, Part I, Chapter 115 - Treason, Sedition, and Subversive Activities.

What the Constitution says: The Fifth Amendment states that no citizen shall "be deprived of life, liberty, or property, without due process of law; nor shall private property be taken for public use, without just compensation."

What the Supreme Court has Done: In addition to the aforementioned property seizure laws, all three branches of government have conspired to circumvent this law under guise of 'eminent domain' laws. Basically, what this means is that even if you are an exemplary, law-abiding citizen, paying your taxes and breaking no laws, the government can take your property and give it to another private entity, simply because they covet it! (Those who believe that the laws of our land are based on the *Bible*, might want to review Commandment #10) The most visible instance of this treasonous, criminal abuse of power was endorsed by the Supreme Court in its 1994 5-4 decision in the case of *Kelo v. City of New London*. Prior to this insidious and blatantly illegal ruling, the power of eminent domain was almost always used to acquire property for facilities clearly intended for use by the public, such as schools, freeways or bridges. Although such eminent domain actions are viewed as distasteful, they are generally accepted because of their overall benefit to the public. In *Kelo v. City of New London,* however, the Supreme Court legalized theft, conspiracy, and graft by endorsing the scenario in which corrupt government officials seized private property from one individual, and gave it to another, not for the good of the public, but for a private, profit-making enterprise. As a result, if someone *wants* your property, they can either purchase it from the owner, or bribe a government official into confiscating it without due process and *giving* it to them.

Crimes Committed: Treason under multiple articles of the Constitution. Denial of due process. Theft. Robbery. Conspiracy. Racketeering.

Typical Penalties: Here again, the sheer audacity of power involved merits any number of severe penalties, but in the final analysis, deprived of due process, the citizen is fully justified in using force to protect their property from the criminals who are attempting to steal it from them.

What the Constitution says: The Sixth Amendment states that in all criminal prosecutions the accused shall have the right to the "assistance of counsel."

What the Supreme Court has Done: The lawyer's cartel (Bar Association), of which all Judges and the vast majority of Politicians in general are members, contrived to have the word "counsel" in the Constitution (mis)interpreted as "Attorney at Law," for the obvious furtherance of their own agendas. The authors of the Constitution were all men of letters, who chose their words with great deliberation. The word 'attorney' was widely known at that time, having been used as early as Shakespeare's Henry V (Act 2). Then, as now, the word "counsel" is well understood, and is defined in every dictionary. In no case is its primary meaning "attorney-at-law." Moreover, the Judiciary Act of 1789, §35, explicitly allows for assistance by *either* "counsel *or* attorneys at law." This *proves* that the term "counsel" is *not* synonymous with the term "attorney at law;" A fact of which our erudite founding fathers would have been well aware. Those judges who rule otherwise have lied in their sworn duty to accurately interpret the law.

Crimes Committed: Judicial incompetence, Treason.

Typical Penalties: Removal from the bench. Stipulated in U.S. Code Title 18, Part I, Chapter 115 - Treason, Sedition, and Subversive Activities.

What the Constitution says: The Seventh Amendment states quite unambiguously (at least to a normal citizen without ulterior motives): "In suits at common law, where the value in controversy shall exceed twenty dollars, the right of trial by jury shall be preserved."

What the Supreme Court has Ruled: In *Bank of Columbia v Okely*, the court ruled that: "Had the terms been, that 'the trial by jury shall be preserved,' it might have been contended that they were imperative, and could not be dispensed with. But the words are, that the right of trial by jury shall be preserved, which places it on the foot of a l*ex pro se introducta*, and the benefit of it may therefore be relinquished."

That is, they're arguing that the Seventh Amendment is *not* guaranteeing a trial by jury, but the *right* to a trial by jury, and hence, are saying it is okay for the bank to take this person's property without a trial. Now, while the Founding Fathers were demonstrably literate, honest, and concise, I would contend that anticipating *this* kind of twisting of meaning by fast-talking weasel lawyers and judges is *not* something any but another scoundrel would ever anticipate. I'm continually reminded of Bill Clinton, caught in lie after lie, under oath, on camera, quibbling over the meaning of the word "is". Moreover, as this chapter demonstrates, this ruling must be seen in the context of the repeated, blatant, deliberate efforts to contradict the Constitution by linguistic slight-of-hand; and hence, can only be interpreted as a conspiracy to completely abrogate every protection of the Constitution through this insidious, stepwise mangling of language.

Crimes Committed: Treason.

Typical Penalties: Stipulated in U.S. Code Title 18, Part I, Chapter 115 - Treason, Sedition, and Subversive Activiti

What the Constitution says: The Eighth Amendment says: " Excessive bail shall not be required, nor excessive fines imposed, nor cruel and unusual punishments inflicted."

What the Federal Government has Done: The concept of what constitutes 'cruel and unusual punishment,' like 'torture', may be open to some latitude in interpretation, however, most normal, sane human beings will know brutal treatment when they see it. In the aftermath of 9/11, a great deal of deliberation was devoted to the definition, the efficacy, and the justifications for torture. Some have argued that, if many innocent lives are at stake, then the torture of a proven terrorist is justified. Others contend that once you empower a force to utilize these techniques, you've paved the way for similar treatment under a variety of pretenses. Since little is to be gained by reiterating these arguments, we will examine just one specific case, in which the suspect is an American Citizen, supposedly protected by the Constitution, and in which *no* lives are dependent upon the extraction of information in a timely manner. This is the case of Pfc. Bradley Manning, who *allegedly* turned over evidence of atrocities committed by American soldiers in Afghanistan to the Wikileaks website. For the purposes of this analysis, we'll ignore the moral issues, such as whether the actions he reported do reflect the will of the American People, are legal, moral, or justified; we'll assume that he has been accused of treason, with no extenuating circumstances, and nothing else. Regardless of any outrage you might feel toward what he did, he has *not* been *convicted* of any crime, and is being held in conditions that 250 top legal scholars have condemned as torture. Laurence Tribe, a Harvard professor who is considered to be America's foremost authority on Constitutional law, has described Manning's treatment as: "not only shameful but unconstitutional." As he awaits court martial in Quantico marine base in Virginia. Manning is kept in solitary confinement for 23 hours a day, checked every five minutes under a so-called "prevention of injury order" and stripped naked at night apart from a smock. Tribe has described this treatment as objectionable "in the way it violates his person and his liberty without due process of law and in the way it administers cruel and unusual punishment of a sort that cannot be Constitutionally inflicted even upon someone convicted of terrible offences, not to mention someone merely accused of such offences." If and when he is found guilty of treason, he will face whatever punishment is prescribed by law, up to and including death. But America does *not* condone torture as a *means of punishment*, even if it is willing to consider it in the interest of public defense. Justice is not synonymous with vengeance. The real thing every American needs to consider here is that if they can do this to one individual simply on their say-so, then they can do it to another citizen by labeling him or her an anti-government, right-wing separatist, a white supremacist, an eco-terrorist, or any other word that, in the final analysis, boils down to a person who opposes the actions of the *Republicrat Junta.* Think about *that* before saying something like: "Hey, the traitor is getting what he deserves." That Constitution is there to protect American Citizens, and once the precedent is set to abrogate that protection for one, purportedly justifiable purpose, that protection is gone for everyone. More importantly, consider this in the light of the overall audacity of this illegal junta in violating *every* Constitutional protection with impunity. As commander in chief, Obama is ultimately responsible for Manning's treatment at the hands of his military jailers. In his only comments on the matter so far, Obama has insisted that the way the soldier was being detained was "appropriate and meets our basic standards". In other words, he is showing himself to be as much of a liar and a hypocrite as every other *Republicrat*.

Crimes Committed: Treason, crimes against humanity.

Typical Penalties: For treason: as stipulated in U.S. Code Title 18, Part I, Chapter 115 - Treason, Sedition, and Subversive Activities. For crimes against humanity: death by hanging.

What the Constitution says: The Ninth Amendment says: "The enumeration in the Constitution, of certain rights, shall not be construed to deny or disparage others retained by the people."

What the Federal Government has Done: What this Amendment means is that Congress can't simply pass laws, willy-nilly, because they are popular with some contingent of their constituency, thereby enhancing their prospect of re-election. As we demonstrate in the next chapter, the ability to pass the most absurd laws imaginable simply means that *any* citizen can be turned into a criminal at the whim of a corrupt government official. At this moment, over 31% of our prison population consists of individuals incarcerated for victimless crimes; that is, behaviors that should reasonably be protected under the heading of "life, liberty, and the pursuit of happiness." *You* may not find these behaviors admirable, but it really isn't your place to judge them, any more than the filthy, vomit-covered drunkard lying on the sidewalk, who is not in jail solely because *his* self-destructive behavior supports a 'connected' provider (the liquor industry, which spent $3 Billion in 2006 alone on lobbying/bribery). Hence, such inmates are, in every sense, political prisoners. The situation becomes even clearer when one realizes that the prison system is itself a big, money-making industry, with lobbying efforts of its own. As of the end of 2009, the prison system contained over 2,297,400 inmates, of which almost three-quarters of a million are there for victimless crimes (actually, *they are* the victims!) The United States has the highest documented incarceration rate in the world at 754 persons in prison or jail per 100,000 U.S. residents (as of 2008). While prison population quadrupled between 1980 and 2003, violent crime rates were relatively constant or declining over those decades. The prison population was increased primarily by *public policy changes* causing more prison sentences and lengthening time served, (e.g. through mandatory minimum sentencing, 'three strikes' laws, and reductions in the availability of parole or early release.) These policies were championed as protecting the public from serious and violent offenders, but instead yielded high rates of confinement for *nonviolent* offenders. Earlier, we examined the crimes of judges involved in the 'Cash for Kids' scandal. It's important to recognize that what these judicial criminals did was, in essence, no different from what every participant in our criminal 'justice' system does every day. Prisons are big business, and the more people you send there, the more money is funneled back to you through your political party. The only difference is that Judges *Conahan* and *Ciavarella* were sloppier, more greedy, more stupid, and got caught. In 2006, *$69 billion* was spent on corrections. That means that, while whining about the state of our economy, and cutting the pay of working people, we are spending $21,311,632,930.00 a year to keep people in prison for behaviors that *should be protected* by the Constitution. You decide, but keep one more thing in mind: If you're a fan of that old *Dukes of Hazard*, television series, these people in prison are like the heroes, and those who are putting them there more closely resemble B*oss Hogg*.

Crimes Committed: Corruption, racketeering, treason.

Typical Penalties: Prison. For treason, as stipulated in U.S. Code Title 18, Part I, Chapter 115 - Treason, Sedition, and Subversive Activities.

What the Constitution says: The Tenth Amendment says: "The powers not delegated to the United States by the Constitution, nor prohibited by it to the states, are reserved to the states respectively, or to the people."

What the Federal Government has Done: State's rights is a touchy topic, as many liberals tend to equate it with Southern secession, slavery, and so forth, but the plain fact of the matter is that the framers of the constitution realized, wisely, the futility of trying to force all people into a single mould. The Constitution covers what each State can or cannot do in terms of adhering to the common principles necessary to make us a unified people. Beyond that, the Tenth Amendment states the objective quite unambiguously. A highly visible application is the recent proliferation of Medical Marijuana laws. *The People* of some states have expressed their will with regard to this topic. It is in no way counter to *any* provision of the Constitution. Nevertheless, a heavy-handed federal government has overruled the will of *the People*, contrary to the Tenth Amendment. Ultimately, what this amounts to is taxation without representation, and should be treated as such by every patriotic citizen. Take your federal tax debt, and turn it over to your state government! The critical thing to realize here is that the motivation for this particular intervention is to protect the pharmaceutical industry, which, once again, purchases its interests from our corrupt ruling junta; hence, it is a clear demonstration of corruption, plain and simple. Legal experts, *ad nauseum,* can debate this argument, but one thing is indisputable: By all legal interpretations, the Constitution is fundamentally a treaty between separate and sovereign nation-states, which those states agreed to support, as opposed to being bound to obey by law. This is a very important point that illustrates the rape of the Constitution, commencing with the administration of Lincoln, who, in his first inaugural address, stated that: "No state upon its own mere motion can lawfully get out of the Union."
Crimes Committed: Corruption, racketeering, treason.
Typical Penalties: Prison. For treason, as stipulated in U.S. Code Title 18, Part I, Chapter 115 - Treason, Sedition, and Subversive Activities.

What the Constitution says: There are several versions of the text of the Second Amendment, each with slight capitalization and punctuation differences, found in the official documents surrounding the adoption of the Bill of Rights. One version was passed by the Congress, while another is found in the copies distributed to the States and then ratified by them. Since we've already seen how such seeming minutia is seized upon by those interested in promoting their own agendas, it is critical that one or the other be selected as a basis of interpretation. Since Congress has already shown itself to be utterly corrupt, any reasonable American should understand that, as the basis of the agreement by which the states ratified the Constitution, that is the version that must prevail. Although the Supreme Court has repeatedly made far more egregious rulings, the notion that a signed contract can be reworded—in effect, renegotiated—without the consent of all signatories, is an affront to all reason. For the sake of completeness, here are the two versions:

- As passed by the Congress: *"A well regulated Militia, being necessary to the security of a free State, the right of the people to keep and bear Arms, shall not be infringed."*
- As ratified by the States: *"A well regulated militia being necessary to the security of a free State, the right of the People to keep and bear arms shall not be infringed."*

What the Federal Government has Done: Obviously, in view of their many documented violations of law and abuse of citizens, this Constitutional right represents a threat that those who commit crimes under the camouflage of law are keen to eliminate. Elements of all three branches have conspired to circumvent this law repeatedly, through blatant sophistry and nitpicking over the meaning of words that are perfectly apparent to any literate adult. Specifically, 'the militia' was *never* intended to refer to a standing force that leaders of an illegal coup could turn against the citizens; rather, it meant just the opposite: the ability *of* the citizens to join forces and *resist*, by force of arms if necessary, *any ruling force that had violated the Constitutional rights* of *the People*.

The Remedies: Thomas Jefferson is quoted as having said: "When the government fears the people, there is liberty; when the people fear the government, there is tyranny." And herein lies the intent of the Founding Fathers for including this critical element in the Constitution.

Let's get something straight from the outset: Gun rights are *not* about hunting furry little critters. They're not even about defending our homes and families from gangbangers or other ne'er-do-wells. The Second Amendment is about keeping power-hungry psychopaths from doing to us what Hitler's minions did to the Jews in Nazi Germany.

If you have any doubts about *this* government's willingness to order its forces to abuse its citizens, or of the willingness of those forces to *follow* those orders without question, you need only examine the evidence: Kent State, Ruby Ridge, Waco Texas, and many, *many* others. Only *one* thing will ultimately keep these hounds at bay, and that's the fear that the next door they kick in might have an armed citizen on the other side.

There is, however, another aspect of this topic.

Passive resistance is certainly the preferable course, when dealing with humane, human adversaries, but it falls far short when faced with a great white shark, or a lion, or a grizzly bear. In India, Gandhi resisted the British—an arrogant, imperialistic, high-handed occupation force, but one comprised, on the whole, of basically well-meaning, high-minded individuals. Would such an approach have been effective for the Jews in opposing the Nazis who were bent on genocide? Was it effective at Sand Creek? (Would you wager your genitals on the answer?)

There is a fundamental problem with trying to reason with committed aggressors that is typified by the apocryphal story of the death of Archimedes. As the story goes, in 212 B.C. during the Second Punic war, Archimedes was in a tent when a Roman soldier crashed through the entrance. The great mathematician tried to communicate with the cretin by drawing mathematical symbols in the sand. The soldier responded by killing him with his sword.

If you believe that rational argument, logic, or reason will prevail against an armed mercenary or government thug of the sort that murdered Randy Weaver's wife and son; or attacked the compound at Waco, Texas with tanks and helicopter gunships, you're in for a rude and probably fatal surprise.

You do not reason with a rabid dog, you destroy it.

How do you talk to someone who is *proud* of being ignorant, aggressive, warlike, and abusive?

Answer: you *don't!*

It's critical to realize that those who misuse power under the color of law will *always* be an existential threat to those who value freedom. This underlines the greatest weakness of many Liberal Americans: they fail to acknowledge that there are times when peace *must be defended.* This is emphatically not the same as preemptive bombing, or claiming we are entitled to torture anyone whom we say deserves such treatment, or that we can imprison anyone, even a citizen, without due process simply by attaching to them a convenient label, such as 'unlawful combatant'. It is, however, a matter of facing reality: those who would attack with force, must be repelled in a similar manner.

But *That's* Against the *Law!*

With the exception of anarchists,[1] most people acknowledge that society requires laws, and laws must be enforced. As children, we're taught that policemen are there to help us in times of trouble, and under the best of circumstances, this is actually the case. Unfortunately, as in so many areas of human endeavor, circumstances aren't always ideal, people aren't always perfect, and reality often falls short of our expectations.

Those of a certain age, or those who appreciate classic television, will be familiar with the always equitable Andy Taylor, Sheriff of Mayberry, his overbearing and bumbling deputy, Barney Fife, and all the other lovable denizens of the *Andy Griffith Show*.

In one episode that stands out in my mind, Andy chides his overzealous deputy about the necessity of cutting a little slack for truck drivers who must exceed the posted speed limit in order to make it up one particularly onerous hill. This seemingly innocuous scene underscores the distinction between the ideal law enforcement officer, and the dogmatic automaton who will always follow orders, even if those orders defy all logic or humanity.

"I don't make the laws, I only carry them out."

"I was only following orders...."

Let's remind ourselves of the most important nuance of any law-enforcement officer's oath:

"...to support our Constitution, to recognize it as the supreme law of our land, and to uphold ***only those laws that are in conformity with the Constitution***."

[1] Actually, anarchists typically aren't adverse to *all* laws, they simply favor strictly *limited* laws.

This often-ignored clause *requires* the officer to apply his or her discretion, to question the law, and means that one cannot exonerate themselves from responsibility with the simple assertion that "I was only following orders."

Failure to recognize this distinction transforms that man or woman in uniform from a servant of the people into an instrument of tyranny; a member of the praetorian guard, the Nazi SS, the strong-arm thug of a fascist regime.

Some time ago, I listened to a lecture by a former FBI drug enforcer. He described having insinuated his way into the trust of a group of teens, and when one passed him a joint (a marijuana cigarette), he arrested him; not only for *possession*, but for *trafficking* (since he had passed it to someone else). The teen was sentenced to *20 years*. Now, to his credit, this person admits the error of his deeds in 'the war on drugs', but that scarcely compensates a citizen deprived of due process, and twenty years of his life.

This goes to the heart of the matter. By and large, police officers take that oath to uphold the law, but very few are willing to question the legitimacy of those laws. If those laws say send a youngster to jail for two decades for extending an act of friendship?

"Only following orders."

How far is this from rounding up Japanese Americans during WW-II because 'the law' says they must be forcibly relocated?

"Only following orders."

How far is it, really, from rounding up Jews in Germany because 'the law' says they must be 'relocated' to concentration camps?

"Only following orders."

How about the brutality of police officers at the Republican National Convention in St. Paul, when they gassed, beat, and arrested peaceful demonstrators, including renowned journalist Amy Goodman and her cameraman, ripping the batteries from his camera so he couldn't document the assault. During the same event, uniformed thugs with M-16 rifles executed a "preemptive" strike against innocent citizens, inside a private residence, because they claimed to believe they might do something illegal!

"Only following orders!"

More recently, during the 2011 Wall Street protest, police have arrested thousands of peaceful protesters, exercising their Constitutionally guaranteed right to free speech and peaceful assembly, and were even caught on camera spraying pepper spray directly into the eyes of female attendees who were doing absolutely nothing to resist.

"Only following orders?"

It's important to remember that in Nazi Germany, helping Jews to avoid death in the concentration camps was against the law. In Communist China, it is against the law *not* to terminate pregnancies in excess of what the government allows, In the Soviet Union, it was against the law to hold religious services. Closer to home, prior to the Civil War, it was against the law to harbor runaway slaves,

This is hardly hyperbole. Not every Nazi private was a war criminal in the sense of Josef Mengela, or Hienreich Himmler. They were idealistic young enforcers of the law, merely *following orders.* I would far prefer to be on my own when it comes to defending myself and my family against an occasional criminal than contend with a highly organized, heavily armed, intransigent, police force, which has shown itself repeatedly to be prone toward abuses of power, cover-ups, and self-serving acts of treachery. This is not 'keeping the peace'. This is not preserving civilization. It is an enforcement of tyranny, plain and simple.

Today, anyone who seriously challenges, or even questions federal authority is threatened, suppressed, driven into poverty, or imprisoned. If they persist, our federal government has repeatedly demonstrated that it will not hesitate to use its tactical forces to kill its opponents. *The Republicrat Junta*, just like its dictatorial counterparts in places like Chile, Peru, Libya, Iran, Iraq, and numerous other places, calls these forces 'law enforcement' personnel. Anyone with eyes and a modicum of honesty can see that they are actually a well-equipped standing army used to exterminate U.S. citizens who dare to threaten federal authority; that is, to question the legitimacy of a patently illicit ruling junta.

We have all seen them. Dressed like Gestapo, in black uniforms, their faces masked, they descend upon and eliminate any opposition to federal authority. These, my friends, are *not* that honest Andy-of-Mayberry style sheriff that you elected to safeguard your community. They are power-drunk mercenaries who would just as soon march you off to a concentration camp, or machine gun you in a trench, as write out a parking ticket. They are totally anonymous, and completely unanswerable.

This is why, to be true to the intent of the Second Amendment, citizens must possess the same kinds of armament that the government can use *against* them! *These* are the enemies, *not* the guys who want to steal your wallet!

'To Protect and Serve'?

At least the Nazis had the COURAGE not to hide their faces!

"I don't make the laws, I only carry them out...."

Since this is so often the mantra of these so-called protectors of freedom, it behooves us to look at some specific laws that they are only too happy to enforce.

Periodically, anyone with internet access is sure to receive one of those chuckler emails listing some 'dumb laws' that remain on the books in one place or another. Some of them are merely amusing: "In Atlanta it's against the law to tie a giraffe to a telephone pole or a street lamp." The serious aspect, often overlooked, is that *any* of these laws can be enforced, selectively, to persecute just about anyone the government decides is becoming too troublesome.

There are several troubling facets to this phenomena:

1. Many laws are passed with the sole purpose of providing law enforcement with a pretext to discriminate against specific segments of the population. For example, marijuana was originally illegalized so southwestern police could use the law to round up Mexicans. Cocaine was illegalized to facilitate persecuting the African-Americans who were its primary users at the time. In Illinois, you may be arrested for vagrancy if you do not have at least one dollar bill on your person. Hence, poverty is made a crime. In Minnesota it is illegal to stand around any building without a 'good reason' for being there.
2. Overbearing, overshooting, despots who believe that they have the right to legislate *their* vision of propriety—usually in direct violation of the spirit and letter of the Constitution—will inevitably do so. Hence, in Florida, it is illegal to engage in sex in any but the 'missionary' position. Oh, and while doing so, it is also illegal to kiss your wife's breasts. In Massachusetts it is illegal for a woman to be on top during sexual activities. In Mississippi, it is illegal to *teach* others what polygamy *is*.
3. Just plain stupid laws are enacted, leading to the general erosion of respect of law. For example, the legislators of Indiana, believing themselves above the laws of physics, have decreed the value of ***pi*** (a fundamental constant of nature) to be 3. In New Jersey, it is illegal for a man to knit during fishing season. It's important to remind yourself that the people who dream this stuff up are doing so on *your* tax dollar!

So, just to provide a cross section of the kinds of laws that are, or were until recently on the books in various places, subject to enforcement at the whim of officials, here are some representative statutes:

Alabama

- It is illegal to sell peanuts in Lee County after sundown on Wednesday.
- You may not have an ice cream cone in your back pocket at any time
- In the town of Anniston, you may not wear blue jeans down Noble Street.
- Men who deflower virgins, regardless of age or marital status, may face up to five years in jail. *(Think this lawmaker was unclear on some critical concept?)*

Alaska

- In the town of Haines, a person may only carry a concealed slingshot if that person has received the appropriate license.
- In Juneau, owners of flamingos may not let their pet into barber shops.
- In Soldotna, persons may not allow "attractive nuisances" to exist.

Arizona

- Any misdemeanor committed while wearing a red mask is considered a felony.
- Donkeys cannot sleep in bathtubs.
- A class 2 misdemeanor occurs if one places a mark upon a flag which is "likely to provoke physical retaliation". *(Is the person engaging in the physical retaliation exonerated thereby?)*
- It is illegal to manufacture imitation cocaine. *(Would that include... salt, sugar, talcum powder.... ")*
- When being attacked by a criminal or burglar, you may *only* protect yourself with the same weapon that the other person possesses. *(Wait while I fetch my green striped dildo....)*
- You may not have more than two dildos in a house. *(Whoops! Would that include my self-defense dildo* and *that being wielded by my assailant?)*
- In the town of Globe, cards may not be played in the street with a Native American.
- In Nogales, one is prohibited from wearing suspenders. *(A pay-off from a well-connected belt manufacturer, perhaps?)*

Arkansas

- The Arkansas River can rise no higher than to the Main Street bridge in Little Rock. *(Arrest that fluid!)*
- A law provides that school teachers who bob their hair will not get a raise.
- A man can legally beat his wife, but not more than once a month.
- Alligators may not be kept in bathtubs. *(Lest it eat your Arizona donkey?)*
- In Fayetteville, it is illegal to kill "any living creature". *(I suppose one could be prosecuted for taking an antibiotic. Is the eradication of Smallpox regarded as genocide?)*

California

- Sunshine is guaranteed to the masses. *(A vote for me is a vote for eternal sunshine....)*
- Animals are banned from mating publicly within 1,500 feet of a tavern, school, or place of worship. *(Does this apply to the human animal as well?)*

Florida

- One may not commit any "unnatural acts" with another person. *(Well, that leaves a lot of latitude for prosecution.)*
- Unmarried couples may not commit "lewd acts" and live together in the same residence. *(And remember, those foreigners hate* ***us*** *for our* ***freedoms****.)*
- A special law prohibits unmarried women from parachuting on Sunday or she shall risk arrest, fine, and/or jailing.
- When having sex, only the missionary position is legal.
- You may not fart in a public place after 6 P.M. *(Hurry, sunrise!)*
- It is considered an offense to shower naked.
- Oral sex is illegal.
- You may not kiss your wife's breasts. *(How about those of someone else's wife?)*

Georgia

- All sex toys are banned. *(Even dildos used in self defense?)*
- Donkeys may not be kept in bathtubs.
- No one may carry an ice cream cone in their back pocket if it is Sunday.

Hawaii

- Coins are not allowed to be placed in one's ears. *(Honest, Judge—that cop dropped the dime in my ear!)*

Idaho

- It is Illegal for a man to give his sweetheart a box of candy weighing less than fifty pounds. *(So, technically, not giving her a box of candy at all is the same as giving her a box weighing zero pounds, right?)*

Illinois

- You may be arrested for vagrancy if you do not have at least one dollar bill on your person. *(Well, that's* ***one*** *way to solve the poverty problem.)*

Indiana

- Anyone 14 or older who profanely curses, damns or swears by the name of God, Jesus Christ or the Holy Ghost, shall be fined one to three dollars for each offense, with a maximum fine of ten dollars per day.
- The value of Pi is 3. (*We don't subscribe to the Constitution OR the laws of physics.)*
- It is illegal for a man to be sexually aroused in public. 
- A man over the age of 18 may be arrested for statutory rape if the passenger in his car is not wearing her socks and shoes, and is under the age of 17.
- You can get out of paying for a dependent's medical care by praying for him/her..

Iowa

- One-armed piano players must perform for free.

Kansas

- If two trains meet on the same track, neither shall proceed until the other has passed.

Maryland

- Thistles may not grow in one's yard. *(Well, if marijuana is illegal, why not thistles?)*
- Oral sex cannot be given or received anywhere.

Massachusetts

- Snoring is prohibited unless all bedroom windows are closed and securely locked.
- Goatees are illegal unless you first pay a special license fee for the privilege of wearing one in public.
- A woman cannot be on top in sexual activities.
- Quakers and witches are banned. *(Freedom of religion be damned!)*

Michigan

- No man may seduce and corrupt an unmarried girl, or else he risks five years in prison. *(Damn, that could certainly cramp one's style.)*
- A woman isn't allowed to cut her own hair without her husband's permission.

Minnesota

- It is illegal to stand around any building without a good reason to be there.
- It is illegal to sleep naked. *(Is it okay to be **born** naked?)*

Mississippi

- It is illegal to teach others what polygamy is.
- Adultery or Fornication (living together while not married or having sex with someone that is not your spouse) results in a fine of $500 and/ or 6 months in prison.
- Vagrancy is punishable by either 30 days in prison or a $250 fine.
- Unnatural intercourse, if both parties voluntarily participate, results in a maximum sentence of 10 years and $10,000.
- It is illegal for a male to be sexually aroused in public. *(Influenced by the powerful codpiece lobby?)*

Missouri

- Single men between the ages of twenty-one and fifty must pay an annual tax of one dollar. *(A tax on what you **are**.)*
-

Montana

- It is illegal to have a sheep in the cab of your truck without a chaperone. *(**Must** have been a good reason for this one.)*
- It is a misdemeanor to show movies that depict acts of felonious crime. *(Wouldn't CSPAN fall within this statute?)*

Nebraska

- If a child burps during church, his parent may be arrested.

New Hampshire

- You may not tap your feet, nod your head, or in any way keep time to the music in a tavern, restaurant, or cafe.
- It is considered an offense to check into a hotel under an assumed name.
- On Sundays citizens may not relieve themselves while looking up.

New Jersey

- It is against the law for a man to knit during the fishing season.
- You may not slurp your soup.

New Mexico

- State officials ordered 400 words of "sexually explicit material" to be cut from Romeo and Juliet.

New York

- Citizens may not greet each other by "putting one's thumb to the nose and wiggling the fingers". *(Extending the middle finger is protected by law.)*

North Carolina

- The mere possession of a lottery ticket is illegal in North Carolina and may result in a $2,000 fine.
- It's against the law to sing off key.
- While having sex, you must stay in the missionary position and have the shades pulled.
- If a man and a woman who aren't married go to a hotel/motel and register themselves as married then, according to state law, they are legally married.
- Couples staying overnight in a hotel must have a room with double beds that are at least two feet apart.
- Oral sex is considered a crime against nature.
- Persons in possession of illegal substances must pay taxes on them.

North Dakota

- It is illegal to lie down and fall asleep with your shoes on.
- It is *legal* to shoot an Indian on horseback, provided you are in a covered wagon. *(No, really—I'm a* ***Sicilian****, not an Indian!)*

Ohio

- Breast feeding is not allowed in public. *(Is* ***having*** *breasts still legal?)*
- It is illegal to mistreat anything of great importance. *(We'll let you know when you do it.)*
- No one may be arrested on Sunday or on the Fourth of July. *(Not even if they're breast feeding, or mistreating something of great importance?)*

Oklahoma

- Females are forbidden from doing their own hair without being licensed by the state. *(Strong hairdresser's lobby?)*
- Dogs must have a permit signed by the mayor in order to congregate in groups of three or more on private property.
- Residents are taxed for the furniture in their homes, and any other personal belongings.
- It is illegal to have sex before you are married.
- Tissues are not to be found in the back of one's car.

Oregon

- It is illegal to whisper "dirty" things in your lover's ear during sex. *("Ooo, Baby—mud, sludge, grease, dust, grime....")*

Pennsylvania

- It is illegal to sleep on top of a refrigerator outdoors.
- Any motorist driving along a country road at night must stop every mile and send up a rocket signal, wait 10 minutes for the road to be cleared of livestock, and continue.
- A special cleaning ordinance bans housewives from hiding dirt and dust under a rug in a dwelling.
- You may not sing in the bathtub.
- No more than two packages of beer at a time may be purchased, unless you are buying from an official "beer distributor". *(State owned, of course)*
- All liquor stores must be run by the state. *(But down with Socialism!)*
- Though you do not need a fishing license to fish on your own land, a hunting license is required to hunt on your own land. *(Private property rights only go* ***so*** *far.)*

Rhode Island

- Exercising any labor, business, or work, or using any game, sport, play, or recreation, or causing any of the above to be done to or by your children, servants, or apprentices on the first day of the week (Sunday) results in a penalty of $5 for the first offense and $10 for the second.

South Carolina

- No work may be done on Sunday.
- Horses may not be kept in bathtubs. *(Save room for the donkeys!)*

South Dakota

- Movies that show police officers being struck, beaten, or treated in an offensive manner are forbidden.
- If there are more than 5 Native Americans on your property you may shoot them *(Hey, Geronimo—party at my place—bring 4 of your friends....)*

Tennessee

- "Crimes against nature" are prohibited. *(You mean, like **polluting**?)*
- Interracial marriages are illegal. *(But inter-**species** relationships are fine.)*

Texas

- One must acknowledge a supreme being before being able to hold public office. *(Does praying to Odin qualify?)*
- Up to a felony charge can be levied for promoting the use of, or owning more than six dildos. *(Five is reasonable, but **six**? Pervert!)*
- A recently passed anticrime law requires criminals to give their victims 24 hours notice, either orally or in writing, and to explain the nature of the crime to be committed.
- The entire Encyclopedia Britannica is banned in Texas because it contains a formula for making beer at home.

Utah

- It is illegal not to drink milk. *(How often?)*
- A husband is responsible for every criminal act committed by his wife while she is in his presence. *(Guess the same applies to multiple wives.)*
- It is a felony to persistently tread on the cracks between paving stones on the sidewalk of a state highway.

Vermont

- Women must obtain written permission from their husbands to wear false teeth.
- It is illegal to deny the existence of God. *(How about fairies, or sprites, or goblins?)*

Virginia

- Not only is it illegal to have sex with the lights on, one may not have sex in any position other than missionary.
- There is a state law prohibiting "corrupt practices of bribery by any person other than candidates." *(Well, at least **these** politicians are **honest** about their corruption.)*
- You may not engage in business on Sundays, with the exception of almost every industry. *(Particularly the ones who make big political contributions)*
- If one is not married, it is illegal for him to have sexual relations. *(Even when alone?)*
- It is illegal to tickle women.

Washington

- No person may walk about in public if he or she has the common cold.
- All lollipops are banned. *(Well **that** sucks!)*

West Virginia

- Unmarried couples who live together and "lewdly associate" with one another may face up to a year in prison. *(Unless, of course, they're brother and sister).*
- It is *legal* for a male to have sex with an animal as long as it does not exceed 40 lbs.
- According to the state constitution, it is unlawful for anyone to own a red or a black flag.

Wisconsin

- Butter substitutes are not allowed to be served in state prisons.
- State Law made it illegal to serve apple pie in public restaurants without cheese.
- Margarine may not be substituted for butter in restaurants unless it is requested by the customer. *(You suppose the dairy lobby might have anything to do with these laws?)*

Wyoming

- You may not take a picture of a rabbit from January to April without an official permit.

Amusing as some of these may be, there is a deadly serious issue here. Our lawmakers have become *so* brazen, and our citizens *so* complacent, that virtually any law, legal under the Constitution or otherwise, is allowed to stand, and can be used to deprive any citizen of their inalienable rights at the whim of the most corrupt people in our society. Is it a stretch of credulity to imagine laws that make it illegal to be, say, Jewish? How about a law that permits incarceration for having parents who were born in Japan?

Everyone wants the security promised by a 'law and order' society, but failure to assess the associated costs is a vote for voluntary slavery, and we have already gone further in that direction than our founding fathers would ever have believed possible.

A sentiment expressed by both Benjamin Franklin and Thomas Jefferson, in several variations, asserts that those willing to trade freedom for security deserve neither and will lose both. ***Amen!***

" The battle, sir, is not to the strong alone; it is to the vigilant, the active, the brave. Besides, sir, we have no election. If we were base enough to desire it, it is now too late to retire from the contest. There is no retreat but in submission and slavery! Our chains are forged! [...] Is life so dear, or peace so sweet, as to be purchased at the price of chains and slavery? Forbid it, Almighty God! I know not what course others may take; but as for me, give me liberty or give me death!"
—Patrick Henry

"Kill the king!" —Ronnie James Dio

"Off the Pig!" —Huey Newton

Platform 2012!

The fact that the Founding Fathers were able to unite people of such divergent interests, beliefs, and perspectives is nothing short of miraculous. Some participants wanted slavery, some did not. Some wanted a king, others felt otherwise. Many remained who still wanted reconciliation with England. If the framers had insisted on a platform that included everything they believed to be right, moral, and important, this nation would have been a non-starter. Today we would likely be former colonies of France, Spain, England, and probably others as well. (In fact, in the Declaration of Independence, as first written by Thomas Jefferson, there was a clause abolishing slavery. However, because of pressure, he was forced to delete the clause.)

It is a tribute to their foresight, vision, and faith in the ultimate goodness of mankind that they were willing to compromise on many items that they almost certainly knew were unjust, immoral, and critically important.

In terms of a single human lifespan, two or three centuries seems like an eternity, but within the history of civilization, it is little more than the blink of an eye. The progress this nation has made since the ratification of the Constitution is a testament to the success of those compromises.

We stand poised at a juncture no less critical than that following our victory over the tyranny of Great Britain. Gradually, insidiously, over a period of a century or more, corrupt, immoral, unpatriotic, despots have infiltrated and usurped every right our progenitors worked so hard to create for us, our children, and countless generations into the future. Nor have *We, The People,* been blameless in this despicable *coup d'état*. They have purchased our compliance with comfort, distraction, and the equivalent of a handful of beads and trinkets. We have accepted their offers, selling our birthright, and that of our children, for empty promises and unrealistic visions of unattainable grandeur.

Are we, the Americans of the twentieth and twenty-first centuries less noble, less able, and less selfless than our forefathers? That chapter has yet to be written, and I fervently pray that we can rise to the challenge.

Those who took up arms against the most powerful nation on earth had far greater obstacles to surmount, and far greater dangers to face. We, even with the few paltry remnants of the power they granted us, may still reclaim our birthrights without resort to violent confrontation; we have only to unclench our fists, take a leap of faith, and, like our Founding Fathers, put our belief in the basic righteousness of our fellow Americans.

Yes, there *are* important issues at stake: The right to life, the right to choose, the rights of people whose ideas, orientations, and values seem so foreign to our own. But at the most basic level, we must accept that the vast majority of or countrymen want exactly the same things: the right to live their lives, fulfill their potentials, make their limited days on earth as meaningful as possible, and, hopefully, allow the next generation to build upon the foundations they establish.

From a practical perspective, it must be obvious to all who can see that unless basic changes are made first, none of the other things are going to happen. It has been wisely observed that those who do not learn from history will be doomed to repeat it. Within the lifetime of every man and woman in this nation, there can be no doubt that, regardless of the transient shifts in administrations and rhetoric, nothing of substance has changed, except, perhaps, for the ongoing erosion of our rights and freedoms.

Consider this: In the year 2008, Americans overcame half a millennia of racial prejudice and elected an African-American to the presidency. While some may have supported him because of his racial background, there were undoubtedly an equal number who did so *despite* that factor. Barack Obama became President because he promised change. Promises, of course, are what *all* politicians offer. Promises, historically, are where they differ from one another, but after they are elected, they typically do exactly the same things. In 2008, the American people dared to *believe*. In 2008, we dared to hope that *this* time it would be different.

The reality has proven us wrong. The reality is that we have, once again, been deceived by empty promises.

With a progressive president, and a progressive congress, did we make a single step toward curbing climate change? Toward healthcare reform that wasn't simply a give-away to the insurance companies? Toward ending a costly and ill-considered war? Toward restoring due process for all? Toward immigration reform? Government corruption? Corporate welfare and give-aways? Stopping the exporting of American jobs? Energy independence? What exactly *has* he accomplished, other than accepting a Nobel Prize, basically awarded to him for not being George W. Bush?

Zip. Zero. Nada! Why did Obama lose that support in the mid-term elections? Because his *actions* proved him to be a spineless, self-serving, scumbag, just like all the others.

Remember that 1970 book by Richard Nelson Bolles entitled *What Color is Your Parachute*? Today we might well ask ourselves: What color is our scumbag?

Wherever you stand on the political, spiritual, theological, or philosophical spectrum, draw upon your personal experience, and ask yourself whether you can realistically expect that any of the choices likely to be offered will ever make the slightest bit of difference? Obama (again)? Newt (export some jobs) Gingrich? Rick (Welcome to Niggerhead) Perry? Michelle (I wouldn't recognize the truth if it crawled up my ass) Bachmann? Mitt (I'm not quite as bad as the others) Romney? Rick (I just hates all queers) Santorum? Give me a break!

Regardless of whether you vote Democrat or Republican, *your* taxes are *not* going to go down. Your property will not be protected. *Rowe V Wade* is *not* going to be rolled back, and a real, fair, universal healthcare program is not going to be implemented. Creationism is *not* going to replace a science curriculum, and people of faith are *not* going to abandon their beliefs. Corporations *will* continue to denigrate the dignity of the working men and women whom they no longer consider useful for exploitation, and will continue to bribe their agents in government into doing their bidding. In other words, things will continue just as they have for the past century, with Democrats and Republicans putting on contentious little displays for your benefit, keeping you riled up, and then doing precisely what they want, and what benefits their corrupt cronies.

We *do* have an alternative; but it is becoming more unattainable every day, as the entrenched *Republicrat Junta* works hard at plugging up the last cracks in the ramparts that protect its hegemony. Already, they have convinced many Americans that their illegal government is, in fact, the natural order of things. They have convinced Americans that third-party candidates are not serious or viable choices, and that a vote for any but a *Republicrat* candidate is a vote wasted; when in fact, precisely the *opposite* is true. Can you truly believe that a choice between Barack Obama and Newt Gingrich, or any of the other scumbags you're likely to be offered is going to get this nation back on its intended noble course?

We must continually remind ourselves that elections were held in the former Soviet Union. Every voter had a choice between candidates who served the same corrupt interests, and would implement the same crooked policies and main the same totalitarian government. In other words, their elections were precisely like ours.

Remember Ross Perot? When they began to see him as a threat to their hegemony, they used their power to threaten him through his family, forcing him to unceremoniously withdraw. Pat Buchanan, a real Conservative, and Ralph Nadar, an honest liberal, were marginalized, their words distorted, until their campaigns were little more than a joke. Who today remembers that the running mate of Pat Buchanan, the supposedly racist conservative, was African-American activist and retired teacher from Los Angeles, Ezola B. Foster; or that his ticket was endorsed by the future Socialist Party USA presidential candidate Brian Moore, who said in 2008 he supported Buchanan in 2000 because "he was for fair trade over free trade. He had some progressive positions that I thought would be helpful to the common man."?

But which are the *real* wasted votes, if not the ones cast for people who lie to get us into wars, or lie by promising 'change', and then, like all of their cronies, toe the line of their corrupt party agendas?

The biggest lie of all, however, is that *we* are not all Americans, but rather, that we are contentious factions with nothing but mutual distrust and animosity toward each other. We will *always* have differences, but we also have significant commonalities, and foremost among them is the capacity for reason, independent thought, and an aversion to being manipulated by those who treat us like idiots.

Slavery *was* a great evil, and because of the compromises of our Founding Fathers, it took a hundred years until it was abolished, but abolished it was. Had the framers of the constitution insisted on a *perfect* constitution, slavery might still be a fact of life today. It took even longer for women to attain the vote, but today they probably enjoy greater equality than most societies in history. No, we're not there yet, but do you honestly believe that insisting on it in that first draft of the Constitution would have advanced that cause rather than delayed it?

There are many, *many* injustices in our society, and these will persist for a while longer *whatever* we do. The innocent will suffer, but suffering will always be an integral part of life. (Jesus suffered, but He did so for a purpose. Shall *we* do any less?) The question that faces us now is whether we can realistically believe that insisting on a solution for *all* problems, all at once, will accelerate their resolution, or whether a more efficacious approach is to stop, build a solid foundation, and continue from there.

Any attempt to build a better society from where we now stand is akin to nailing two boards together, stepping back, and asking whether it's a house yet. If it is not, we nail on another board and repeat the process. The prospects of ending up with a safe, solid shelter by this methodology is practically nil.

The Republicrat Junta has worked long and hard to convince us that we have absolutely no common ground. If this is indeed the case, than the United States of America is already doomed. However, as I have argued throughout this book, I am convinced that this is a carefully calculated deception.

We *can* overcome their treachery, and we *can* take back our nation, simply by building on the common ground that we *do* have. My proposal is simple and straightforward: Put aside, for the time being, all of the admittedly important, compelling, and contentious issues that will not be resolved over the next 4 or 8 years *anyway*, identify those items on which we *do* concur, and use those as a foundation for restoring the Constitutional government that is our birthright, and that of our children.

Will there be hardships? Certainly. But are we not enduring hardships *now*? When someone tells you that there will be *no* discomfort, no sacrifice, no hardship, there is only one thing of which you can be certain: that person is ***full of shit!***.

For lack of a better term, I shall refer to this mechanism for ousting the illegal *Republicrat Junta* as:

C.O.P.
The Coalition of Opposition Parties

Since the monumental effort of overcoming the numerous procedural hurdles to even competing in a national election have already been surmounted by several established 'third parties', the most efficacious approach would be if one of them would graciously agree to a stripped-down platform of essentials, behind which all or most of the others would be willing to lend their weight. Personally, I believe that *The Reform Party*, having hosted so great a range of ideologies, from Ross Perot to Pat Buchanan, would be a natural, and probably has the least political baggage to overcome, but others would do as well. The main thing to keep in mind is that this ***C.O.P.*** movement is a *temporary* one, whose primary agenda is to oust the lock grip of *the Republicrat Junta,* and allow other, more principled parties to actually have some prospect of success in the future. In other words, *it is what the Tea Party movement could have been, and should have been,*

This platform will seek to get government under control, eliminating major sources of corruption, while ensuring *minimal disruption* on the lives of individuals, existing programs and commitments, and the economy. ***It will guarantee focus on 10 simple items that every voter can understand, digest, and decide whether or not to support.***

As stated above, this will mean that many topics of great importance to many passionate, sincere individuals will be put on hold, but since the vast majority of such topics are hopelessly deadlocked anyway, the only loss will be the soapboxes for screaming about issues everyone has already heard, and about which the vast majority of individuals have already formed steadfast positions.

In return, those who support this platform are guaranteed that these, and *only* these items will be addressed.

Candidates running on this platform will agree to a single term only.

Candidates running on this platform will agree to pursue only these agenda items, except as demanded by national emergencies:

1. All current laws, policies, statutes, and international commitments, except those specifically identified in this platform statement, are to be left untouched until the platform items have been accomplished.

2. The first priority of the C.O.P. government will be the immediate banning of the Republican and the Democratic parties, based on provable acts of deliberate exclusion, and the willful abrogation of Constitutional precepts. While these offenses might ordinarily rise to the level of treason, a general amnesty will be applied to any who do not challenge or interfere with this process.

3. Any former Republican or Democrat who has broken party lines in at least *one* vote during his or her political tenure will be eligible to seek public office as an Independent or 'third-party' candidate. Other former Republicans and Democrats will be prohibited from holding public office for the remainder of their lives.

4. Immediate impeachment of all members of the Supreme Court, and replacement with individuals who have not participated in direct political activities favorable to Democrats or Republicans. Impeachment proceedings will be presided over by qualified legal professionals who either are not members of any Bar Association, or who are willing to renounced membership in the American Bar Association.

5. No individual who derives more than $1 Million per year from investment holdings in any single company, or who possesses an off-shore bank account, may hold federal office, elected or appointed, for a period of 3 years after divesting themselves of such holdings and/or accounts.

6. In order to meet current obligations, and keep the government and programs operational until a new budget can be established, a flat-rate tax will be instituted, at such a rate as is necessary to reach the aforementioned funding goal. There will be no deductions, no loopholes, no exemptions for individuals or businesses.

7. In order to protect life, health, and wellbeing until a comprehensive energy program can be established, a substantial usage excise tax will be levied on all recreational devices that employ oil products for their usage. This includes, but is not limited to, RVs, motor homes, recreational trailers that are towed on public highways, power boats used primarily for recreational purposes, private aircraft, jet-skis, ATVs, radio-controlled, gas-powered models, toys, etc., and snowmobiles not primarily employed for rescue or emergency use. The proceeds of this tax will be used to subsidize

a) fuels used exclusively for heating purposes, in non-commercial private domiciles of under 5000 square feet, owned by persons with a net annual family income of under $250,000.00, or renters of properties qualified as above who are solely responsible for the cost of heating.

b) fuels used in emergency vehicles,

c) fuels used for the transport of foods and other essentials that are distributed within 500 miles of the point of production.

8. An emergency law will be passed making it a federal crime to defraud the government and the people of the U.S. by any unqualified usage of fuels sold under the provisions of item #7, the penalty for which will be not less than 10 years in prison, without possibility of parole, time off, sentence reduction, or amnesty by subsequent administrations.

9. All lobbying, as presently practiced, will be temporarily suspended until comprehensive safeguards and limitations can be defined. Until then, every company, organization, interest group, advocacy group, etc., will be permitted a set number of official petitions annually, that number to be defined, each to be within a strictly defined size limit to be determined. These will be reviewed, compiled, and considered. Any additional efforts to further specific interests will be defined as attempted bribery, and will be punishable by the same term described in item #8.

10. The full effort of the administration will be dedicated to collecting, collating, analyzing, and documenting all official petitions, priorities, and suggestions collected from the public, and by organizations under item #9. The resulting list will be analyzed by the (new) Supreme Court to determine which items are required or prohibited by the Constitution. The remaining items will be presented to the public, with an approximate price tag normalized as per-capita cost, for prioritization and approval.

After 4 years, all individuals elected under this platform will agree not to seek re-election.

This, my fellow Americans, is truly change you can trust!

In order to facilitate this ambitious effort, I am providing a rallying point at:

http://www.KickThemOut.org

PART IV

THE BACK BURNER

Overview

The purpose of this section is not to be a prescription for any particular issue, but rather, to suggest some ways in which these very important topics might be approached so as to at least permit some productive dialog between sincere, concerned individuals. As illustrated throughout this book, however, it should be clear by now that no such meaningful discussion, and certainly no real solutions will be possible until we first oust the current unresponsive, and irresponsible *Republicrat Junta,* and return power to *the People*.

These are manifestly not simple, one-dimensional issues. They are complex, nuanced, and highly important to all concerned, and must be approached as such. If anything should be clear by now it is that they will *never* yield to the simplistic, rule-based, silver-bullet approaches that those in power have tried to peddle to us in the past.

For the most part, these observations represent my own current mode of thought on each particular issue, arising from many decades of going back and forth, listening to the thoughts of people whom I respect from numerous points of view. And therein lies the best advice I can give for moving forward and making real progress: Judge each source, and each issue as a single cell in a matrix. Allow yourself to respect each individual on the basis of their honesty, sincerity, and intelligence overall, even if you believe they are dead wrong on a particular issue; and from that perspective, force yourself to consider the possibility that they *might* at least be *partly* right on that issue as well. Maybe they won't change your mind, but perhaps they just might soften the edges a bit, and even suggest some viable middle ground between you.

Hands clasped in friendship are far more productive than fists clenched in rage.

Respect for the Constitution

The Constitution ***is*** the foundation of this nation. It is not perfect, and its authors were neither prophets nor saints; but it nevertheless contains the mechanism for its own correction and evolution. That mechanism is described in Article V:

The Congress, whenever two thirds of both Houses shall deem it necessary, shall propose Amendments to this Constitution, or, on the Application of the Legislatures of two thirds of the several States, shall call a Convention for proposing Amendments, which, in either Case, shall be valid to all Intents and Purposes, as Part of this Constitution, when ratified by the Legislatures of three fourths of the several States, or by Conventions in three fourths thereof, as the one or the other Mode of Ratification may be proposed by the Congress; Provided that no Amendment which may be made prior to the Year One thousand eight hundred and eight shall in any Manner affect the first and fourth Clauses in the Ninth Section of the first Article; and that no State, without its Consent, shall be deprived of its equal Suffrage in the Senate.

The procedure described *is* difficult, as it was *intended* to be.

The proliferation of frivolous, intrusive, contentious, and contradictory laws under which we currently suffer is precisely the burden which our Founding Fathers sought to avoid. If something is sufficiently important, *and* sufficiently obvious to a majority of the people in *all* of the states, then it should be *considered* for inclusion under the purview of the federal government. If not, then it has no place being imposed upon them. *That* is how this nation was formed, *that* is how it was intended to operate, and *that is what it **is.***

Permitting congress to pass laws, willy nilly, in furtherance of their own interests, and in direct violation of the Constitution, is an invitation to the corruption we are now faced with undoing, and must not be allowed to happen again.

State's Rights

This is an extension of the topic discussed in the last chapter: *Respect for the Constitution.* The Tenth Amendment says:

" The powers not delegated to the United States by the Constitution, nor prohibited by it to the states, are reserved to the states respectively, or to the people."

The homogenization of the United States serves the sole purposes of furthering the interests of big businesses and moving power into the hands of the federal government. This comes at the expense of the rights of the People to live in a manner of their choosing, under laws consistent with their values and principles, within the limits set forth in the Constitution.

This latter point means that, no, states are *not* free to implement slavery, deprive women of the right to vote, or force anyone to belong to any particular church, or any church at all. On the other hand, it means that people who want to express their religious beliefs are free to do so, providing they don't force anyone else to participate.

Immigration Reform

Unrealistic idealism and wishful thinking is most frequently associated with the most liberal segment of our society: Wouldn't it be wonderful if we lived in a world without war, a world with no guns, and no hunger… maybe if we all join hands and sing *Kumbia*….

However, Conservatives are just as unrealistic when they insist that "Nobody should be rewarded for breaking the law…." Hey, our business leaders, politicians, judges, and even our clergy have been repeatedly rewarded for breaking the law, so how about a moderate dose of realism? No, we're not going to welcome in violent criminals with open arms, but the people who have been here, picking our fruit, cleaning our homes, and grooming our estates *are* here, have been here, and that's just reality. If we could allow amnesty for Nixon, and a plethora of other criminals whose misdeeds often cost thousands of lives, we can do the same for those whose 'crimes' merely facilitated our low grocery prices and lavish lifestyles.

It's informative to read John Steinbeck's classic *Grapes of Wrath,* or view John Ford's movie interpretation, and note that the treatment of the American migrant farmers was in every respect identical to our current attitudes toward 'illegals'. Some people *are* simply ugly and mean-spirited. What does the Bible say about the treatment of strangers? What about the parable of the 'Good Samaritan'?

We also have to consider the *reality* that many of them have children who, having been born in the United States, *are* citizens thereof. You may not *like* that clause of the Constitution. You may not *agree* with it, but you are *not* empowered to disregard it, or change it without formal amendment. Even *if* you did so, you would *also* have to amend the clause prohibiting the passage of *ex post facto* laws, or all those *already* born here, would *still* be citizens. Do you *realistically* believe there is sufficient support in this country to pass *both* of these Amendments? Are you prepared to break up families, whose only crime is working for Americans, by deporting parents? Are you prepared to accept the support of their children?

So, let's be *realistic*, shall we? Anyone who has been working here for a certain amount of time should be able to fast-track into citizenship, start paying taxes, and become subject to our laws.

Is this unfair to those who 'played by the rules'? Undoubtedly, but as so many Conservatives have so often observed: "life ain't fair!" In the meantime, all immigration is put on hold until we can tighten our borders, expel criminals, and implement a fair, realistic, workable, and enforceable immigration system.

No Hablo Inglés? No Ciudadanía!

(Don't Speak English? No Citizenship!)

What makes a society *a society?* Commonality of purpose, the ability to work together in a coordinated manner—all of these things demand some basic communication ability, and that means a common language. Sorry, all my liberal friends, but that's just common sense.

Remember the hostage-rescue mission carried out by the Israel Defense Forces at Entebbe Airport in Uganda on 4 July 1976? A week earlier, on 27 June, an Air France jet with 248 passengers was hijacked by Palestinian terrorists and flown to Entebbe, near Kampala, the capital of Uganda. Shortly after landing, all non-Jewish passengers were released.

When the hijackers threatened to kill the hostages if their demands were not met, a rescue operation was planned. The operation took place at night, as Israeli transport planes carried 100 elite commandos over 2,500 miles to Uganda for the rescue operation. The hostages had been moved to the main hall of the airport building, directly adjacent to the runway. Upon entering the terminal, the commandos shouted: "Stay down! Stay down! We are Israeli soldiers." in both Hebrew and English. A 19-year-old Frenchman named Jean-Jacques Maimoni—who had chosen to identify himself as an Israeli Jew to the hijackers even though he had a French passport—stood up, and was killed by the Israeli commandos, who mistook him for a hijacker.

Nobody wants to destroy anyone else's culture, nobody's saying that accommodations should not be made for those who have not yet become fluent in English, but if someone yells: ***"FIRE!"*** all within earshot should be heading for an exit, not passing the *Grey Poupon*.

This was mentioned earlier, but bears repeating. Wherever I've lived in this great nation, I've always managed to fit in and establish lasting friendships among those who had lived there for generations. I attribute this success to having made an effort to fit in and respecting *their* ways, rather than trying to compel *them* to conform to *mine*. If you love Mexico that much, or Italy, or France, or Russia, then that's where you should be speaking those respective languages. Sorry if that comes across as strident or jingoistic, but I believe it's the way a majority of Americans feel, and I believe that, in this case, the majority is completely correct. People don't want to feel as if immigrants are here solely to serve their own interests. Acceptance is a two-way street, and if you want *me* to accept *you* as my neighbor, you need to show me that *being* a neighbor is important to you as well.

I believe Theodore Roosevelt spoke for most Americans when he said: "we should insist that if the immigrant who comes here in good faith becomes an American and assimilates himself to us, he shall be treated on an exact equality with everyone else, for it is an outrage to discriminate against any such man because of creed, or birthplace, or origin. But this is predicated upon the person's becoming in every facet an American, and nothing but an American…There can be no divided allegiance here. Any man who says he is an American, but something else also, isn't an American at all. We have room for but one flag, the American flag…. We have room for but one language here, and that is the English language... and we have room for but one sole loyalty and that is a loyalty to the American people."

Like every other aspect of life, with every privilege comes corresponding responsibilities. You can't demand the first and refuse to accept the second.

Defund the CIA

The Central Intelligence Agency (CIA) was created by Congress with the passage of the National Security Act of 1947, and signed into law by President Harry S. Truman. Its primary function included collecting information about *foreign* governments, corporations, and individuals, and advising public policymakers. Although also empowered to engage in covert activities (when ordered by the President of the United States), these activities have become so egregious as to qualify as war crimes and crimes against humanity by any objective standard. Moreover, there have been numerous documented instances when, in direct violation of the National Security Act, they have been used *against* United States citizens *within* the Unites States, as well as against other branches of the United States Government (as was the case in Watergate). This makes them an illegal, subversive organization. Since we now have other agencies, such as the NSA, responsible for the intelligence-gathering functions that were really the only Constitutionally justifiable function of the CIA, its continued existence should no longer be tolerated.

The Defense Department just released its mammoth budget for the next fiscal year. Much of the proposed spending is fairly detailed—identifying exactly how many helicopters the Pentagon plans to buy and how many troops it plans on supporting. But about $56 billion goes simply to "classified programs," or to projects known only by their code names, like "Chalk Eagle" and "Link Plumeria."

That's the Pentagon's *black budget*.

The CIA has been called into question repeatedly for some of the tactics it employs to carry out its missions. At times these tactics have included torture; funding and training of groups and organizations that would later participate in killing of civilians and other non-combatants and would try or succeed in overthrowing democratically elected governments; deadly human experimentation, including some on American citizens, and targeted killings and assassinations.

The CIA has repeatedly been shown to be ineffective in its basic mission of intelligence gathering, in favor of engaging in misconduct operations that have little to do with that legitimate mission, such as assassination attempts and human rights violations. The CIA has also been charged with having more than 90% of its employees living and working within the United States, rather than in foreign countries, which is in direct violation of its charter. The CIA has also been shown to lack financial and whistleblower controls, which has led to waste and fraud.

Research by Dr. Alfred W. McCoy, Gary Webb, and others has pointed to CIA involvement in narcotics trafficking across the globe, During the Cold War, when numerous soldiers participated in transport of Southeast Asian heroin to the United States by the airline Air America, the CIA's role in such traffic was reportedly rationalized as "recapture" of related profits to prevent possible enemy control of such assets. Gary Webb and other researchers have reported on similar operations during Reagan's Contra War against the democratically elected government of Nicaragua, U.S. involvement in Afghanistan during the Cold War, and current CIA involvement with Pakistan's ISI intelligence agency, which allegedly has links to the refining of Afghan heroin in Pakistan.

When some unscrupulous politicians say that they "want the government to operate more like a business," *this* is undoubtedly what they mean.

Whether or not the intelligence available to, or presented by, the Bush Administration justified the 2003 invasion of Iraq, or allowed proper planning (especially for the occupation) is quite controversial. However, numerous CIA employees claimed that Bush administration officials placed undue pressure on CIA analysts to reach conclusions that would support their stated policy positions with regard to Iraq. Hence, it is indisputable that the CIA has become, in practice, the unanswerable, secretly funded, enforcement arm of the *Republicrat Junta*, in every sense identical to the German Gestapo.

More recently, we've seen the CIA, *a civilian agency*, extensively engaged in overt warfare, particularly in the use of unmanned Predator Drones. While the technology involved presents its own issues, the use of a civilian agency in this manner blurs the lines between legitimate and illegal combatants, in essence, justifying retaliations against civilian targets by our enemies. Stated differently, we cannot endorse this kind of action on one hand, and then condemn attacks like 9/11 on the basis of their effect on 'innocent civilians'.

Like the justification of torture, we cannot claim the moral high ground while engaging in these practices, regardless of the transparent sophistry we use to justify our actions. In the long run, it's a self-defeating, short-term, morally bankrupt tactic that will inevitably come back to haunt us.

Extensive research has proven that normally civil individuals will engage in aggressive, even vicious behaviors when shielded by the anonymity of their automobiles, from whence the other person is conceptually dehumanized. Cases of 'road rage' have resulted in thousands of deaths or injuries, almost always involving actions that the individuals involved would never even consider in a face-to-face encounter.

It requires no stretch of imagination to comprehend the analogy of remote controlled drones. When some empowered but unanswerable video-game-enthusiast, sitting in the comfort of his cubical in Langley, coffee mug conveniently within arm's reach, framed photo of wife and kids decorating his desk, can manipulate a computer mouse and annihilate a wedding party halfway around the world, we have made an abject mockery of what was once "The land of the free and the home of the brave."

In the 1975 movie *The Wind and the Lion,* Mulay Ahmed Muhamed Raisuli the Magnificent, Lord of the Riff, Sultan to the Berbers, and Last of the Barbary Pirates (and, parenthetically, a Muslim), played by Sean Connery, says: " I prefer to *fight* the European armies, but they do not fight as men—they fight as dogs! *Men* prefer to fight with swords, so they can see each other's eyes! Sometimes, this is not possible. Then, they fight with rifles. The Europeans have guns that fire many times promiscuously and rend the Earth. There is no *honor* in this—nothing is decided from this."

While our enemies have been portrayed as craven, ignoble cowards, devoid of any trace of dignity or honor, this self-congratulatory distortion does not hold up to unbiased scrutiny. Are these not the *same* people whose bravery and valor we praised when they stood up against the *Soviet* invaders? Have *they* changed their principles, or the culture they have embraced for a thousand years? Do we expect them to respect as noble enemies those who murder them from the comfort of their offices, thousands of miles away? Which of us truly *are* the spineless, craven cowards?

From a practical perspective, how long do we imagine it will be until someone figures out that similar weapons can be easily constructed by combining readily available smart-phone technologies, off-the-shelf hobbyist aircraft components, and home-made explosives? No longer will angry individuals have to sacrifice their own lives by flying planes into IRS buildings, police barracks, or other targets. (As I revise this chapter, just such a plot was recently foiled.)

When the citizens of the United States give this kind of *Carte Blanche* to government, closing their eyes to crimes committed in their names, they forfeit any expectation of being treated as innocent civilians, and become legitimate targets of military retaliation. Like the Germans living within the shadows of the smokestacks of Treblinka, we can't on one hand say: "I don't want to know what's going on," and later excuse our complacency and complicity by saying: "I didn't know what was going on."

Foreign Affairs

Ideology aside, from a purely practical perspective, we have made hundreds of military commitments that we can never possibly honor. We maintain military presences overseas that we can no longer afford to support. Moreover, none of these can be reasonably justified in terms of our national defense. The fact that *we* are the *only* remaining superpower means that we can ensure our security without these nineteenth-century displays of uniformed forces. Indeed, these presences serve no practical purposes except to enrich the coffers of corporate war profiteers, while fueling resentment that ultimately erupts in the kinds of attacks that cannot be countered by either our standing armies or our technological strategic weapons.

In today's reality, nobody who is capable of delivering a weapon of mass destruction via conventional means (e.g., ballistic missiles), has anything to gain by doing so. Conversely, those who *might* be so inclined, would have to do so through some alternative means: in a shipping container, smuggled across our borders, etc. If they were successful, would we be morally justified in retaliating by obliterating innocent civilians elsewhere? And if so, where?

Would it not be more effective to redeploy our forces currently scattered all across Europe, Asia, and the Middle East, and instead, put them to work protecting our home soil, where the threat actually exists? For the cost of maintaining these strutting, ineffective, and expensive displays of machismo, could we not patrol our borders, inspect incoming freight containers, and, in the process, reduce the hatred, resentment, and animosity that are most likely to *motivate* such an attack in the first place?

I do not *know* the answer to these questions. I am not a military tactician, nor am I an international diplomat; however, I find it disturbing that nobody is even asking or considering these kinds of questions.

Redefine Foreign 'Aid'

Helping people in need is not the same are bribing regimes in furtherance of self-serving political agendas, or arming factions in destructive skirmishes. America should not be the weapons dealer for the entire world. When a survivor sees a scrap of metal marked "*Made in the U.S.A.*" amidst the scattered body parts of friends and family, we have just created another enemy; another 'terrorist'. Who is truly the 'cowardly terrorist'; the one who sacrifices his life striking back at an overwhelming enemy, or the 'hero' who directs a Predator Drone from his posh office space, killing a few hundred civilians before taking his morning coffee break?

If and when we have the resources to direct toward foreign aid, how about helping those who need a source of potable water? How about teaching those who are starving to develop sustainable farming practices? How about working toward eliminating the deprivation that *leads* to factional warfare, rather than arming our preferred side, as if we were betting on a sporting event? How about using foreign aid in a way that will make us the nation that people don't *want* to attack? It might not work, but it's certainly not something we have ever actually tried!

Capital Punishment

American 'people of faith' have been very selective about which passages from the Bible they choose to embrace under any particular circumstance. Are we primarily *New Testament* devotees, or *Old Testament* zealots? Is it "an eye for an eye," or "vengeance is mine, saith the Lord?"

We can go around and around forever trying to determine whether or not the prospect of a death penalty actually deters crime, and will probably never agree on an outcome, so perhaps we should simply approach the issue from a practical perspective.

We have seen, and continue to see, hundreds of instances in which men and women are proven to be innocent after serving years, or even decades in prison. Sometimes these are the results of honest mistakes, sometimes deliberate subversion of justice by unscrupulous police, prosecutors, or witnesses. Regardless of the cause, we can still mitigate the resultant injustice by returning to the *victim* what remains of his or her life. However, once we take that irrevocable step, no such mitigation is possible.

The indisputable evidence shows that our system is imperfect. People are imperfect. Can we, in view of this manifest imperfection, justify so final a punishment? Does not even one such injustice counterbalance all of the other instances in which the ultimate penalty seems so satisfying to our sense of retribution? I personally find the whole concept of officially sanctioned homicide repulsive, as does most of the civilized world, but I would be willing to support capital punishment, if, supporters were prepared to tell me that they could unequivocally guarantee that a miscarriage of justice will never occur. How about this: suppose all citizens be required to register as pro- or anti-capital-punishment. In the event that a miscarriage of justice does occur, ten death-penalty supporters will be selected at random, humanely executed, and their organs harvested and sold, the proceeds going to compensate the family of the victim unjustly executed. Let those who are so sure of themselves and our system of justice put their lives where their bloodlust is. Sounds fair to me!

From a theological perspective, is it not just a little bit presumptuous to take the position that the eternity of torment in *God's* sentence is *inadequate*, and needs to be extended by 10 or 20 years by *us*? Seems pretty arrogant to me!

Finally, unless we are prepared to resort to elimination of all due process, and simply hang suspects from the nearest tree, then the expense of allowing death-row inmates all possible avenues of exoneration costs more than life without parole, which, once again, *can* be reversed if we discover we have made a terrible mistake.

Reproductive Rights

Homicide in general comes in many flavors—some justified or even encouraged, others frowned upon. To put a blanket judgment on every woman's situation or reasons for, as some choose to phrase it, killing a baby, is inconsistent. In the final analysis, if the religious view of cosmic justice is correct, then the woman will be judged by one with far greater perspicacity than Oral Roberts, and the infant will we welcomed by the angels without the necessity of earthly suffering.

The flip side, for those advocating unqualified 'right to choose', is that *no* right is *absolute*. What makes you think that a woman doing something with her own body that causes the death of another entity should be exempted from any constraint whatsoever?

There is a continuum between using a spermicidal jelly and Andrea Yates drowning her children, and failure to recognize how, at some point on that spectrum, killing another human being for your own convenience is simply wrong, is to display the utter callousness toward human life that so offends many groups of people characterized as 'pro-life'. Abortion is not, or should not be, the first-choice form of birth control, yet it is frequently treated as such.

Still, it is somewhat incongruous that the same group who would force *every* mother to bear *every* child, would then deny that child proper nutrition, a decent education, an even chance to compete in an equitable playing field, and would then advocate the harshest punishments if desperation leads them to employ means for survival outside the constraints of laws that are themselves often unjust.

And one thing of which both sides are equally guilty is an absurd desire to put *everything* under the auspices of the government, and total consternation when everyone fails to agree with *their* priorities.

Regardless of how strongly you might feel about a woman's right to choose, is it so difficult to comprehend why some people would find it morally objectionable to *fund* what they see as *murder*? How do *you* feel about your tax dollars going toward spraying napalm on infants, or providing lethal injections to prisoners who sometimes turn out to be innocent, or performing illegal syphilis experiments on foreigners and United States citizens alike?

Moral outrage is not limited solely to *your* sensibilities.

There is no mandate in the Constitution for the federal government to provide healthcare for *anyone*, let alone fund controversial procedures, be they the termination of an unwanted pregnancy, or cloning Donald Trump for spare parts so he can live forever. The only proviso is that the law be applied to all citizens equally.

So what if we say, for the sake of argument, that women will not be prohibited from terminating any pregnancy except those that could, by the current state of medical technology, produce a viable living entity (i.e., if that thing inside the mother can be kept alive outside the mother, than it *must* be); however, the government is not going to pay for it? If it's *that* important an issue to enough people (and I believe it *should* be), then set up foundations to provide funding. Is that *so* unreasonable?

Conversely, abortion opponents need to recognize that we do not live in a perfect world. Women have *always* terminated unwanted pregnancies, and to prohibit them from doing so will only result in prohibiting them from doing so in a safe manner. Perhaps some feel that it is an abomination worthy of a death sentence, but that death sentence is *not* yours to impose.

It's difficult to blame the government for overreaching when we continuously demand that they take more and more of the responsibilities that should belong to the individual, and it's even harder to then complain about how much it costs, and the way it's being carried out.

Incomprehensible to me are the outraged objections to any suggestion that a person seeking an abortion be required to undergo some psychological counseling. I personally know one woman who, after undergoing her second legal abortion, suffered an infection that necessitated a complete hysterectomy. After over forty years, it remains the greatest regret of her life. I do not believe she is unique in this respect. Like the death penalty, some decisions cannot be undone, so does it not make sense to ensure that those decisions are given due consideration; *especially* when those involved are young and inexperienced?

As a father of two daughters, this is a topic to which I have devoted some deep soul searching. Ultimately, I decided that if such a situation ever came to pass, I would do my best to convince my child to carry the child to term, while assuring them of a support structure that would make it possible to do so without negatively affecting her entire life. If that meant supporting her, and, if necessary, the child's father, and caring for the child so she/they could complete their education, that would have to be part of the package. However, the decision would ultimately be hers/theirs to make, and whichever decision they made, I would assure them of my love and support.

Public Worship

The First Amendment of the Constitution states: "*Congress shall make no law respecting an establishment of religion, or prohibiting the free exercise thereof;....*"

Sixteen words. Only the most corrupt, litigious attorneys could take these sixteen words, which any honest, literate citizen should be able to comprehend, and turn them into a topic for endless debate and litigation.

Nowhere in the Constitution does anyone say anything about Christianity, Judaism, Islam, Paganism, Wicca, Satanism, or some aboriginal dung-worshiping cult. Want public schools to require a prayer to *Crom*[1] every morning? If not, then you have to live with not promoting *your* preferred cult either.

And for those on the more liberal side of things, seeing someone's religious icons in a public place may make you uncomfortable, but, in itself, it does not deprive you of the ability to worship, or not, as you choose. Your freedom is guaranteed by the constitution. Your comfort under any circumstances, however, is not.

If the majority of people in your state want a picture of their favorite myths in a courthouse, and so long as an equal right is extended to any other group willing to put forward, defend, and finance a display, you have not been diminished, and your discomfort should not represent sufficient cause to deprive others of their preferences. Sometimes, being a good neighbor, and fitting in, is a surer route to acceptance than fighting perceived slights at every turn.

So long as nobody forces you to worship, or prevents you from worshipping as you please, the Constitution is working as it was intended.

[1] Crom is a fictional deity imagined by L. Sprague de Camp and appearing most prominently in the Conan the Barbarian stories.

Gay Rights

A great deal of governmental gridlock could be eliminated by adhering to one principle: *mind your own business.* The gay marriage issue is a prime example. First of all, marriage isn't a right, or a requirement of life. It's a societal custom, one which is, or should be, symbolic in nature only; that is, there should be no legal benefit or ramification to being married that is not available to adult, single-partner, domestic cooperatives, regardless of the genders, sexual practices or sexual orientations of the participants. Declaration of a cohabitive cooperative relationship should be akin to forming a corporation—declaring a new collective entity—and no more expensive or complex than obtaining a marriage license.

Hence, any discrimination is eliminated, leaving only those issues related to the word 'marriage', and any ritualistic accoutrements your favorite non-binding sanctioning body might care to confer.

As most people know, and a few are committed to enforce, free speech is a guarantee, and if you want to insist that your hamster is married to your goldfish, that's nobody's business but your own. On the flip side, if you crave membership in an ultra-orthodox organization, and that body refuses to recognize the pairing of your choice, well, sorry…life ain't perfect, and all we can do is ensure that it's at least as fair as possible.

For gay people, you deserve to live your lives as you choose, You are entitled to equal rights, and equal treatment under the law. However, if your neighbors want to reserve the word 'marriage' for a traditional pairing, sorry, *you* have to compromise too.

So, if you don't like the idea that the folks down the street have a squirrel married to a spaniel, with a certificate from the Church of Gospel Critters to prove it, you'll just have to learn to deal with that, perhaps by employing your God-given neck, and looking a different way. You have a right to determine who can be a member of your private organization, including, by the way, on the basis of race, religion, amount of body hair, color of eyes…(however, as an 'exclusionary group', don't expect government support, tax exemptions, or any kind of protection, or any ability to profit from government contracts, or support by most reasonable people.)

The issue of *adoption* by gay partners is an entirely separate one. To my knowledge, no same-sex pairing has ever resulted in offspring, so it's impossible to argue that such a family situation is or isn't detrimental to children. Adoption isn't a right, it's a privilege. Some male-female partners are reasonably prevented from adopting—I'll not offer any examples lest they be misinterpreted as suggesting an unfair and negative comparison—all I'm saying is that those charged with ensuring the interests of children deserve considerable latitude in making those determinations. Adoption is reasonably interpreted as a surrogate for situations in which those seeking to adopt would ordinarily be capable of producing their own offspring.

I don't necessarily believe this is right, perfect, or ideal, but it is at least a reasonable non-arbitrary place to draw a line. There are undoubtedly others, and I would be perfectly willing to hear and consider them. Nevertheless, I believe that if same-sex couples were allowed to benefit from the same protections as others, and avoid hatred and other discriminations, this would be a fair and reasonable trade off.

Public Education

During a brief period when I attended public elementary schools, one afternoon each week, classes ended early so those who were so inclined could attend religious instruction. Similarly, if you feel so strongly about your kids praying for so many hours each day, is it unreasonable for you, the parent, to take responsibility for making that happen somewhere other than that 6 to 8 hours they spend in school?

A similar argument applies to sex education. People have been managing to learn the gist since the beginning of life, and I daresay life will continue without the government sticking its long nose into the mix. *You* might not like the way *those* people are instructing *their* children, but you know what? *They* don't want *you* teaching their children either, so how about learning to mind your own business?

Children *can* be taught the notion of tolerance toward alternative sexual orientations without giving them an encyclopedic coverage of sexual practices throughout the history of the world.

The framers of the Constitution foresaw that there would be differences in tastes, priorities, lifestyles, and desires, and wisely chose to limit federal responsibility to those specific areas where only a unified approach is feasible, such as providing for the common defense.

The problem is, when anyone thinks about the homogenization of America (that is, making everyone the same, not making everyone a homosexual), what they envision is making everyone just like *them*. When it turns out that some other group may have yelled louder, or bribed more heavily, then it becomes government overreaching.

Free Trade

As suggested earlier, if the aim is to implement a fair, workable solution that serves the needs of the nation and its citizens, rather than those of greedy business criminals, many avenues might be explored.

"For example, we might define the amount of imports we're willing to take without matching exports. This will handle critical import categories such as oil, rare earth metals, etc. that aren't really available at the required quantity in this country. Every import above that must have a matching export credit. These are dollars paid to U.S. manufacturers, or service providers, that are used to offset the cost of the exports. Those wishing to import additional goods to the U.S. must buy these export credits from the product/service providers, thus driving down the cost of the exports and hence increasing the export volume. There's lots more details but that's the basic idea. Works like the energy cap and trade concept but for imports."

No doubt there are other possibilities as well.

PART V

CONCLUSION

America Divided?

It should be obvious to anyone with a modicum of intellectual honesty that, in the vast majority of cases, our politicians, regardless of party, speak loudly and passionately about topics designed to polarize their constituencies, then, behind the closed doors of government, strike deals that bear no resemblance whatsoever to their professed creeds, or their solemn promises. There is an often repeated joke that goes something like this:

Q: How can you tell when a politician is lying?
A: His/her lips are moving.

Conversely, true Statesmen speak the truth as they see it, unconcerned about who might agree or disagree, or whether the result will ultimately benefit their own careers. A prime example is Thomas Jefferson, who wrote: "I have the consolation of having added nothing to my private fortune during my public service, and of retiring with hands clean as they are empty." Would that the same could be said of even a handful of our current so-called 'leaders'. Since I have argued throughout this book that the image of Americans as disagreeing on virtually every important topic is contrived, erroneous, and perpetuated by those whose aim is to breed dissent, I will conclude this book with some quotations from some men I consider great Americans. In order to avoid the influence of the many distortions, misquotations, and propaganda associated with some of them, I shall identify each by number only, and reference each at the end. Read them with an open mind, and decide for yourself if Americans are truly as divided on all important issues as we are being misled to believe, and then, ask yourself whose interests this artificial animosity serves. While, obviously, there are a great many issues upon which we do and shall always differ, the fact that we can agree on at least *some* of the very important topics identified here illustrate that the deliberate and insidious distortions promoted by members of *the Republicrat Junta* are by no means true. (In addition, I'm including some quotes from *Republicrats* themselves—see how easily you can spot the lies without even knowing who uttered them!)

1. "The most effective way to restrict democracy is to transfer decision-making from the public arena to unaccountable institutions: kings and princes, priestly castes, military juntas, party dictatorships, or modern corporations"
2. "The ideal is to create a completely fragmented atomized society where everybody is totally alone, doing nothing but trying to pursue created wants."
3. "By the end of the Reagan era, the U.S. shoe industry had lost 88 percent of its home market.... by the time he became president in 1981, Ronald Reagan had been converted to free trade, but in earlier years.... [he said that] workers can't compete against goods sold at below-production cost.... what will happen to the American worker? How will he and his family get along?"
4. "When people talk about capitalism it's a bit of a joke. There's no such thing.... [Under the Reagan Administration] the entire dynamic economy in the United States is based crucially on state initiative and intervention.... Run through it, and you find massive rip-offs of the public, meaning, a system in which under one guise or another the public pays the costs and takes the risks, and profit is privatized. That's very remote from a free market."
5. "...the idea that such entities [corporations] have special rights, over and above persons, has been strongly advocated. The most prominent examples are Bolshevism, fascism, and private corporatism.... There is no alternative to the emerging system of state corporate mercantilism disguised with various mantras like globalization and free trade."
6. "...free trade theory is first cousin to socialism and Marxism.... free trade is truly a betrayal of Middle America and treason to the vision of the Founding Fathers."
7. "The 'corporatization of America during the past century has been an attack on democracy—and on markets, part of the shift from something resembling 'capitalism' to the highly administered markets of the modern state/corporate era. A current variant is called 'minimizing the state,' that is, transferring decision-making power from the public arena to somewhere else: 'to the people' in the rhetoric of power; to private tyrannies, in the real world."
8. "Free Trade is a myth. Foreign countries subsidize their manufacturers, which enables them to undercut United States companies and take the jobs of American Workers...this is not competition—it is a stacked deck, stacked against the American Worker.... If we pursue the policies that have gone on for the last few years, we're going to be a completely service nation."

[You want fries with that, Sir?]

9. [Response to statement that consumers will be the big winners from a GATT agreement.] “If you mean by ‘consumers’ rich ones, yes. Rich consumers will gain. People who have lost their jobs, for example—and that will be true both in the rich countries and the poor—obviously are not going to be better consumers.”
10. “Leadership means standing up against the voices of isolation and protectionism.”
11. “The dominant propaganda systems have appropriated the term ‘globalization’ to refer to the specific version of international economic integration that they favor, which privileges the rights of investors and lenders, those of people being incidental. In accord with this usage, those who favor a different form of international integration, which privileges the rights of human beings, become ‘anti-globalist.’ This is simply vulgar propaganda, like the term ‘anti-Soviet’ used by the most disgusting commissars to refer to dissidents. “
12. “I think it only makes sense to seek out and identify structures of authority, hierarchy, and domination in every aspect of life, and to challenge them; unless a justification for them can be given, they are illegitimate, and should be dismantled, to increase the scope of human freedom.”
13. “Neoliberal democracy. Instead of citizens, it produces consumers. Instead of communities, it produces shopping malls. The net result is an atomized society of disengaged individuals who feel demoralized and socially powerless. In sum, neoliberalism is the immediate and foremost enemy of genuine participatory democracy, not just in the United States but across the planet, and will be for the foreseeable future.”
14. “No free man shall ever be debarred the use of arms.”
15. “When the people fear their government, there is tyranny; when the government fears the people, there is liberty.”
16. “I suppose that, at some point, the ruling class will simply strike back by force, and there has to be defense against that force, and that probably means violent revolution.”
17. “The strongest reason for the people to retain the right to keep and bear arms is, as a last resort, to protect themselves against tyranny in government.”
18. “The European reaction to Obama is a European delusion.”
19. “Israel’s ‘secret weapon’…is that it may behave in the manner of what have sometimes been called ‘crazy states’ in the international affairs literature.”
20. “There are only two groups that are beating the drums for war in the Middle East—the Israeli defense ministry and its ‘amen corner’ in the United States.”
21. “I see no anti-Semitic implications in denial of the existence of gas chambers, or even denial of the holocaust.”

22. "And though it has received $100 billion in U.S. arms and aid over the past thirty years.... Israel suborned the traitor Jonathan Pollard to loot our vital secrets, lied about it, and then sold the technology for our Patriot and Python missiles, and the AWACS and F-16, to Communist China.... Israel looks out for Israel first,"
23. "Jews in the US are the most privileged and influential part of the population... privileged people want to make sure they have total control, not just 98% control. That's why anti-Semitism is becoming an issue."
24. "I hope we shall crush in its birth the aristocracy of our moneyed corporations which dare already to challenge our government to a trial by strength, and bid defiance to the laws of our country. "
25. "Ours is a system of corporate socialism, where companies capitalize their profits and socialize their losses...in effect, they tax you for their accidents, bungling, boondoggles, and mismanagement, just like a government. We should be able to dis-elect them."
26. "If one's allegiance is to the world, who cares if America is the dominant power? To a citizen of the world, a hollowing out of America's industrial power is an inconsequential, even a positive, development. It matters deeply only to American patriots."
27. "The only difference between the Republican and Democratic parties is the velocities with which their knees hit the floor when corporations knock on their door. That's the only difference."
28. "The idea that a congressman would be tainted by accepting money from private industry or private sources is essentially a socialist argument."
29. "Newt Gingrich...quite demonstrably is the leading welfare freak in the country.... His own district in Cobb County Georgia gets more federal subsidies than any suburban county in the country, outside of the federal system itself."
30. "Unlike members of Congress, Big Business knew what the WTO [World Trade Organization] agreements contained. That's because corporate lobbyists helped draft them."
31. "I think one of the great problems we have in the Republican Party is that we don't encourage you to be nasty. We encourage you to be neat, obedient, loyal and faithful and all those Boy Scout words, which would be great around a campfire but are lousy in politics."
32. "The new Republicans represent a kind of proto-fascism. There's a real sadism. They want to go for the jugular. Anybody who doesn't meet their standards, they want to kill, not just oppose, but destroy."
33. "The time has come to tell the truth about the corruption of the government employee unions in this country."

34. "the Democrats know that no matter how many GATTs, NAFTAs, empty OSHAs, and other betrayals...they heap on those labor leaders, they can be had because, once again, the Republicans are deemed worse."
35. "No one has deputized America to play Wyatt Earp to the world."
36. "The basic idea which runs right through modern history and modern liberalism is that the public has got to be marginalized. The general public are viewed as no more than ignorant and meddlesome outsiders, a bewildered herd."
37. "Why did Osama bin Laden target America? Not because we are a democracy, but, by his own testimony, because he wanted the American infidels off the sacred soil of Saudi Arabia that is home to Islam's holiest shrines. The terrorists were over here because we are over there"
38. "We fight them over there so we don't have to fight them over here."
39. "Better a foreign war than an internal upheaval."
40. "In the final hours before war was declared, it became clear Spain was casting about for an honorable way to capitulate, even if it meant ceding Cuba to the United States."
41. "It's entirely possible that bin Laden's telling the truth when he says he didn't know about the [9/11] operation."
42. "We Americans have been behaving like the Roman Empire. Between 1989 and 1999, we invaded Panama, smashed Iraq, intervened in Somalia, invaded Haiti, launched air strikes on Bosnia, fired missiles at Baghdad, Sudan, and Afghanistan, and destroyed Serbia. We imposed embargoes and blockades on Libya, Iran, Iraq, and dozens of other states. The Iraqi sanctions may have caused the deaths of 500,000 children. When Madeleine Albright, secretary of state under President Clinton, was asked if all this horrific toll of Iraqi children was justified, she replied, 'We believe the price is worth it.'... Now millions see the United States as an arrogant empire that flaunts its power, props up corrupt dictatorships, and spreads its ungodly culture among their young. How can we call a policy that reaps such a harvest of hatred a success?"
43. "You don't need today's defense budget to defend the United States; you need today's defense budget to lead the world."
44. "If a nation's power fails to cover its commitments, its foreign policy is bankrupt."
45. "With little discussion or dissent, America has undertaken the most open-ended and extravagant commitments in history. With the expansion of NATO, we have undertaken the defense of Eastern Europe, forever, as well as Central Europe from Norway to Turkey. American troops are, for the first time in history, policing the Balkans. We have undertaken the 'dual containment' of Iran and Iraq and the ground and naval defense of the Persian Gulf. These new war guarantees have been added to old Cold War commitments to the security of Israel in a hostile Arab world, to the defense of Korea, Japan, Australia, and the SEATO pact nations of South Asia, not to mention every Latin American member-state of the Rio Pact. Voices can even be heard in Washington

asserting a 'vital U.S. interest' in preventing Russia and Iran from dominating the south Caucasus.... The Clinton administration claims that NATO expansion will cost us only $1.5 billion over ten years. Whom are we deceiving? Does anyone believe a U.S. protectorate over Eastern Europe can be bought for less than the price of a B-2 bomber?"

[Whom indeed? Is it any wonder we can't seem to balance our budget?]

46. "A wise and frugal government, which shall restrain men from injuring one another, which shall leave them otherwise free to regulate their own pursuits of industry and improvement, and shall not take from the mouth of labor and bread it has earned. This is the sum of good government."
47. "If there is one principle more deeply rooted in the mind of every American, it is that we should have nothing to do with conquest."
48. "Today the large organization is lord and master, and most of its employees have been desensitized much as were the medieval peasants who never knew they were serfs."
49. "The tree of liberty must be refreshed from time to time with the blood of patriots and tyrants."
50. ***There Will Be Blood.***

1. Noam Chomsky, *Z Magazine*, May 1998
2. Noam Chomsky, Speech on eve of Iraq War.
3. Patrick J. Buchanan, *The Great Betrayal-How American Sovereignty and Social Justice Are Being Sacrificed to the Gods of Global Economy*, Boston, Little Brown. 1998, p38-39.
4. Noam Chomsky, Talk titled "Sovereignty and World Order" at Kansas State University, September 20, 1999.
5. Noam Chomsky, *Rogue States* , South End Press, 2000.
6. Patrick J. Buchanan, *The Great Betrayal-How American Sovereignty and Social Justice Are Being Sacrificed to the Gods of Global Economy*, Boston, Little Brown. 1998, p44.
7. Noam Chomsky, *Profit Over People: Neoliberalism & Global Order*, Seven Stories Press, 1999.
8. Pat Buchanan—quoting George Meany [AFL-CIO President, 1977 ("Amalgamated Clothing and Textile Workers Union Press Conference Transcript," News From the AFL-CIO, Oct. 31, 1977, pp 1, 6.)].
9. Noam Chomsky, *Keeping the Rabble in Line: Interviews with David Barsamian,* Common Courage Press, 1994.
10. George H.W. Bush, Remarks at the 1996 Republican Party National Convention, San Diego, California, August 12, 1996.
11. Noam Chomsky: Interview by Snježana Matejčić, June 2005.
12. Noam Chomsky, *Language and Politics,* AK Press, 1998, p775.
13. Noam Chomsky (unsourced).
14. Thomas Jefferson, *Jeffersonian Cyclopedia* published in 1900 by Funk and Wagnalls and edited by John P. Foley, p 51.
15. Commonly attributed to Thomas Jefferson, but probably John Basil Barnhill in *Debates on Socialism,* published in 1914.
16. Noam Chomsky, Interview, Black Rose, No. 1, 1974.
17. Uncertain, but attributed to Thomas Jefferson.
18. Noam Chomsky, interview with *Der Spiege*, Oct 13, 2008.
19. Noam Chomsky, *Fateful Triangle* [rev. ed., Pluto Press, 1999], pp. 468-9.
20. Patrick J. Buchanan, *McLaughlin Group*, 8/26/90.
21. Noam Chomsky, *Quadrant*, Australia, October 1981.
22. Patrick J. Buchanan, *A Republic, Not an Empire-Reclaiming America's Destiny,* Regency Publishing, 1999, p xiii.
23. Noam Chomsky, *Anti-Semitism, Zionism and the Palestinians*, 11 October 2002.
24. Thomas Jefferson (unsourced).
25. Ralph Nader, http://www.nader.org.
26. Patrick J. Buchanan, *The Great Betrayal-How American Sovereignty and Social Justice Are Being Sacrificed to the Gods of Global Economy*, Boston, Little Brown. 1998, p68.

27. Ralph Nader, Bill Moyers interview, 2004
28. Newt Gingrich, "Master of Disaster," by David Beers, *Mother Jones*, October 1989.
29. Noam Chomsky, Talk titled "Education and Democracy" at Michigan State University, March 28, 1995.
30. Ralph Nader, *The Good Fight: Declare Your Independence and Close the Democracy Gap*, Regan Books, 2004.
31. Newt Gingrich.
32. Noam Chomsky *The Progressive,* March 1996.
33. Newt Gingrich.
34. Ralph Nader, *Crashing the Party: Taking on the Corporate Government in an Age of Surrender,* St. Martin's Press, 2002.
35. Pat Buchanan, Source: NY Times, p. A22 Dec 17, 1999.
36. Noam Chomsky, *Class Warfare: Interviews with David Barsamian,* Common Courage Press, 2002.
37. Patrick J. Buchanan, *A Republic, Not an Empire-Reclaiming America's Destiny,* Regency Publishing, 1999, p xi.
38. George W Bush.
39. William McKinley—justifying the Spanish American war.
40. Patrick J. Buchanan, *A Republic, Not an Empire-Reclaiming America's Destiny,* Regency Publishing, 1999, p 157.
41. Noam Chomsky, *9-11,* Seven Stories Press, 2001, p. 60.
42. Patrick J. Buchanan, *A Republic, Not an Empire-Reclaiming America's Destiny,* Regency Publishing, 1999, p xi.
43. Newt Gingrich, *Los Angeles Times*, July 19, 1995|, "Gingrich Proposes U.S.-Led Force for Bosnia", by Norman Kempster.
44. Patrick J. Buchanan, *A Republic, Not an Empire-Reclaiming America's Destiny,* Regency Publishing, 1999, p 27.
45. Patrick J. Buchanan, *A Republic, Not an Empire-Reclaiming America's Destiny,* Regency Publishing, 1999, p 67.
46. Thomas Jefferson, First Inaugural Address In the Washington, D.C., Wednesday, March 4, 1801.
47. Thomas Jefferson, *Jeffersonian Cyclopedia* published in 1900 by Funk and Wagnalls and edited by John P. Foley.
48. Ralph Nader (unsourced).
49. Thomas Jefferson, letter to William Smith in 1787.
50. Paul Thomas Anderson (2007 movie title).

Individuals quoted in this section (presented alphabetically)

Patrick Joseph "Pat" Buchanan is an American conservative political commentator, author, syndicated columnist, politician and broadcaster. Buchanan was a senior adviser to American Presidents Richard Nixon, Gerald Ford, and Ronald Reagan, and was an original host on CNN's Crossfire. He sought the Republican presidential nomination in 1992 and 1996. He ran on the Reform Party ticket in the 2000 presidential election. He co-founded The American Conservative magazine and launched a foundation named The American Cause. He has been published in Human Events, National Review, The Nation and Rolling Stone. He is currently a political commentator on the MSNBC cable network including the show *Morning Joe* and a regular on *The McLaughlin Group*.

George Herbert Walker Bush is an American politician who served as the 41st President of the United States (1989–1993). He had previously served as the 43rd Vice President (1981–1989), a congressman, an ambassador, and Director of Central Intelligence.

George Walker Bush is an American politician who served as the 43rd President of the United States from 2001 to 2009. Before that he was the 46th Governor of Texas, serving from 1995 to 2000.

Noam Chomsky is an American linguist, philosopher, cognitive scientist, and social activist. He is an Institute Professor and professor emeritus of linguistics at the Massachusetts Institute of Technology. Chomsky is well known in the academic and scientific community as one of the fathers of modern linguistics, and a major figure of analytic philosophy. Since the 1960s, he has become known more widely as a political dissident and an anarchist, referring to himself as a libertarian socialist. Chomsky is the author of more than 150 books and has received worldwide attention for his views. Chomsky has written numerous books and lectured widely on what he considers the antidemocratic character of American capitalism and its pernicious influence on the country's politics and foreign policy, mass media, and academic and intellectual culture.

Newton Leroy "Newt" Gingrich, born Newton Leroy McPherson, is an American politician who served as the 58th Speaker of the United States House of Representatives from 1995 to 1999. Time magazine selected him as the Person of the Year for his role in leading the Republican Revolution in the House, ending 40 years of the Democratic Party being in the majority. During his tenure as Speaker, he represented the public face of the Republican opposition to President Bill Clinton.

Thomas Jefferson was the third President of the United States (1801–1809) and the principal author of the Declaration of Independence (1776). An influential Founding Father, Jefferson envisioned America as a great "Empire of Liberty" that would promote republicanism. Jefferson's revolutionary view on individual religious freedom and protection from government authority have generated much interest with modern scholars. He was the eponym of Jeffersonian democracy and the co-founder and leader of the Democratic-Republican Party, which dominated American politics for 25 years.

William McKinley, Jr. was the 25th President of the United States (1897–1901), and the last veteran of the American Civil War to be elected to that office. He was the last President of the 19th century and the first of the 20th.

Ralph Nader is an attorney, author, lecturer, political activist, and four-time candidate for President of the United States, having run as a Green Party candidate in 1996 and 2000, and as an independent candidate in 2004 and 2008. Areas of particular concern to Nader include consumer protection, humanitarianism, environmentalism, and democratic government. Nader came to prominence after publishing his book *Unsafe At Any Speed,* a critique of the safety record of the Chevrolet Corvair automobile. In 1999, an NYU panel of journalists ranked *Unsafe At Any Speed* 38th. among the top 100 pieces of journalism of the 20th. century. In 1990, Life magazine named Nader one of the 100 most influential Americans of the 20th. century.

Index

Symbols

A

B

C

D

G

H

I

J

K

L

M

P

Q

R

S

T

U

V

W

Y

Z

Demonic gods do not die easily.

Tatian, Oratio15.14

Born in 1952, author J.P. Befumo grew up in the Bensonhurst section of Brooklyn, NY during the turbulent sixties. Dropping out of high school at age seventeen, he spent several years working on the docks in Red Hook, ultimately working his way up to management positions at American Export Lines, then the world's third largest ocean freight company.

At age twenty-seven, dissatisfied with the direction his life had taken, he left his job, took the high-school equivalence exam (achieving the highest score ever recorded at that time), and enrolled in Brooklyn College, majoring in physics, mathematics, and computer science.

His activities working in the university's Dynamitron (8.75 MEv proton accelerator) lab gave rise to the conviction that advanced relativistic quantum effects had profound ramifications for mystical and spiritual concepts.

After graduating college (summa cum laude), he went to work at Digital Equipment Corporation's Advanced Semiconductor Development facility, where he participated in development of the DEC-Alpha, then the world's fastest super-microprocessor chip. After a stint at AT&T Solutions, as leader of their Center of Excellence for Estimating Metrics, and Quality, he became a Senior Client Partner at Clarity Development, LLC., a South Carolina high-tech consultancy, where he still serves as a part-time consultant. In early 2000, he semi-retired from consulting to devote full-time attention to writing.

His novels include Ariadne's Clew, Survival Skills, and The Apothecary Chest. Nonfiction works include Exotic Scales: New Horizons for Jazz Improvisation, and Faith and Physics, which, draws together his conclusions regarding the intimate connections between modern physics and Western spirituality in a presentation aimed at the popular audience. Another novel, By Mutual Consent, nears completion.

In addition to his work in science and literature, Befumo has participated in amateur theater, remains a serious amateur musician and performer, and is a talented artist, whose award-winning works have been displayed in the Springfield Museum of Fine Art, the Mari Gallery, and other prestigious venues.

The following web sites may also be of interest to you:

www.RepublicratJunta.com
www.befumo.com
www.KickThemOut.org
www.PleasantMountPress.com
www.AndFreedomToo.com
www.FaithAndPhysics.com

Other works by J.P. Befumo:

Fiction

The Apothecary Chest
Ariadne's Clew
The Orgone Experiment
Survival Skills
By Mutual Consent
The Sibylline Prophesies

Nonfiction

Faith and Physics – The Scientific Basis for Spiritual Belief
The Book of M.O.R.O.N.—Wicked Scriptures, Evil Folks
Exotic Scales – New Horizons for Jazz Improvisation
Boxes Beyond the Blues: A Pattern Approach to Jazz Improvisation
A Heritage of Hypocrisy – Why *'They'* Hate Us

Humor

Why Did the Prophet Cross the Road?
(To Wage Jihad Against the Crusading Infidel!)

Made in United States
Troutdale, OR
11/03/2026

56844489R00196